# REVOLUTIONARY NEW YORK

A. J. Schenkman

Globe
Pequot

Guilford, Connecticut

# Globe
# Pequot

An imprint of Globe Pequot, the trade division of
The Rowman & Littlefield Publishing Group, Inc.
4501 Forbes Blvd., Ste. 200
Lanham, MD 20706
www.rowman.com

Distributed by NATIONAL BOOK NETWORK

British Library Cataloguing in Publication Information available

Library of Congress Cataloging-in-Publication Data

Names: Schenkman, A. J., author.
Title: Patriots and spies in Revolutionary New York / A. J. Schenkman.
Description: Guilford, Connecticut : Globe Pequot, [2020] | Includes
  bibliographical references and index.
Identifiers: LCCN 2021028613 (print) | LCCN 2021028614 (ebook) | ISBN
  9781493047048 (hardcover) | ISBN 9781493047055 (epub)
Subjects: LCSH: New York (State)--History--Revolution, 1775-1783. |
  Revolutionaries--New York (State)--History--18th century. | American
  loyalists--New York (State) | Spies--United States--History--18th
  century. | United States--History--Revolution, 1775-1783--Secret
  service. | United States--History--Revolution, 1775-1783--Social
  aspects.
Classification: LCC E263.N6 S28 2020  (print) | LCC E263.N6  (ebook) | DDC
  973.3092/2747--dc23
LC record available at https://lccn.loc.gov/2021028613
LC ebook record available at https://lccn.loc.gov/2021028614

*Dedicated to*

*Lorraine*
*Your belief in me is undying; even when I don't believe in myself.*

*Barbara*
*There are no words that can adequately express my appreciation.*

***In Memory of***
*Michael Schenkman (1938–2016)*

# Acknowledgments

I would like to thank the following. If I have forgotten anyone, I am genuinely sorry. It was not intentional.

J.J. Blickstein;
Peter Shea;
National Portrait Gallery, Washington, DC;
Town of New Windsor Historian,
    Glenn T. Marshall;
Library of Congress;
New York State Archives;
Historic Huguenot Street,
    Carrie Allmendinger;
Kara Augustine;
Erin Beasly of the National Portrait Gallery, Washington, DC;
my editor Amy Lyons;
Jessica Blaustein-Marshall;
Rowman & Littlefield;
New York History Blog;
Carol Johnson;
Mary Etta Schneider;
Marybeth Majestic;
Town of Gardiner, New York;
my students;
Cindi Pietrzyk;
Gretchen Weerheim, Rosalie Spire, Michael Schenkman, Christine Hein;
New York Historical Society;
Globe Pequot;
Uncle Ron and Uncle John for all their support;
and of course my wife as well as my son, who at age five can't believe I have so many words in my head. Hi Jonah!

# CONTENTS

# INTRODUCTION

I never really liked studying the American Revolution. When I was a student, before college, it was just a series of facts with the start of the American Revolution beginning after the French and Indian War, which Europeans called the Seven Years War. The war had its origins in the Ohio Valley with a conflict between the French and the English, more specifically, Virginia, which sent a twenty-one-year-old major named George Washington by order of Lieutenant Governor Robert Dinwiddie in 1753 to tell the French to get out of the valley. A year later young Washington was sent back to the Ohio Valley as a lieutenant colonel. Washington's subsequent actions ignited the French and Indian War. Most students, and I was no exception, learned that the English won the war, vanquishing France from the Ohio Valley as well as most of North America. England and France signed the Treaty of Paris in 1763, officially ending the war. The Road to Revolution began after the war ended, as England looked for a way to pay for the war. They naturally looked toward their North American colonies.

Waging so many wars, both colonial and "Indian" wars, left England in a great deal of debt. Pontiac's War resulted in the Proclamation Line of 1763, which forbade Americans from settling on the Western side of the Appalachian Mountains. England believed this would end the conflict with the Native Americans in the west. The Proclamation Line, of course, enraged the Americans, especially the flurry of legislation passed by Parliament aimed at raising revenue to pay off England's debt. Students are still taught that the colonists resisted. No one can forget the slogan, "No taxation without representation." Civil strife lead to the first battles of the American Revolution, including Lexington and Concord and what was called the "shot heard around the world." Even after the colonists declared independence in 1776, it looked as if they would lose the war.

The Battle of Saratoga is considered the turning point by most school textbooks. After this victory, the United States formed a valuable alliance with the French and later Spain. France helped the United States win the Siege of Yorktown, which effectively ended the war. Other than the 1783

Treaty of Paris, little was mentioned about this in most textbooks when I was a student. When I took my first college class, my view of the American Revolution dramatically changed.

Once I graduated from high school, I took a class that provided a lot of information on the American Revolution. This class featured New York's role in the war, which was substantial. I fell in love with the history of the war. There was so much information that had been left out in years of education and even on television shows. There were places such as Newburgh where Washington set many precedents for the new nation, including his circular letter to the governors of the colonies. I learned about the Newburgh Conspiracy, when the country faced a genuine threat; the great chain and boom across the Hudson; the burning of Kingston, I did not even know that Kingston was the state's first capital; and finally the betrayal of West Point by Benedict Arnold. This lead to my next area of fascination.

Once I started delving into the American Revolution in college, I also learned about the cast of characters who gave depth and color to the war. Toward the end of college, I took jobs at various New York State historic sites, where I learned about people like Deborah Sampson, Peggy Shippen, and Major Andre.

There were numerous men and women who not only participated in battles but spied for both sides throughout the war. There were mutinies by unhappy and unpaid troops, assassination plots against General Washington, and other forms of intrigue. In short, a sweet, gentlemen's war was, in some ways, as brutal as the American Civil War. It completely uprooted the social fabric of society and pitted American against American, or Englishman against Englishman if you prefer. It was a destructive civil war not only in the white man's colonies but also in the Native American world as they were forced to take sides in the battles.

I remember while in middle and high school, I always thought of the American Revolution as a dignified war. Historians commonly viewed it as a gentleman's war. As my education and understanding of the war grew, I began to see it as anything but. In many ways, it was a guerrilla-type war. Officers and soldiers utilized hit and run tactics using the woods as cover, fighting more like the Native Americans than the British.

Additionally, the war resulted in massacres of both soldiers and non-combatants. Some historians, such as Carol Berkin, wrote of violence perpetrated against women on both sides of the conflict. These threats sometimes forced women to become "camp followers" as a way to stay safe. These were not prostitutes like during the American Civil War. Camp followers were many times family members or girlfriends of soldiers or officers. They took care of the men, doing the laundry and cooking as well as other tasks. Sometimes women posed as camp followers, but in reality, were spies. One of the most intriguing aspects of war were the spies, traitors, and even assassins, of both sexes, on both sides of the conflict.

This book will explore, as the title suggests, *Patriots and Spies in Revolutionary New York*. Some of the individuals described in this book are well-known, but I present them in a different light. Still other individuals are not as well-known outside New York, such as Daniel Taylor who is well-known in Ulster County, but not so much in the rest of New York.

The genesis of this book occurred in 2015 with a story entitled, "Is it time to grant Benedict Arnold Clemency?" The article, featured on North Carolina Public Radio, proposed, just as the title suggests, granting clemency to the man whose name is synonymous with treason. It prompted me to look into other notorious individuals who tried their best to undermine the American Revolution or, in some cases, manipulate events to further their gains. I found no shortage of individuals to explore. Unfortunately, during the subsequent four years I picked up my research only to be distracted by other projects. The biggest distraction being my father's untimely death. He was killed in 2016 while riding his bicycle in Queens, New York. I was in a deep state of grief for the next year or so. I continued to read but did not write much. I realized that my father always supported me in my writing. It was while cleaning out his home that I found all my books in a neat corner of his office. I started writing again.

I hope you have as much fun reading this book as I had writing it.
Sincerely,

A. J. Schenkman
Gardiner, New York

# THE MOHAWK VALLEY

# Tories and Mohawks Raid
# New York's Western Frontier

*Such Deadness of Military Spirit I never saw before. I think an Inquiry into such conduct ought to be made.*[1]

LEVI PAWLING

By July 1781 the American War for Independence was in its sixth year, and about to take a new turn winding down to its conclusion. The French Army joined Gen. George Washington and his army at Dobb's Ferry, New York. Washington hoped to launch an attack against the British-held New York island; however, intelligence apprised him in August of the arrival of a French naval fleet that would be sailing into the Chesapeake Bay from the West Indies in August/October. American plans to attack New York City were abandoned and eventually morphed into the Siege of Yorktown, which was the last major battle of the Revolutionary War.

During the summer of 1781, again the Iroquois attacked New York's vulnerable western frontier one more time. Their target was the town of Wawarsing in western Ulster County, roughly one hundred miles north-west of New York City. This area was under an almost constant threat of attack during the American Revolution, from both British Tories and the Iroquois. Historian Colin G. Calloway wrote that Native Americans, "allied with the Crown as the best hope of protecting their homelands from the encroachments of American colonists and land speculators . . . Indians knew that the Revolution was a contest for Indian land as well as for liberty."[2] Many of the incursions originated from the Mohawk Valley, which was considered an Iroquois stronghold. As a whole, the scope of the attacks was so impressive that as early as "1779, New York Governor George Clinton was reporting that the frontier of New York would be pushed back to the Hudson River if these raids were allowed to continue."[3] After Generals Sullivan and Clinton's Campaign of 1779 broke the power of the Iroquois, attacks noticeably declined but did not entirely cease. Once again they started up in 1781.

The purpose of some raids was to capture supplies, while others served to instill terror in citizens loyal to the American cause. Their target this time was a string of forts located throughout Ulster County and the surrounding region erected to protect settlers from these raids. Colonel Albert Pawling commanded these forts, though they often were no more than blockhouses or fortified homes with gun ports protected by citizens. Colonel Pawling often found himself expected to defend a large area with roughly one thousand soldiers at his disposal. If the alarm came at harvest time, the number might be considerably less.

Colonel Pawling's pension application, submitted by his widow Eunice on October 20, 1830, states that Pawling had been on the frontier since "the summer of 1779 [when] he was appointed Colonel Commandant of Levies annually raised for the defence of the frontier of the State of New York and remained in that service till the end of December 1781 ..."[4] Although the attack on Wawarsing was primarily considered unsuccessful, it reminded citizens just how vulnerable the frontier was.

A group of three hundred Iroquois joined ninety members of Butler's Rangers to execute the raid on Wawarsing. They launched their attack on August 12, 1781, after marching for eighteen days. The Niagara Falls Museum describes Butler's Rangers as consisting of eight companies of mainly Loyalists. Lieutenant Colonel John Butler, originally from Connecticut, relocated when still a child to the Mohawk Valley. When hostilities broke out between America and the British, he stayed loyal to the King of England. He formed the Rangers, which specialized in guerrilla warfare, in 1777. Butler's Rangers made an effort to learn not only Native American culture, but their languages and their fighting techniques. What settlers found particularly frightening was that many times, the Tories and Native Americans managed to be undetected by the settlement until the actual attack was in motion.

William Caldwell, a captain in one of Butler's eight companies, often led attacks against these frontier settlements. Born in County Fermanagh in Northern Ireland, Caldwell, according to *Canadian Biography*, immigrated to the North American colonies in 1773. He quickly became involved in military affairs with a campaign against the Native Americans on the Pennsylvania and Virginia frontiers.

When war broke out between England and its colonies, there was no question in the mind of Caldwell which side he would take. He declared himself a Loyalist and fought with Lord Dunmore the Governor of Virgina, in attacking Norfolk, Virginia. The British army shelled the harbor town and eventually put it to the torch. Dunmore was ultimately defeated and forced to flee Virginia along with a severely wounded Caldwell. Both men sailed for British-controlled New York City. After healing, Caldwell continued from New York City to Fort Niagara, which stood at the mouth of the Niagara River, a fort the British would retain for the duration of the war with America; for Caldwell, it served as a base of operations.

Caldwell became a hated individual by colonists, especially after he participated in the Wyoming Valley Massacre in Pennsylvania, in which a force of about 1,000 Loyalists and Native American allies massacred some 360 women and children. "In September 1778 (Caldwell) led an attack on German Flats (Herkimer) in the Mohawk Valley of Central New York, where he destroyed all of the buildings and grain in the area."[5] Many colonists wanted to see him brought to justice. Caldwell and his Native American allies' predations on settlements, as well as massacres on the western frontier, forced Washington to send a large military force against the Iroquois.

General Washington wanted to end the ability of the tribes to wage war against the United States by destroying not only their principal villages, but their food supplies. The officer he chose to lead the expedition against the Iroquois was Major General John Sullivan, and the second in command was Brigadier General James Clinton. Almost five thousand troops were committed to this campaign, a very substantial number of troops to commit to one operation. It showed how important a problem the Native Americans posed to the American frontier.

Also joining Butler's Rangers on the raid against Wawarsing was a Mohawk named Joseph Brant and some of his warriors. Known to his people as Thayendanegea Brant was born sometime around 1742 in the Ohio Country. He spoke English having attended school and also converted to Christianity in accordance with the Anglican Church. His sister, Molly Brant, eventually married Sir William Johnson, the British Superintendent for Northern Indian Affairs. Johnson held this title from 1756 until his death in 1774. Brant followed Johnson during the French and Indian War and was also made an officer by Sir William's successor, Guy Johnson. When hostilities broke out between the colonists and England, Brant fell firmly with the Crown. A very influential leader, he terrorized settlements along the frontier in New York as a Mohawk War Chief.

There are more than a few accounts of what transpired on the morning of August 12, 1781, when the combined forces of Tories and Mohawks attacked. One of the more well-known is by way of Silas Bowker Jr.'s 1832 pension request. According to his affidavit, Bowker enlisted with his father, of the same name, in Poughkeepsie on April 1, 1781. They both had served in the militia before, but this time they enlisted in the Continental Army for a term of nine months. Shortly after enlisting, the father and son paid a visit to George Clinton, then Governor of New York State, and requested to be transferred to the frontier of Ulster County. During that visit, the men signed a contract to join Colonel Albert Pawling's regiment, which patrolled Western Ulster County. Their wages were increased to $16.91.

With the agreement, father and son went to Wawarsing, where they stayed for five days. From there, they went to Peenpack, where they were enlisted as "Indian Spies." Along with others, they were stationed in the woods along the Delaware River, sometimes for ten to twenty days at a time. When the time elapsed, the spies returned to the regiment to report on their findings. Bowker Jr. stated in his pension affidavit, that "sometimes they were between 40 and 50 miles from settlements or the regiment."[6] Their primary mission was to watch the various Native American footpaths along the Delaware where they believed an attack might originate.

While on one such mission Bowker Sr. was in the woods watching a trail when he, along with fellow militia member Philip Hines, were caught by surprise and captured by a Mohawk raiding party. The hostages gave up information that allowed the Mohawks to "learn where our Guards were ordinarily stationed & were enabled to pass them in the night & gain the settlement early in the morning without being discovered."[7]

After the guards were captured, Captain Caldwell focused his assault on the house of Captain Andries Bevier in Napanoch, which doubled as a place of refuge for citizens in the area. Caldwell and Brant abandoned their objective of attacking the Bevier home in Napanoch because they were told the blockhouse, which was also Bevier's home housed a small cannon with plenty of deadly grapeshot available. This left the Bevier home spared. Little did the raiding party know, the gun was not in working order and the fort had not yet been completed. It was also drastically undermanned. Caldwell and Brant decided not to attack the fort and turned their attention to less fortified settlements as far away as modern-day Kerhonkson. The objective of the attack was to stir up fear, which it succeeded in accomplishing. They brought back prisoners and valuable supplies.

According to local stories, the home of Peter Vernooy was attacked first but deemed too well defended. It could be taken, but only with a significant loss of life. The attacking party did succeed in lighting Cornelius Bevier's dwelling on fire when they were repulsed by the defenders of the home. Then they decided to turn their attack on Cornelius DuPuy's home. Once again, the defenders repulsed the raiding party.

When the attack was underway, alarms sounded up and down modern-day Route 209. Captain J. L. Hardenbergh was visiting the home of John G. Hardenbergh, near the junction of modern-day Routes 44/55 and 209 when they heard the alarm of cannon and gunshots. They struck out from the house to confront the attackers. Making their way to the home of John Kettle, who was not there at the time, they created a concentrated defense. Kettle was, at the time, tending to matters at the home of another prominent family from the area, the Bruyns, who had removed from the frontier to the other side of the mountain in search of safety, leaving their home vacant. Kettle needed to attend to matters at the vacant home. Some accounts tell of him being a caretaker of sorts while the family was away. Others believe he was checking on some property that belonged to him. When Kettle heard the alarm, he hurried back toward his family home to help, but was shot dead and scalped by the Native American raiding party. Silas Bowker Jr. confirmed his death. Meanwhile his home was protected by his brother, the Hardenberghs, and some other individuals, as they fought the onslaught of the Loyalists and Iroquois.

One of the first to apprise Governor Clinton of the attack was Colonel Levi Pawling from the Third Ulster County Militia. Levi was the father of Albert Pawling. A letter written by the colonel, contained in Clinton's Papers (a collection of the governor's public papers), arrived from Marbletown, New York. Marbletown, also located in Ulster County, was a short distance from the incident. According to Pawling's letter, Caldwell's raid occurred at nine o'clock in the morning. He continued that Colonel John Cantine, also of the Third Ulster County Militia, was at "mumbakers" (probably a reference to Mombaccus, which is the present-day Rochester, New York, located near Wawarsing).

Pawling's letter went on to explain that as events unfolded Cantine sent a messenger to Colonel Albert Pawling to alert him that "the enemy" was attacking Wawarsing. Cantine reported that he heard gunfire and saw smoke coming from the vicinity of several houses in the distance. Albert Pawling rushed his troops to the besieged settlement. Cantine also sent an express to Levi Pawling, imploring him to contact Major Adrian Wynkoop emphasizing that the situation was dire. The attack concluded in about an hour.

Two days after the battle, August 14, 1781, Clinton wrote to Major General Philip Schuyler that the soldiers "took to the houses"[8] to defend the settlement in Wawarsing. Though these soldiers had been no match for Caldwell's superior forces, Clinton felt that this maneuver saved the settlement from destruction. Two hours after the attack, Wynkoop had finally assembled troops to march to the relief of Wawarsing. Perhaps cognizant of the fact that a more significant force of Patriot militia was on their way, the Tory-led raiding party retreated.

In a letter from Colonels Cantine and Pawling to Governor Clinton, the officers told the governor of a deserter who said to them that the forces were closer to four hundred and under the command of Captain Caldwell. The prisoner identified himself as "Vrooman"[9] and shared with his American captors all of the information he knew at the time. Bowker,

Jr., in his pension application, remembered that Vrooman included not only the size of the war party, but the fact that they needed supplies for the journey back to Fort Niagara where the war party originated. When the deserter was interrogated about how the party was able to attack the settlement without being detected, Vrooman confirmed that the raiders had captured two scouts named Burgher [Bowker] and Hine posted near the Delaware River.

In an express letter issued to Levi Pawling from Albert Pawling, details started to emerge about the scope of the attack. Several houses had been torched, including the homes of Johannes G. Hardenbergh, as well as, "Benjamin Bruyn, 2 other Bruyn houses, Rubin DeWitt and several others." John Kettle was the only known casualty on the Wawarsing side, though the raiders stole some fifty horses, cattle, and sheep from the settlement. On the opposing force, several men were wounded and/or killed.

Although urged to pursue the offending party, both Cantine and Albert Pawling decided that it would be prudent to await reinforcement troops. Albert Pawling sent a letter to Levi Pawling requesting he use his influence to convince Colonel Johannes Snyder to help them by dispatching his regiment without delay. Again, according to Clinton's Papers, Cantine and Albert Pawling also reached out to other area officers, including a Colonel Jonathan Elvindorph (Elemendorph), for assistance. "If Elvindorph could arrive quickly enough, all soldiers would set off at about the [time of the] rising of the moon."[10] The plan to pursue Caldwell's war party needed to be delayed; however, due to heavy rain; it was also reported to be a very dark night.

In a letter to Clinton, Levi Pawling complained about the lack of support from Elvindorph and Snyder. He explained that some soldiers arrived, but there were not nearly enough soldiers for the mission. Levi Pawling also questioned the motivation of these men, saying he was unsure of their intentions regarding marching in pursuit of the war party. He wrote, "Such Deadness of Military Spirit I never saw before. I think an Inquiry into such conduct ought to be made."[11] Meanwhile, the war party kept moving to place greater distance between pursuing troops and themselves.

Sometime during the morning of August 13, 1781, additional reinforcements arrived from both Marbletown and Rochester. Cantine's already exhausted soldiers were bolstered by some two hundred fresh troops, with other men journeying over the mountain from New Paltz. According to historian Ralph LeFevre, the total forces contained about four hundred soldiers.

They struck out in pursuit of Caldwell and his Native American allies. At one point they came within striking distance of the fleeing raiders and Silas Bowker Jr., reported that the troops were victorious in reclaiming some of the plunder. However, rather than give up the horses or cattle, the Native Americans shot them all. Bowker reported that they again caught up with the fleeing raiding party at the Beaver Kill, but Caldwell and his confederates successfully eluded them yet again. Clinton, meanwhile, kept apprised of the unfolding situation. In a letter to General Schuyler he again warned that the members of the war party were probably well-provisioned. He thought that they might attempt more mischief along "the frontier." Clinton also sent separate letters to other leaders. In the letters, he issued the following request ordering out part of a brigade to Schoharie "until we have certain advices that this Party have left our frontiers."[12]

Silas Bowker Sr. and Philip Hines were taken back to Montreal where they were kept prisoners. Fearing they were going to be killed by their captors, they hatched a plan to escape. According to at least one source, they took turns digging a tunnel out of the cabin where they were imprisoned. They hid their work by covering the hole with lose floorboards. Eventually they were able to make a run for it. More than a year after his capture, Silas Bowker Sr. entered a tavern then located at the corner of modern-day Route 209 and Mettacahonts Road in Accord, New York, in Ulster County. He walked into a town meeting that was being conducted and, needless to say, many of his neighbors were surprised to see him. Today, there is a New York, State Education Department (NYSED) historic sign commemorating the event. The year 1779 is wrong. With his regained freedom, Silas Sr. left the Rochester area in Ulster County. According to Margaret Thompson's article on Silas Bowker, and Joanne Doster's account in *Pioneer Families of Barry County, Michigan*, he moved to Norwich, New York where he died in 1789. He is buried in Kirkwood Cemetery.

Silas Bowker Jr., continued to serve on the frontier. When his current enlistment expired, he signed up again on March 1, 1782, in Colonel Cantine's regiment. He continued to work as a spy in the same general area where his father had been taken hostage. After the war, Silas married and eventually moved to bounty lands in Cayuga County. He died in 1834, two years after his pension application. His wife Amy filed to claim her late husband's pension.

Caldwell's partisan attacks lasted well into 1782 when he was victorious at Upper Sandusky in Ohio. During this battle, Caldwell was severely wounded again, shot through both legs. The Revolutionary War came to an end for Caldwell with the signing of the Treaty of Paris in 1783.

After the war, Caldell was granted lands in Upper Canada along with other Loyalists. Eventually, he became a merchant in Amherstburg in Ontario, Canada. He served England again during the War of 1812. After the Treaty of Ghent, he continued his life as a merchant until his death on February 20, 1822, in Amherstburg.

Shortly after the attack, people living in the area of the modern-day Kerhonkson bridge reported seeing the ghost of John Kettle. Locals stated that it was during a full moon with a slight breeze, and almost only in the summer. How do we know it is Kettle? Those who remembered him in life recognized him. Most of the time, he appeared on the western side of the bridge that spans the Rondout. It seems that Kettle is trying to cross the Rondout Creek, perhaps trying to get to safety.

# A Massacre at the Hands of
# Mohawk Chief Joseph Brant

*Our future security will be in their inability to injure us . . . and in
the terror with which the severity of the chastisement they receive will
inspire them.*[13]

GENERAL GEORGE WASHINGTON

"Dear Sir, I am sorry to inform you that this morning just as I was marching my Regt., From this place I Rec'd an acc't that several Houses were
burnt at the Fantine Kill."[14] The opening letter from Colonel Philip van
Cortlandt of the Second New York to Governor George Clinton in Newburgh did not paint an encouraging picture. Colonel van Cortlandt wrote
his letter from the frontier of Western Ulster County in the Rondout Valley. The attack, it was believed, had been carried out by a Mohawk raiding
party under Thayendanegea, better known as Joseph Brant.

Brant became a close ally of the British before the American Revolution. His brother-in-law was Sir William Johnson, the British Superintendent of Indian Affairs for the Northern District, a position he held
from 1756 until his death in 1774. Sir Johnson made every effort to not
only learn the language of the Mohawks but their customs as well. When
his first wife died, Johnson married into the Mohawks by taking Molly
Brant, Joseph's sister, as his wife.

Molly continued to solidify the alliance between her people and England. It is believed she even worked as a spy funneling information to the
English in order to help them crush the colonial rebellion. Molly most
likely had knowledge of her brother leaving the Mohawk Valley toward

George Clinton / National Portrait Gallery, Washington, DC

Ulster County on a raiding expedition in Wawarsing, New York. He had between thirty and forty warriors with him.

Wawarsing in 1779, considered part of the frontier in New York State, had various local militia and Continental Army patrolling the frontier in the hopes of thwarting or even preventing attacks. "The raids crippled the

American Continental Army by depriving it of food and manpower and spread terror by destroying frontier settlements and taking prisoners."[15] This forced some settlements to be abandoned for a time. One of the more notorious raids occurred in the morning on May 4, 1779, in the small settlement along the banks of the Fantine Kill Stream. Some believe the attack on Fantine Kill was an attempt by Brant to keep the Continental Army from attacking those Iroquois settlements loyal to the British.

New York Governor George Clinton was concerned about the state of the frontier in Ulster County. In a letter to General George Washington in October 1778, he pleaded for more help from Washington.

*I find it impossible to secure the Frontier Settlements against the Depredations of the Enemy by the utmost Exertions I am able to make with the Militia and I am lead to fear that unless some effectual Check can be given to their Operations, exclusive of the Distresses which they bring on Individuals (who more immediately suffer by them) they will sensibly affect the Public as the last Settlements they have destroyed usually afforded greater Supplies of Grain than any other of equal Extent in the State.*[16]

Colonel Philip van Cortlandt commanded the Continental Army's Second New York Regiment. Later, he also would be part of Sullivan's Expedition against the Iroquois during the summer of 1779. Colonel van Cortlandt wrote in his memoir that because of the threat to the frontier, his troops stationed on the east side of the Hudson River, in Poughkeepsie, New York, were ordered to march to Western Ulster. The colonel started transporting troops across the Hudson and from there marched to Rochester in Ulster County. They continued to Laghawack and ultimately to a blockhouse for safety. His orders changed again when General Washington instructed him to advance to Fort Penn where he would report to Major General John Sullivan. Colonel van Cortlandt waited at the blockhouse until Colonel John Cantine's militia relieved the Second New York and continued protecting the frontier.

Colonel van Cortlandt, on May 4, 1779, called in his guards. Soldiers were striking their tents for the long march. Their destination was the

Wyoming Valley. Once there they were to await further orders. In his journal, Lieutenant John Leonard Hardenbergh an officer in the Second New York recorded that May 1 was a Saturday in 1779. Two days before the attack, his troops were emerging from winter quarters in Wawarsing. His troops spent the winter in a field near a local's home. On May 3, he ordered his troops to draw provisions to prepare for a march to the Wyoming Valley in Pennsylvania, but before they could leave for the Wyoming Valley, where the year before there had been a massacre of Patriots by Loyalists and their Native American allies, an express arrived with word of the attack on Fantine Kill. The express stated, "the savages were murdering the inhabitants at Fantine Kill, about five miles in our front."[17] Hardenbergh figured the raiding party came by way of Grahamsville and from there moved on the tiny settlement along the banks of the Fantine Kill. Colonel van Cortlandt led the expedition to rescue the besieged settlements. He would also take the lead in the pursuit of the raiding party. A fatal mistake for the party is that they believed the soldiers were already on the march. Hardenbergh's journal clearly spoke of the mistake.

Just before dawn on May 4, 1779, the Bevier family slept in their home. In a slaveholding family such as this, it was not unusual for the slaves to be up before the family to begin the day's work of cooking as well as other chores. One of the Bevier slaves named Robert heard some commotion outside. When he opened the door to investigate, he saw the raid unfolding before his eyes. The Bevier home, as well as the nearby Sax family, was under attack. His instinct told him to run, which he did. Local stories say that a Native American hurled a tomahawk at the man, hitting him. Severely wounded, Robert continued to run even after being additionally wounded by musket shots. The screaming and gunshots woke both the Sax and Bevier families.

Widow Bevier and her sons were victims in the attack. Her daughter, Magdalene, somehow escaped detection fleeing with another individual to the safety of the home's cellar. Feeling they might survive the attack, they huddled in the cellar but became alarmed when they smelled smoke. The alarm became panic as they felt the heat of a fire. They quickly realized that the raiding party had torched the home. Only through quick thinking did the two women escape, climbing through a cellar window and finding safety in some woods nearby. After setting Widow Bevier's house ablaze, the Mohawks turned their fury on the home of Michael Sax.

Local sources place the blame for the attack on Abraham Jansen and his father. His neighbors were always suspicious of him as a possible loyal subject to the King of England. They believed that he tipped the raiding party off and to the vulnerability of the settlement. This is because his home, which was close to the raid, escaped harm. Finally, the family was conspicuously absent during the raid as if they knew it was going to happen. Most of this information is anecdotal in nature and can't be proven or disproven one way or the other. Some reported that they believed Jansen's daughter-in-law also had advance notice of the attack. Neighbors remembered that days before the attack, she was conspicuously absent from the settlement, which seemed unusual. Additionally, many neighbors reported seeing Native Americans on more than one occasion at the elder Jansen's home. It was believed by Jansen's neighbors that the family were Loyalists. It was never confirmed, and most of the information is anecdotal. They wanted the rebellion in the colonies to be crushed in order to restore English rule. We shall see in later chapters that English recruiters sometimes made promises to citizens who helped the king. This ranged from money to land.

Colonel van Cortlandt also suspected that a spy gave intelligence to the attacking party that descended on Fantine Kill. He believed someone must have given Butler's troops advance notice that the settlement was relatively undefended, and that that information was passed on to Brant. He believed it was two unnamed men who had deserted from the American militia. There is no reason to believe that he thought it was Abraham Jansen and his father who betrayed the settlement.

When Brant attacked, he believed the troops guarding the settlements and patrolling the frontier had been gone for several days. Instead Colonel van Cortlandt marched to the relief of Fantine Kill. In a letter to Governor Clinton, Colonel van Cortlandt wrote that he saw the enemy two times and got close enough to personally identify Brant. In the same letter on the day of the attack, van Cortlandt wrote that he believed that the raiding party contained roughly thirty to forty individuals. His information was elicited from a settler taken prisoner by the party and later released. When the soldiers were seen approaching Fantine Kill, the Mohawk raiding party fled.

The next day the soldiers pursued the warriors. Colonel van Cortlandt eventually overtook Brant and his warriors but was unable to surround them because they were on a mountain. He told Governor Clinton that they "exchanged several long shots with them, but they made their escape."[18] Willima L. Stone, in his book entitled *Life of Joseph*

Joseph Brant (Thayendanegea) / National Portrait Gallery, Washington, DC

*Brant-Thayendanegea*, described that while in pursuit of the warriors, van Cortlandt decided to take a break to figure out his next move. He chose to stand in the shade of a large pine tree not realizing that Brant, a short distance away, could easily see him. Brant called for one of his warriors, whom he knew to be an excellent shot with a rifle. Brandt pointed out the colonel standing next to the pine tree, and, taking careful aim, the Mohawk warrior fired. At that moment, van Cortlandt slightly moved his head. He remembered the rifle ball missed his head by roughly three inches.

Realizing that the raiding party remained close, they renewed the chase. It finally ended when the retreating Mohawks detoured through a vast swamp, which made it impossible for the troops to pursue them. Frustrated, the Second New York returned to camp. While still in retreat, the Mohawk raiding party stopped to attack Woodstock, New York, also in Ulster County. They reportedly burned several houses and obtained badly needed provisions for their journey back home.

On May 5, 1779, van Cortlandt finally left for Wyoming Valley, allowing Colonel Cantine, who arrived the same day of the massacre, to take up the chase as well as the defense of the Ulster frontier. Unfortunately, Colonel Cantine's troops were slow in arriving. Even with Cantine's troops, they were dangerously understaffed. In response, Governor Clinton ordered: "1/4 part of Hardenbergh's & McClaughy's Regt to join Col. Cantine & the like proportion of the three northern Regts of Orange to such posts on the frontiers."[19]

Growing frustrated with the depredations of the Native Americans and Loyalists, Washington wrote the following to General Sullivan on May 31, 1779,

> *The Expedition you are appointed to command is to be directed against the hostile tribes of the Six Nations of Indians, with their associates and adherents. The immediate objects are the total destruction and devastation of their settlements, and the capture of as many prisoners of every age and sex as possible. It will be essential to ruin their crops now in the ground and prevent their planting more.*
>
> *I would recommend, that some post in the center of the Indian*

*Country, should be occupied with all expedition, with a sufficient quantity of provisions whence parties should be detached to lay waste all the settlements around, with instructions to do it in the most effectual manner, that the country may not be merely overrun, but destroyed.*

*But you will not by any means listen to any overture of peace before the total ruinment of their settlements is effected. Our future security will be in their inability to injure us and in the terror with which the severity of the chastisement they receive will inspire them.*[20]

Command of the expedition was given to General Sullivan, with General James Clinton serving as his second in command. "The fact that four brigades of Continental troops totaling around 4,469 men were earmarked for this expedition underlines just how important the Americans felt this enterprise was."[21] The purpose was to stop the attacks by Loyalists and their Native American allies. Sullivan executed the total war on the Iroquois, forcing many Iroquois to retreat to Canada for safety. After his campaign, their power was mostly broken.

Meanwhile, after the Fantine Kill attack, the bodies of those slain were gathered up and buried in common graves, "on a hill above the Fantinekill." The *Kingston Daily Freeman* recorded, in 1903, "roughly lettered slabs of blue stone [were] placed at the graves."[22] Prior to 1903, the cemetery became overgrown through neglect. Some of the headstones disappeared including one that was incorporated into a sidewalk. In 1903, most of the original stones were located and reset where people believed the originals had been. A piece of Shawangunk Conglomerate was cut for a monument with a bronze plaque commemorating the massacre and those killed.

# THE UPPER HUDSON

# The Convention Army Travels South after Saratoga

*Is it not enough that I give you shelter, ye wretched royalists?*[23]

COLONEL JONATHAN HASBROUCK

Lieutenant-General John Burgoyne surrendered to Major General Horatio Gates on October 17, 1777, at Saratoga. It was the first time a British officer surrendered his sword to the rebels. The three-pronged attack to defeat the Patriots came crashing down on that day. General Washington, who was not present, was elated. In a letter to Gates, he wrote:

> *Sir: By this Opportunity, I do myself the pleasure to congratulate you on the signal success of the Army under your command, in compelling Genl. Burgoyne and his whole force, to surrender themselves prisoners of War. An Event that does the highest honor to the American Arms, and which, I hope, will be attended with the most extensive and happy consequences.*[24]

After the defeat, the terms of the surrender needed to be ironed out. This surrender was to become known as the Convention, and the army that came under the terms of surrender became known as the Convention Army. It consisted of some five thousand British soldiers plus camp followers.

"The troops under Lieutenant-General Burgoyne, to march out of their camp with the honours of war, and the artillery of the entrenchments, to the verge of the river where the old fort stood, where the arms and artillery are to be left; the arms to be piled by word of command from their own officers"[25] read the first article of the Convention. It continued, "a free passage to be granted to the army under Lieutenant-General Burgoyne to Great Britain, on condition of not serving again in North America during the present contest; and the port of Boston is assigned for the entry of transports to receive the troops, whenever General William Howe shall so order."[26] General William Howe was the commander in chief of the land forces for the British. His brother Admiral Richard Howe was Admiral of the Fleet for England.

These articles of capitulation included more than two thousand Hessians. The Convention Army marched under an American guard to Boston and then Cambridge. While America and Britain continued to work out the details of the articles of capitulation, which continued well after the battle. An early issue occurred when British ships arrived outside Boston Harbor to ferry the defeated British troops back to England were refused entrance to the harbor by Boston authorities. In fact, at the local level, Boston did not want the Convention troops to be housed in Boston because of the still simmering anger over the Siege of Boston. On the broader national level, there were problems with ratifying the Convention. This is because the English and the Americans did not trust each other to sign the document in good faith. By 1779, British troops, including the Hessian forces, were sent south through Connecticut, New York, New Jersey, Pennsylvania, and eventually exited in Virginia. The account of the Hessians' ordeal found a voice in the diary of Lady Riedesel, wife of Major General Friedrich von Riedesel.

Frederika Charlotte Louise von Massow, Lady (Freifrau) Riedesel was born on July 11, 1746, in Brandenburg in what is today Germany. She was born to "Hans Jürgen Detloff von Massow, a lieutenant-general in the Prussian army and commissary-in-chief under Frederick II, King of Prussia, and Miss von Crausee."[27]

The baroness met her future husband Friedrich Adolph Riedesel when she was thirteen years old and he was twenty-one years old. According to several biographies, it was an arranged marriage. Adolph was "a captain in the Brunswick cavalry and aide-de-camp to the Duke of Brunswick." The couple would have nine children, of whom three did not reach maturity.

According to one of her servants, and quoted in *Canadian Biography*, the baroness was "very young, very good-looking."[28]

What brought the baron to America were the colonies, which were, by 1776, in full rebellion, but had not declared their independence yet from England. King George III hired soldiers who "were principally drawn from the German state of Hesse-Cassel [Hessians], although soldiers from other German states also saw action in America."[29] One of those other German states was Brunswick where Riedesel was part of the army. He left his wife and young children behind to sail to Canada in the winter of 1776. His wife left four months later for England to eventually join her husband, bringing with her three young children, including a newborn. Knowing she to be forceful and not afraid to speak her mind, her husband wrote to Frederika shortly before she left for America, "You have the best character in the world . . . but often are so unreasonable as not to hide the hate which you have for important men, and you speak in the presence of everybody . . . you know that we have many enemies and people profit by your frankness and intrigue against you and me."[30]

She would be detained in England for almost a year before finally catching up with the army in August 1777, in time to accompany her husband during the ill-fated Burgoyne Campaign. She would witness firsthand the Battle of Saratoga. By this time, the baron had been promoted to Major General.

What became known as the turning point in the American Revolution started on September 19, 1777. The baroness recorded in her diary,

> *When we marched on I had a large calash [light carriage] readied, with room for myself and the three children and my two maids; thus I followed the army right in the midst of the soldiers, who sang and were jolly, burning with the desire for victory.*[31]

When the Battle of Freeman Farms commenced, she recorded, "I saw the whole battle myself, and, knowing that my husband was taking part in it, I was filled with fear and anguish and shivered whenever a shot was fired. . . ."[32] During the battle, she not only comforted wounded soldiers and officers, but their wives, if with them, who also needed support.

John Burgoyne / National Portrait Gallery, Washington, DC

On September 19, 1777, Burgoyne's columns collided with part of General Gates's army near the abandoned farm of Loyalist John Freeman. During the long afternoon, the British were unable to maintain any initiative or momentum. Pinned in place, they suffered galling American gunfire as they strove to hold their lines. Late in the day, reinforcements of German auxiliary troops turned the tide for Burgoyne's beleaguered forces. Driven from the battlefield, the British had suffered heavy casualties and Gates's army still blocked Burgoyne's move south to Albany. On this same day, Reidsel and his forces attacked Gates's troop's right flank. It is because of Reidsel that the British won the first day of fighting.

Lieutenant General Burgoyne needed to make a move soon. His supplies were running low and the morale of the troops was beginning to be affected. Meanwhile, in the American camp, Gates's and the American army were behind fortifications on Bemis Heights, which gave them an excellent position. He argued daily with Major General Benedict Arnold, who believed they should attack the combined forces of the Hessians and British. Gates demurred, and out of frustration, relieved Arnold of his command. The second Battle of Saratoga known as the Battle of Bemis Heights commenced on October 7, 1777, when the British tried to break through the American lines. Early in the battle, Brigadier General Simon Fraser was shot by one of Colonel Daniel Morgan's Virginia riflemen. These frontiersmen known as Morgan's riflemen were crack shots with a rifle. They were used as sharpshooters picking off British and Hessian officers to spread confusion in the British ranks. Mortally wounding Fraser is credited with helping to turn the tide at Saratoga in favor of the Americans. Fraser would be cared for by the baroness and Fraser's wife.

The baroness was sent by her husband to the Marshall House, which was part of a family farm. It was owned by the Lansing family in 1777. The family built the home about 7 years earlier. It was purchased by the Marshall family in the nineteenth century. The baroness was sent to the home for protection from the American bombardment. The house would be turned into a makeshift hospital as wounded came flooding in, overwhelming the doctors. Frederika was "ever relieving and comforting the sick the wounded and the dying." In the basement of this house, she sought protection from American shelling for six days. She wrote about the Marshall house in her diary:

> We were at last obliged to resort to the cellar for refuge, and in one corner of this I remained the whole day, my children sleeping on the earth with their heads in my lap; and in the same situation I passed a sleepless night. Eleven [cannon balls] passed through the house, and we could distinctly hear them roll away. One poor soldier who was lying on a table for the purpose of having his leg amputated, was struck by a shot, which carried away his other; his comrades had left him, and

*when we went to his assistance we found him in a corner of the room, into which he had crept, more dead than alive, scarcely breathing.*[33]

The home was heavily bombarded because the American's saw a lot of activity around the home. They believed it was part of the British defense and began shelling it. Several cannon balls went straight through the home.

On October 16, 1777, it was inevitable that the British and their Hessian allies were going to surrender. This finally came on October 17, 1777. After the surrender at Saratoga, the baroness was invited to the American headquarters to dine with Burgoyne and Gates along with her husband. It is here she met Major General Philip Schuyler. He insisted she and her family stay at his home in Albany along with General Burgoyne. She remained there for two days when by way of Schuyler's coach, she made the journey to Boston. In her diary, the baroness wrote of how she found herself overcome with emotion that General Schuyler had opened his home to the very army that burned his country house after being occupied by the British during their retreat. After a brief stay in Boston, the baroness and her whole family moved to Cambridge located outside Boston when ratification of the Convention started to break down. This was

Philip Schuyler House / HABS/HAER Library of Congress, Washington, DC

due to mutual distrust between the American and the British. Burgoyne left for England, in the spring of 1778 in order to move the process forward leaving the Convention army in and around Boston.

The Riedesel family made their way, in December 1778, to Fishkill where they crossed the Hudson River with great difficulty and anxiety. Before crossing, they stayed at the house of the boatman. Frederika complained about the lack of necessary supplies that added to her comfort such as tea, coffee, or sugar. Adding to their misery, they had to wait to cross the Hudson because of a bad storm, and the boatman believed it not safe to make the crossing during the storm, possibly in respect to the boatman's wife. Colonel Robert Troup, a veteran of the Battle of Long Island in 1776, served under General Gates in Saratoga as his aide-de-camp. He was chosen by Gates to escort the Convention army south. He also protected the baroness from the populace that held a lot of anger toward the Hessians. Troup wrote in a letter to General Gates of the difficulties with the local populace. According to David Head, an historian affiliated with Mount Vernon Historic Site, it was because the Hessians were known to plunder the Americans. It "made the Hessians unpopular with Americans."[34] He continued that "Hessian plundering often pushed neutral or indifferent Americans to the Patriot side." Troup accompanied the defeated British army as far as New Jersey when another officer continued south with the army.

When they were able to cross the Hudson, it took almost five hours. Once finally across the river at Newburgh, "We were still obliged to wade up to the knees through a morass, still we came to the home of a Colonel Harbon[Hasbrouck]—a very rich man, where we were to lodge."[35] She arrived at Colonel Jonathan Hasbrouck's home on December 19, 1778. Colonel Hasbrouck's brother Abraham, who lived north of Jonathan in the state capital of Kingston wrote in 1778 that it was the coldest winter on record mostly because of the temperature being so low for so long and also accompanied by large snow falls. Locals took to calling it "the Cold Sabbath." The winter of 1777–1778 would become known as one of the coldest on record in Newburgh as well. When she and her family finally made their way to the fieldstone home, she reported being soaked to the bone.

The winter deepened on January 26, 1778, when the Hudson River froze for much of the winter, and the brutal winter caused much hardship and suffering among the population in Newburgh already making tremendous sacrifices because of the war. The baroness wrote in her diary that many roads were almost impassable, and storms made travel miserable.

The room that would be her quarters, which she shared with her three children and two maids, was small by her standards. Her husband had remained across the Hudson River with his troops until they all made the crossing. The family was also forced to share their lodgings throughout the day with "the adjutants who had to take breakfast, dinner and tea" in the room. This would be in addition to the Hasbrouck family and their slaves.

The room she described was most likely the Hasbrouck parlor, which was about "20 feet square." The parlor is the newest part of the Hasbrouck house built about 1770. Historians know this because there is a date stone outside the front door. It was a formal English-style parlor with the "east wall consisting of wood paneling, paneled doors, and a moulded wood mantel . . . the fireplace was English."[36]

The baroness and her family stayed at the Hasbrouck home for about eight days to give the troops time to cross the Hudson River. It took so

Hasbrouck House (Newburgh) Parlor / HABS/HAER Library of Congress, Washington, DC

long because many of the boats were not considered sturdy and there were not enough of them for the job at hand. They also had to dodge ice floes as the Hudson was probably beginning to freeze over from the intense cold.

Robert Boyd Jr. was an early member of of the New Windsor Committee of Safety and Observation. He also was the chairman of the County Committee for Ulster County. In a letter to Governor George Clinton on December 25, 1778, Boyd wrote that he did not know the cause for the delay. He explained to Clinton in regard to the delay in the Hessians leaving the area, "the reasons for his delay I do not know."[37] When he composed the letter, they had been at the Hasbrouck home for almost a week. Boyd, like many Patriots, was anxious to see the troops, especially the Hessians leave as soon as possible.

There remains some controversy about whether the Hessian family did in fact stay at the Hasbrouck home. The issues revolve around the interpretation of the name Hasbrouck. In the baroness's diary, it appears as Osborn, which there was a Doctor Osborn across the Hudson near Fishkill. However, in *The Public Papers of Governor George Clinton*, a letter between Boyd and Governor Clinton reads, "There is a certain Hessian Genl. belonging to the Convention Troops, who came on to Fish [kill] about two weeks ago...." Boyd wrote the message on December 25, 1778, which would mean they arrived around or on December 12, 1778, which in turn would mean his wife remained on the Eastern Shore of the Hudson River for some five days before crossing to the home of "Colonel Hausbrock's,"[38] which is the name that Boyd uses in his letter to Clinton.

Those historians who believe the Lady Riedesel and her family did reside for a time at the Hasbrouck house have made the stay a focal point of the history of the home. It is often written about out of interest, as well as to offer insight into the persona of Jonathan Hasbrouck.

Hasbrouck was from a prominent family who founded New Paltz in the 1670s. Born in 1722, he was one of the early founders of the Committee of Safety in Newburgh. When the Patriot militia came together, he was appointed a Colonel of the Fourth Ulster Regiment by the New York Provincial Congress on October 25, 1775. Frequently, Hasbrouck worked on the fortifications at Fort Montgomery or was stationed at Fort Constitution as well as locations such as Sidman's Bridge. In addition to his soldiering, Hasbrouck also was a wealthy merchant who owned a large amount of property, storehouses, and sloops on the Hudson River within view of the Hudson Highlands and across from Fishkill Mountain. Finally, Hasbrouck owned mills. His farm and mills, according to Conraedt J. Elemedorph, Assistant Commissary of Purchases for the District of the Counties of Ulster and Orange in the Northern Department, Hasbrouck provided large amounts of supplies.

When Hasbrouck met the Riedesels, he was recovering from an illness that prevented him from marching to the relief of Kingston when it burned in 1777. In his brother Abraham's diary, he recorded that the illness was due to exposure at Fort Montgomery. Because of his failing health, he resigned his commission as a Colonel in the Ulster Fourth Militia in May 1778. One thing for sure, Jonathan harbored no love for the Hessians who were about to invade his domicile.

The Riedesel family was instructed to stop briefly at the Hasbrouck home and continue as soon as possible on their journey south. Boyd, in the same letter from December 25, 1778, to Governor Clinton, wrote that he was becoming quite alarmed at the behavior of the baron while in the area. If we are to believe the word of Boyd, the baron was attempting to stir up the Tories in the area. After an appeal for direction from General Washington, the decision was made for the family to be ushered along as quickly as possible. Most accounts of the Riedesels' stay at the Hasbrouck's home focus not on the tense situation of having a very charismatic officer in the area and his attempts to stir up trouble, but on the interaction between the baroness and Jonathan Hasbrouck.

Lady Riedesel was anything but impressed when she first met Jonathan Hasbrouck, although he was listed as one of the wealthiest men in Newburgh. When she met him, he was well enough to not only walk around the house but also to be out and about managing his properties and business interests. His improving health must have come about shortly before her arrival, because as of October 1777, he had not been well enough to visit with Governor Clinton at Fort Montgomery nor had he been well enough to march to the relief of Kingston.

When the baroness first saw Colonel Hasbrouck, she believed he had just arrived from working in the fields. She remembered he was wearing "coarse cloth garments," He had a long beard, and clothing looking sweaty as well as dirty. She felt he looked more like a bear than a person. His appearance rather unsettled her, and "we trembled before him."[39] Men during this period were expected to be clean-shaven, especially officers. Many men wore what was considered a work shirt that also doubled, in some cases, as a nightshirt. Many times, a waistcoat was worn over the work shirt to avoid the display of stains. Either Hasbrouck did not expect there to be guests in the house or he did not respect them enough to change into proper attire.

After Hasbrouck left the parlor, he continued to the other side of the house where, upon entering his kitchen, saw the baron's aides-de-camps warming themselves in front of the Dutch Jambless fireplace. According to Walter C. Anthony, a local Newburgh historian and descendant of Hasbrouck, when the baroness wished to change or wanted privacy, the German officers went into the kitchen. This is where they first met Colonel Hasbrouck. He stood there a moment looking upon them with complete disdain. Whether she witnessed it or was told about it later, she describes a six-foot, four-inch Hasbrouck walking up to two of the aides and grabbing them by their arms stating, "Is it not enough that I give you shelter, ye wretched royalists?"[40] Some accounts have Hasbrouck kicking the men before throwing them out of the house.

The accounts of Hasbrouck and Tryntje DuBois, his wife, were primarily from the viewpoint of the baroness. In all of the statements about the Riedesels' stay at the house, the interaction between Hasbrouck and the baroness was anything but cordial. She wrote of him with contempt and thought him below her in social standing; however, this did not thwart Hasbrouck's attempts to win her affection, which seemed to be sparked in Hasbrouck when the two first met. His wife, Tryntje, on the other hand, she praised.

When the baroness and Hasbrouck meet again, it was in the parlor. The parlor, when not being used as a bedroom for the family, was used for eating and drinking. According to historian A. Elwood Corning, one time when Tryntje and the baroness were having coffee in the parlor, Hasbrouck stormed in. Remembering his behavior from the day before, the baroness sought to avoid confrontation and tried to excuse herself from the room. As she attempted to exit into the hallway, Hasbrouck blocked her exit, and in the process shut the door. After he shut the door, he observed how uncomfortable she seemed and asked if she was afraid of him?

"Yes sir; but I wish to avoid new incivilities," she continued, "Instead of waxing wroth, he softened; and taking me by the hand, he begged me to sit down again, next to his wife."

Hasbrouck, still holding her hand, continued, "I am not so rude as you imagine," said he, "I like you, and if I were not married, I cannot tell, but I might fall in love with you."

Taken aback by Hasbrouck's forwardness, she retorted, "Do you believe that I would encourage your affection?"

Undeterred, Hasbrouck spoke again, "As for that, we should see. I am very rich; this whole estate is mine; my wife you see, is old; you will do well, therefore, to remain here."[41]

It is essential to point out that his wife Tryntje remained in the room the whole time. There is no record of her reaction or if she tried to step between the two individuals.

There are no other recorded entries about the Hasbrouck family in the baroness's diary. As the winter became colder and snowier, Lord Riedesel formally requested to stay for the winter at the Hasbrouck home, but the Americans denied his request. The feeling being that because of his high rank, social standing, and the fact that he could not control his inflammatory speech, it would be better for him to be forced to continue his journey. Denied his wish to remain in Newburgh, the baron took his family "over the Wallkill . . . to engage Winter Quarters among the High Dutchers; from what I have been inform'd concerning this Gentleman's conversation, since in this neighborhood I think him a dangerous Man."[42] High Dutchers is a reference to those people who originated from the mountain region of Germany.

Governor Clinton took up Boyd's cause in a letter to General Washington. In the letter, he informed Washington that the baron and baroness are fourteen miles west of New Windsor. They hoped to winter among the Germans in the area. Clinton thought, like Boyd, this was a bad idea. In the end all agreed they should continue their journey south.

After leaving the Hasbrouck's home, the family lodged with a "German, where we were well lodged and well fed."[43] They reached "Colle in Virginia," after passing through Connecticut, New York, New Jersey, Pennsylvania, and Maryland, traveling some "678 English miles"[44] in twelve weeks. In the summer of 1779, they were moved from Virginia to New York City. It was while in Virginia they stayed at a farm a short distance from Thomas Jefferson's Monticello.

Early in April 1779, by way of British Major General William Philips, Jefferson was invited to dine with the Riedesel family. They struck up a friendship with the Sage of Monticello. In a letter, the baron thanked Jefferson for all that he did for their family, and he hoped to return the favor one day. Much to their relief, the Riedesel family finally arrived back in their homeland in 1783. The same year the war came to its conclusion and some six years after Saratoga. The baroness published the diary of her time during the American Revolution after her husband had died in 1800. She died eight years later in March of 1808, in Berlin.

This would not be the last distinguished guest the Hasbrouck family would host. In July 1779 another German, one who was strongly aligned with the Patriot cause, stayed at the house. The guest was Baron von Steuben, the drillmaster for the Continental Army. Hasbrouck also hosted Timothy Pickering, the Quartermaster General and his family. Jonathan Hasbrouck did not live long enough to see Washington arrive at his home. He died on July 31, 1780. The ailment that contributed to Jonathan's death is not known for sure. During this time, they treated more symptoms. He could not pass his urine and, because of this, died even after numerous efforts to help him. We know this because his brother Abraham was by Jonathan's bedside as he was dying. In 1782, Tryntje, now a widow, moved out of her home for General George Washington. It is not known for sure where she stayed while General Washington was headquartered in her home. Some believe she occupied a tenant house near the family mills or she returned to her family in New Paltz, New York.

# *Nous y Voici* (We Are Here)

*Nous y voici, and nothing now between us but Gates. I sincerely hope this little success of ours may facilitate your operations.*[45]

GENERAL HENRY CLINTON

The Hudson River begins its journey from Lake Tear of the Clouds atop Mount Marcy in New York's Adirondack Mountains. It ends its 315-mile trip at New York Harbor. The river is navigable only from Albany to New York City. During the eighteenth century, it was a vital waterway linking colonies, towns, and villages. Merchants such as Abraham Hasbrouck of Kingston, his brother Colonel Jonathan Hasbrouck, and countless others used the waterway to ship goods to New York City, and from there, products sometimes continued to the West Indies. This superhighway gained importance during the American Revolution. Both sides saw the river as vital in their efforts to win the war.

Washington realized early that the fate of the war would be decided by whoever won control of the Hudson River. It is a primary reason that Washington attempted to capture New York City during the summer of 1776, an impossible task because he lacked a formidable enough navy. The Continental Army was soundly defeated, and the following year, 1777, Britain launched an ambitious plan to seize the entire Hudson River, which proved to be a disaster.

During the fall of 1777, a three-pronged plan was put into motion to take control of the Hudson. "British troops led by Lieutenant General John Burgoyne planned to drive south from Montreal to Albany, NY along the historic water route of Lake Champlain, Lake George, and the Hudson River."[46] Burgoyne hoped to join forces with two other British commanders: troops coming from New York City under the command of General William Howe and, from the east along the Mohawk River, troops commanded by Brigadier General Barry St. Leger. Once the three forces met in Albany, they would sail down the Hudson River taking control of it. Once under control, the colonies could be divided.

The British believed that the rebellion would collapse if New England could be isolated because they thought that New England was at the heart of the rebellion. Also, the middle colonies being the breadbasket of the colonies contributed large amounts of food and other supplies to New England. Finally, many roads to New England originated near the Hudson River. So, with the Hudson River controlled by the British, New England could be starved out, bringing the war to a quick conclusion. The campaign, however, had problems from the beginning.

General St. Leger was occupied with the siege of Fort Stanwix, which he attacked on August 2, 1777. American Brigadier General Nicholas Herkimer, accompanied by several hundred militiamen and Oneida warriors, marched to the fort's relief. Hearing of the approaching troops, Leger "dispatched Sir John Johnson and about 100 Loyalist light infantry, supplemented by about 400 Mohawks to attack the militia" before it could relieve Stanwix. On August 6, Herkimer and his troops were still several miles from the fort when Johnson with his Mohawks surprised them. During the battle, Herkimer was mortally wounded. Militiamen placed him under a tree from where he continued to direct troop movements. When the campaign concluded, "Herkimer [had] lost almost half his men." A drenching rainstorm placed a halt to the fighting, allowing the general to reorganize his troops. The battle commenced after the downpour stopped.

A messenger arrived at Fort Stanwix describing the urgency of the battle raging about six miles from the fort. "American Lieutenant Colonel Marinus Willett led 250 men out and proceeded to raid the unoccupied British camp,"[47] which created a panic among the Native American allies who retreated to protect their own camp. Once they departed, the attack fell apart. The siege was finally lifted on Fort Stanwix about three weeks later with Major General Benedict Arnold leading a relief party to the fort. Another essential aspect of the attack unraveled, spelling disaster for Burgoyne's expedition.

The Saratoga Campaign was the brainchild of Burgoyne, and one of two plans proposed to Lord George Germain, Secretary of State for the American Colonies. General William Howe suggested another plan. Unfortunately, Germain approved both plans without telling Burgoyne, a decision that had dire consequences for the success of the Campaign of 1777.

Originally, as previously noted, Burgoyne proposed a three-pronged attack whereby St. Leger and Burgoyne would march from Canada. St. Leger would make his way through the Mohawk Valley, meeting Burgoyne in Albany. British General William Howe would sail from New York City up the Hudson, rendezvousing with the other two in Albany. However, in Howe's alternate plan, a small force would remain in New York City under the command of General Sir Henry Clinton, while Howe headed toward Philadelphia with the hopes of distracting Washington from the main armies forming the British attack. This became known as the Philadelphia Campaign. His rationale being that sacking the rebel capital might demoralize the rebels, especially if the force captured members of the Continental Congress. Sir Henry, under Howe's plan, would, it was hoped, create a diversion for Burgoyne. Troops in Saratoga would rush south to meet the threat posed by the British.

Under Burgoyne's plan General Howe was supposed to travel by way of the Hudson River, destroying the first chain across the river and in the process, conquer the twin river forts and rendezvous with Burgoyne in Albany. They would then be in complete control of the Hudson from Albany to New York City.

However, Howe moved ahead with his own plan, deciding to create the diversion by marching toward Philadelphia hoping that Washington would divert troops there, because he would naturally want to protect the American Capital. Howe took the city of Philadelphia in September 1777. Meanwhile, in New York City, he left General Sir Henry Clinton in charge of a relief party for Burgoyne. While the Saratoga Campaign unfolded, work continued by the Americans obstructing the Hudson River.

Fort Montgomery, named after Major General Richard Montgomery, who fell during the invasion of Quebec, was located "adjacent to the creek flowing through Popolopen Gorge." Fort Clinton was situated, according to Jan Sheldon Conley, a local historian and author "across the gorge of the Popolopen,"[48] and afforded Montgomery added protection. Fort Clinton was named in honor of Brigadier General and current New York State Governor, George Clinton. Governor Clinton was placed in charge of both fortifications. However, his brother James commanded Fort Clinton. Lord Stirling, also known as William Alexander, was a Major General in the Coninental Army

He wrote to General Washington in June 1776,

*Fort Montgomery is situated on the West Bank of the River, which is there about half a Mile broad, & the Bank 100 feet high, on the opposite Shore is a point of Land called Anthony's nose which is many hundred feet high, very steep & inaccessible, to any thing but Goats or men, very expert in Climbing; a Body of Riffle Men, placed here would be of very great use, in annoying an Enemy as the Decks of every Vessel that passes, must lie open to them.*[49]

In addition to what was referred to as the twin forts, a chain and boom were strung across the Hudson from the creek to the base of Anthony's Nose, a peak in the Hudson Highlands. This was to keep the British in New York City from sailing up the Hudson River. The area of the River was too wide and the tides would be too strong to support it during an attack. Finally, engineers strategically placed *cheval-de-frise* in the Hudson in case ships were able to sail past the chain. These were large structures filled with rocks, with harpoon-like points jutting out just above the waterline. In theory, they would puncture the hull of a passing ship.

A constant problem in constructing forts involved the use of the militia. There were rarely enough men. When terms of service expired, they left. As articulated by Brigadier General George Clinton, overseeing the construction of the fort, around harvest season the rate of desertion skyrocketed, leaving the fort dangerously understaffed. One such letter written from Fort Montgomery on July 9, 1777, showed this frustration,

*The Militia which I ordered to this Post & who came in with great Expedition almost to a Man according to Custom begin to be extreamly uneasy. They want to go Home, their Corn is Suffering, their Harvest coming on.*[50]

George's brother, James Clinton, was equally in a state of despair over the constant need for troops. Both officers spoke of the stress of the soldiers who, while they were away from their farms and families, were left open to attack by partisans or their Native American allies. When the Saratoga Campaign began to unfold, the forts were far from completed and dangerously undermanned. Although Fort Clinton was built to protect Montgomery, the back of Fort Montgomery, where the terrain was treacherous, was left mostly unguarded. Additionally, with a combined force of six hundred soldiers, both forts were underdefended by troops.

In September 1777, General Sir Henry Clinton dispatched Lieutenant Daniel Taylor to apprise Burgoyne of his intention to attack both Forts Clinton and Montgomery in roughly ten days. As Dean Snow writes in his book, *The Tipping Point*, on Saratoga, the message was coded. A unique hourglass cover needed to be placed over the letter to expose the intelligence from Clinton. He continued that the communication that Taylor carried undoubtedly made him a spy. The belief during this time is if you were in uniform you were a gentleman. If you were caught in civilian clothing you were a spy. Taylor knew that if he was caught and the message deciphered, the Americans would certainly execute him. The information he carried not only was committed to memory but written on a piece of paper encased in a silver "bullet" about the size of a small musket ball. It included two halves that fit nicely together and secured with a screw in the middle. Taylor concealed the capsule in his jacket pocket. Usually, more than one express made such a dangerous trip leaving at different times and using various routes to increase the chances of success. Once given time to eat and rest. Taylor made the return to the Highlands.

Burgoyne became hopeful that British General Sir Henry Clinton's foray up the Hudson would draw troops away from American General Horatio Gates's troops massing near Saratoga. He felt with so much at stake to the south, Gates would have no choice but to divert resources to protect Albany and the Hudson River. Once again, as several historians have pointed out, Sir Clinton did not have that large of a force, Howe had taken most of the troops toward Philadelphia.

On October 5, 1777, British troops "made several landings below Peek's Kill,"[51] as Major General William Heath recorded in his memoirs. British troops feigning an attack placed General Israel Putnam on the defense at nearby Fort Independence. Anticipating an attack, Putnam refused to send requested reinforcements to American General George Clinton, who was in command of Fort Montgomery. When it became apparent that Forts Clinton and Montgomery were the intended targets, it was too late for Putnam to send relief to the forts. His brother James Clinton was commanding defenses at Fort Clinton. Heath also points out that the flank of Fort Montgomery still needed to be completed.

The attack occurred in the late afternoon and early evening of October 7, 1777. Richard Severo, a journalist, writes the battle was particularly nasty. A combined force of three thousand British regulars, Loyalists and Hessians, marched over the unprotected west flank of Forts Clinton and Montgomery. The superior British forces quickly overtook the woefully limited American troops. Once the British overpowered the forts, troops moved to destroy the chain across the Hudson. The *cheval-de-frise* that acted as a secondary defense failed as the British warships passed over unscathed. The Hudson between New York City and Albany now belonged to the British.

Many of the soldiers fled to escape capture when the twin river forts capitulated. Those who died were dumped in a pond by the British. General George Clinton wrote the following to General George Washington after the battle,

*My Brother Wounded with a Bayonet many Officers and Men, and myself, having the Advantage of the Enemy, by being well acquainted with the Ground, were so fortunate as to effect an Escape under cover of the Night, after the Enemy were possessed of all the Works. I was so happy as to get into a Boat, crossed the River, and immediately waited on General Putnam, with a View of concerting measures for our future Operations, to prevent the Designs of Genl Clinton and impede his Progress in facilitating the Movements of Burgoyne from the Northward.*[52]

The fleeing troops ultimately made it to Little Britain where the Clinton brothers lived. They were headed to Falls House, which was owned by George Clinton's cousin. Those "troops who escaped from the forts as well as the militia of the district that had not been engaged, were rendezvoused in the vicinity and re-organized prior to their march for the defence of Kingston."[53]

Falls House was located in an area known as Little Britain Square because four public roads created a square. The home, according to Benson John Lossing, a nineteenth-century historian on the American Revolution, occupied the right side of what then was called the New Windsor Road, at the southeastern angle of the square. Still, later troops named it Washington Square in honor of George Washington. The home belonged to Mrs. Falls and her first husband Alexander who tragically died while inspecting his mill. Sometimes the home was referred to as the Wood's House because she remarried. On Simeon Dewitt's 1783 map the home is labeled the Wood's House.

After the destruction of Forts Montgomery and Clinton, Henry Clinton sent two messengers to Burgoyne, who was encamped near Saratoga. It was probably in reply to Burgoyne's frantic plea for reinforcements. The two men sent were Captain Campbell and First Lieutenant Daniel Taylor of Stewart's Company of the Ninth Royal Regiment. According to one account, Taylor, on October 10, 1777, approached the advanced American guard on horseback that were reorganizing at the Falls House. As Taylor approached on his horse, he did not show caution because he thought the advanced guard belonged to the British. Little did he know, that the these soldiers had stolen British uniforms and had not changed the color from red. The guards who asked Taylor to stop were, in fact, Americans dressed in British uniforms. Fooled by the uniforms and believing they were members of Sir Henry Clinton's troops, Taylor responded: "I am a friend and wish to see General Clinton."[54]

Complying with his request, the American guards marched Taylor in to see General George Clinton. One can only imagine Taylor's surprise when he realized the dreadful mistake he made confusing the American George Clinton with Sir Henry Clinton. There were so many Clintons even soldiers became confused. Realizing the position, he was currently in, thinking quickly, Taylor pulled the silver bullet with the encoded message from his pocket and swallowed it. George Clinton, witnessing this attempt at hiding the silver bullet, sent for Dr. Moses Higby to come to the Falls House. Higby lived nearby and the home still stands at the current intersection of Union and Cedar Streets in New Windsor, New York.

When Higby finally arrived, he forced a potent tartar emetic down Taylor's throat. It worked, and the prisoner violently threw up the ball. He scooped it up quickly and again swallowed the capsule. Enraged, Clinton advised Taylor that if he did not give up the capsule that he would order him hanged and disemboweled. Clinton asked him which he preferred. The emetic again or disembowelment? Taylor decided to swallow Higby's emetic yet again. He produced the capsule and this time, he allowed the officers to look at what it contained.

Clinton opened the capsule, it read:

*nous y voici, and nothing now between us but Gates. I sincerely hope this little success of ours may facilitate your operations. In answer to your letters of the 28th Sept., by C.C., I shall only say, I cannot presume to order, or even advise, for reasons obvious. I heartily wish you success. Faithfully Yours H. Clinton*[55]

General Clinton demanded his prisoner come clean with all the information he had. While integrating Taylor he tricked him into believing that American forces had already caught Captain Campbell, also sent by Henry Clinton, but by another route. The American general hoped to compare the information and see if there was any more to be gleaned from Taylor. Taylor hoped, perhaps, to save his own skin and decided to start cooperating with Clinton.

Daniel Taylor was cognizant of the fact that as an officer apprehended with a message, and not in uniform, he likely would be considered a spy.

Once tried, he would most likely hang, but there was always the chance of mercy. Taylor pleaded that he was ordered by Sir Clinton to avoid the American camp. In his confession in General George Clinton's papers, Taylor stated, "I left Fort Montgomery in the evening, with a charge from General Clinton to go to General Burgoyne and acquaint him that he had landed about five miles below the fort. . . ."[56] Taylor continued that the obstructions in the river were almost all removed, and that Burgoyne could go forward or back. He also emphasized again to his interrogators that he was instructed to avoid the American camp and that he only entered the camp by accident when he saw the American's in British uniforms. So, by his logic, it was he who was tricked. If he knew they were part of an American guard, clearly, he would have avoided them as ordered. Taylor asserted numerous times he was a messenger and not a spy.

American forces decided to confine Taylor to the Falls House. He tried to escape but was quickly apprehended. George Clinton ordered the prisoner be placed under a heavy guard. Where he was lodged in the house is not stated. On October 14, 1777, a general court-martial assembled on the heights of New Windsor. According to the New Windsor town historian Glenn T. Marshall, this would have occurred on the east side of the present-day State Route 9W above the old village of New Windsor. Colonel Lewis DuBois presided over the court-martial.

*Lurking about the camp as a spy from the enemy, confined by order of General Clinton, was brought before said court, and the above crime the prisoner plead not guilty. But confessed his being an Express from General (Sir Henry) Clinton to Burgoyne to General Clinton, and was taken in the camp of the army of the United States, near New Windsor, NY, Taylor likewise confessed his being a first Lieutenant in Captain Stewart's Company in the Regiment of the British troops, and but one man in company when taken . . ."[57]*

Taylor pled not guilty and testified to the assembled officers that he was not lurking when taken as a prisoner by the Americans. Quite to the contrary, he continued, Clinton instructed him to stay far away from the American camp. The court deliberated and came back with the verdict.

*The court, after considering the case, were of the opinion that the pris-*
*oner is guilty of the charge brought against him, and adjudged to suffer*
*death, to be hanged at such time and place as the General shall direct.*[58]

Around the time of the court's decision as to the fate of Taylor, General Putnam's reinforcements arrived at George Clinton's headquarters at the Falls House. The troops then marched to the relief of Kingston. Along with several other prisoners, Taylor walked with the Americans toward the New York State capital. Once in North Marbletown, on October 16, 1777, the same day Captain Campbell arrived too late to be of any help to Burgoyne, George Clinton set up his headquarters in the Oliver House on present-day Route 209. The appointed date of execution for Daniel Taylor George Clinton wrote, "when the troops are paraded and before they march to-morrow morning"[59] or October 17, 1777. However, the execution would need to be delayed again until October 18. The troops remained in North Marbletown located outside Kingston, New York, because they saw the plumes of smoke and realized they were too late to save the new capital of New York State.

Clinton ordered his troops to continue their march to Hurley just on the outskirts of Kingston, where they again saw smoke as well as flames. Meanwhile, the British warships under the command of Lieutenant General Sir John Vaughan continued up the Hudson River to Livingston's Manor where they burned the home of Margaret Livingston. She was the widow of Robert Livingston who died in 1775. "The British army destroyed Clermont and all the other buildings on the estate as retaliation for the family's support of the Revolution. Margaret and her children, still residing at home, escaped earlier to a relative's house in Connecticut before the burning."[60]

Once in Hurley, Clinton confined Daniel Taylor in the Dumond home, known to later generations as the Guard House. Legend tells us that Taylor was imprisoned in the basement of the home because it was a more secure place for prisoners. However, it is not known for sure. In his diary, Nathaniel Webb wrote that he spent time with Taylor, as did the Rev. Romain. Webb recorded that the two men spoke to Taylor, and when the time of execution arrived, they brought him to the gallows remaining with him as a source of comfort. Taylor must have known after witnessing and hearing about the destruction of Kingston, there was little chance of his life being spared.

Troops arrived shortly before noon at the Dumond home to march Taylor a short distance to the site of his execution. Local historian Ralph LeFevre wrote that an apple tree served as a scaffold with a "large limb about ten feet above the ground."[61] It was from this branch that Taylor was hanged. Legend states that the location of the tree was about halfway down present-day School House Lane. Again, according to legend, Taylor took his place on a hogshead. The executioner, reported the *Kingston Daily Freeman* in 1904, was Jack Ketch. He agreed to be the executioner with the stipulation that after Taylor was pronounced dead, he could have the man's boots. Taylor was brought to the barrel, with his hand's tied. He was helped onto the stand as the noose was placed around his neck. Some sources report that just before the executioner kicked the barrel out from under the prisoner, "He [Taylor] fainted" and "thus had an apparently easy death."[62]

After being hanged, his body was not cut down immediately. "The body hung from the tree for a least two days, during which time all the units of General Clinton's Army were paraded by the body as a lesson to any British sympathizers among them as to what their fate would be if found out. The body was buried at the edge of the road. It was later removed by relatives and taken to a private burial location."[63] Local historians write that the apple tree lived into the mid-nineteenth century before it finally died.

One hundred and twenty-four years later, Taylor was once again on the minds of residents living in Hurley. A newspaper article written in 1901 reported that a body was accidentally dug up by laborers working near a railroad bed. Some locals believed it to be the remains of the spy. No one recalls what happened to the bones or if it was, in fact, the remains of Taylor.

The second messenger sent by Henry Clinton, Captain Campbell, successfully reached the beleaguered British troops in Saratoga two days before the execution, too late to be of any help. The day before Taylor's execution British Troops surrendered to Horatio Gates in Saratoga. Sir

Henry Clinton was ordered by General Howe to return to New York City. When he arrived there, he was to send troops to Howe. Meanwhile, Saratoga, of course, went down in history as the turning point in the American Revolution. With the success of the Americans, France and, later, Spain decided to join them as allies against their common enemy.

The Dumond House still stands in Hurley. It is more well-known as the Spy House or the Guard House because of its notorious guest, Daniel Taylor. During Stone House Day every summer, those interested in history can tour the historic home and basement where Lieutenant Daniel Taylor spent his last days.

# THE MID-HUDSON

# The Pennsylvania Mutiny of 1783
# and the Newburgh Connection

*[Y]ou are a meer composition of obstinacy & fat contented ignorance*[64]
LIEUTENANT JOHN SULLIVAN

Lieutenant John Sullivan of Colonel Millard Moylan's regiment arrived in Newburgh, New York, in August 1779. A mounted unit, Sullivan's troops needed pasture for their horses. He saw Elnathan Foster's meadows and decided to place his horses there without asking for permission. Sullivan probably hoped for Colonel Jonathon Hasbrouck's meadows, but the Continental Army currently rented it out for cattle. Perhaps Foster might not have minded if he had been compensated for Sullivan taking his pastures or, at the very least, asked. However, this was not the nature of Sullivan who did not feel obligated to consult or pay for this service. Foster and Sullivan in 1779 were on a collision course.

As it states in *Washington's Headquarters, Newburgh's Historic Structure Report*, "Beginning in 1779, increasing amounts of military stores were collected at Newburgh from other places. In June, General [Nathanael] Greene ordered all lead which came from Claverack or Fishkill to be sent to Newburgh."[65] The Hudson River was a highway on which much-needed supplies moved between the Middle Colonies and the New England Colonies. Because of the vital military stores at Newburgh, the Continental Army, as well as the quartermaster department, maintained a continuous presence in the town.

On September 13, 1779, General George Washington ordered "all uniforms and winter clothing, including blankets, shirts, and shoes to be sent to Newburgh because of its convenient location." What brought Sullivan to Newburgh was the order by General James Wilkinson on October 10, 1779, to Moylan to take charge of the clothing at Newburgh. Colonel Moylan's regiment was stationed at Hasbrouck's Mill for two weeks of making clothing. The mill and the house there were the most convenient for making clothing. It was also protected, being inland enough to be safe from the British.

Again, according to the historic structure report for *Washington Headquarters*, written by Waite and Huey write, that the manufacture of clothing became one of the most important activities at Newburgh, and on June 28, 1780, Justice Abel Belknap personally informed Colonel Hasbrouck that some men from Colonel Moylan's regiment were to spend two weeks making clothing at "your house at the Mill."[66]

As more and more soldiers found themselves stationed in and around Newburgh, altercations were bound to happen. General Clinton's papers illustrate this issue with a petition concerning the Quartermaster Department in Newburgh, led by Timothy Pickering. The petition asserted that the army was interfering with civil authority. The significant military presence also impacted commerce because of their proximity to the public dock and ferry located on the Hudson River.

When "Lieutenant John Sullivan of Col. Millard's [Moylan's] Regiment of Light Dragoons"[67] took possession of Foster's pastures, Elnathan approached the officer attempting to handle the situation in an amicable manner. He explained he did not want the horses on his property not to mention they were causing a lot of damage to his field. Sullivan ignored repeated requests to find somewhere else for the horses. Feeling as if he was getting nowhere with the obstinate Sullivan, Foster filed a complaint with Justice Belknap. In the complaint, Foster alleged that Sullivan was "forcibly pasturing several horses in his meadow without his consent"[68] in violation of the law.

Belknap summoned Foster before the court located at Weigand's Tavern. Foster explained to the justice that he filed the complaint after trying to resolve the situation by repeatedly approaching Sullivan requesting him to remove the horses from his pasture. Instead of removing the animals, Sullivan became belligerent toward him, which made Foster fear for his own personal safety. In addition to the animals being removed from his land, Foster now wanted compensation for what he viewed as significant damage to his field by the horses.

Belknap patiently listened to the complaint by Foster in the upstairs portion of the old tavern overlooking the Old Town Burial Ground. After Foster finished his description of the events, the judge decided to swear out a warrant on August 22, 1780, for Sullivan to appear before the court in order for the court to hear the officer's side of events. According to George Clinton's Public Papers, Sullivan opted to have his viewpoint heard before Justice John Nicoll, Esq., though Nicoll asked for Belknap to be present at the hearing.

After listening to both sides, the court justices deliberated over the facts presented. They rendered their verdict, which sided with Foster, and instructed Sullivan to remove the horses from Foster's property. Following state law, the justices required the services of an appraiser to determine the scope of the damages to Foster's property. Once the appraisers calculated the costs, Belknap instructed Sullivan to pay the owner for the expenses. He also ordered that until more suitable pastures were found for the horses, Sullivan needed to pay Foster for the use of his field. Although he took the judgment in stride on the outside, Sullivan exploded inside at the judgment. He saw the judgment as unpatriotic and unfair. There would be no way he could adhere to the opinion.

A new location for the horses was acquired on August 24, 1780. A justice sent word to the quartermaster's department that a meadow had been located, and instructed that Sullivan, in accordance with the court's judgment, needed to move the horses to the new pasture. Belknap had no idea how events would shortly spiral out of control. When word reached Sullivan, he flew off the handle in a complete rage.

Sullivan decided to ignore both the judgment to pay Foster for damages and the order to remove the horses from the pasture. He believed that during wartime everyone needed to make sacrifices. Foster was no friend of the Patriot cause. Elnathan turned again to the court for help in order to rid himself of Sullivan and his horses. In response, Belknap issued a second warrant and demanded an explanation for Sullivan's contempt. He ordered the lieutenant to answer in person. Sullivan did not come; instead, he dashed off a letter lecturing the justice. In the letter, he scolded Belknap asserting that during wartime civil authorities were subordinate to the military. He questioned Foster's patriotism as well as the justice's patriotism. Finally, Sullivan attacked Belknap's character on August 25, 1780.

*Sir, you ought to be asham'd of such conduct; so inconsistent with the character of an honest and a good magistrate, that had the interest of his country at heart, to propose to send those horses in the country again, when you know their shoes have been taken off; and were rode to such a degree by the inhabitants, as to render'd them in a manner unfit for service this campaign.*

Sullivan surmised that Belknap's conduct toward him must be due to a personal "aversion" to the army. He further berated the judge, referring to him as "illiterate" and "hot-headed"[59] feeling it futile to talk face-to-face with Belknap; thus, he continued in his letter:

*For indeed no man of sense could hear you five minits with patience, as you are a meer composition of obstinacy & fat contented ignorance your ungentleman like behavior in regard to me, would I assure you Sir, have met with its desert, were you worthy the attention of a gentleman.*[69]

Cooler heads temporarily prevailed. Sullivan attempted to move the horses to a new pasture. Someone told him that the local farm contained adequate pasture and that Coleman was not averse to keeping the horses. It is not clear if the officer or one of his subordinates paid a visit to the Coleman family. Coleman's wife explained that they did have a pasture for horses, but it was located at least three miles from Foster's land. Sullivan in a letter addressed to the court strongly felt that the horses needed to be close to the soldiers. It would be easier for taking care of the animals or in case they were needed quickly.

Word was sent to Belknap that the Coleman pasture was inadequate, explaining that the horses were unshod and in need of rest. Sullivan told

Belknap that the horses, as well as his soldiers, would be gone in two days. In his opinion, moving the horses was just not worth the effort and they would remain at Foster's. One can only imagine the frustration felt by Justice Belknap at not only being ignored but continuously insulted by the military officer.

It was later ascertained that Coleman later backtracked during testimony that the army did ask him for use of his pasture. However, Coleman felt that without any way to be compensated he did not want the horses on his lands.

The court issued a third warrant on August 26, 1780. Realizing that dealing directly with Sullivan was futile, Justice Belknap tried another tactic. He swore out a warrant against a caretaker of the horses named William Denton. He ordered the local constable to remove the horses from Foster's land and bring them to the court being held at the tavern. They were also to arrest Denton and bring him before the court. Belknap thought it prudent, because of Sullivan's explosiveness, for the constable to bring additional men with him for protection. They were to be armed with both guns and a copy of the warrant.

According to later testimony by Benjamin Birdsall who assisted the Sheriff, when the men arrived they found that Sullivan had purposely locked himself in the "clothing store."[70] When the sheriff ordered Sullivan to come out, he refused. Nor would he accept the subpoena from the sheriff. It was decided to forget about the lieutenant, and the sheriff and his men attempted to secure the five horses, along with Denton. As they approached the horses, however, three soldiers leveled their pistols at them, telling them to let the horses go or they would shoot. The sheriff showed the soldiers the court order signed by Justice Belknap. One of the soldiers looked over the paperwork and, satisfied that the legal papers were authentic or perhaps feeling they did not want to risk entanglement with the law, they holstered their pistols. When Sullivan was sure the sheriff and his men had left, he emerged from the building. Once he emerged, he was told that the horses and Denton were gone, and he went into a tirade. He ordered his men to follow him to the courthouse to take the horses and Denton back.

The constable arrived, just as a David Brooks stormed into the court. Brooks "who has some care of the public clothing, burst into the courtroom yelling at Belknap and swearing about how badly the court treated Sullivan." Brooks was the Assistant Clothier at Newburgh. He walked with the assistance of a cane and swung it at the justices now assembled to conduct court. As he wildly swung the cane, Brooks yelled "that he was afraid of no man." In his opinion, the justices of the peace were "no friends of the army or the war." The justices were undeterred and ordered Brooks to settle down or be placed in jail. Brooks settled down long enough to be deposed by the court.

He then explained to the court that he felt they had no right to tell Sullivan to remove the horses. He also warned the court justices that they would shortly hear from Sullivan for "insulting the honor of both an officer and a gentleman." No one, of course, mentioned how Sullivan had abused Justice Belknap or the integrity of the court. Just as Brooks predicted, "Sullivan with a guard of 10 men, under arms, with fixed bayonets," burst into the courtroom shouting insults and threats at the justices particularly toward Belknap. The justice later stated that the lieutenant "abused me with the most menacing, abusive language, pointing his drawn sword at me, calling me a dam'd rascall &c." Brooks later admitted that he gave the men firearms to be used to take the court hostage in order to take the horses back to the pasture.

Sullivan then turned his anger against the constable who stood there in the court with the warrant still in his hand, and slapped him across "the face with the flat part of his sword."[71] A stunned constable's face erupted in blood. He stood there in stunned disbelief as the warrant was swiped out of his hand by Sullivan who promptly ripped it up and threw the pieces on the courthouse floor. Sullivan had both his gun and sword still drawn, Sullivan ordered Denton to take the horses back to the pasture. He instructed his soldiers to stay behind with explicit orders to bayonet the first person who tried to intervene or follow Denton. Just before Sullivan exited the court, he accused all in the courtroom of being enemies of their country and Tories. Foster left the area shortly after his outburst in Weigand's Tavern.

An inquiry held to look into the conduct of Sullivan on August 29, 1780, lasted into early September 1780. Depositions were taken from witnesses as to the events that had unfolded. Among those collecting this information were Justices Wolvert Ecker [Acker] and Abel Belknap. A local by the name of Thomas Palmer testified before Ecker on August 29. Lieutenant Jedidiah Stickney filed his deposition with Belknap on September 6. Stickney, who was guarding the stores of clothing where Brooks was stationed, testified that Sullivan asked him for some firearms for a guard. When asked why he needed them, he responded that he wanted to deal with some "bad fellows."[72] Cornelius Hasbrouck, the son of the now late Colonel Jonathan Hasbrouck, testified that he witnessed Sullivan level a pistol at the chest of the constable before assaulting him.

Some three years later, Sullivan's contempt for authority would land him in hot water again. This time his conflict did not involve civil authorities, but the Commander-in-Chief General Washington, who, interestingly enough, had his latest military headquarters at the Hasbrouck House in Newburgh a short distance from where the earlier events had transpired.

This latest episode with Sullivan occurred in June 1783, as anger regarding back pay simmered among some Pennsylvania troops. The army started to furlough soldiers as the war came to an end, and soldiers feared back pay might be ignored by Congress. According to a history of the U.S. House of Representatives, the Pennsylvania troops in Philadelphia and Lancaster were among some of the unhappiest in the army. "On June 20, 1783, about 80 Lancaster officers and militia mutinied."[73] The Lancaster militia hoped to rendezvous with roughly five hundred soldiers already in the city and menacing Congress. On June 20, 1783, the soldiers already in the nation's capital surrounded the State House where Congress met. They refused orders to disband and demanded their back pay.

Fearing an attack on the legislators, Alexander Hamilton asked President of the Executive Council John Dickinson to call out the state militia to protect Congress. The latest crisis exposed one of many weaknesses in the Articles of Confederation, namely that Congress relied on the states for protection. Dickinson did not call out the militia. This refusal, plus the actions of the mutinying troops, forced Congress to flee to Princeton,

New Jersey, for their safety. General Washington found out about the mutiny and responded by sending troops, under Major General William Heath, to crush the rebellion. When word reached the protesters that 1,500 soldiers were on their way to disperse them, the resistance collapsed quickly. An immediate investigation was launched to find the individuals who instigated the mutiny; arrests followed. Several officers were court-martialed, and though some of the soldiers involved were sentenced to death, they were eventually pardoned.

Historians have proposed many names over the years as to who the instigators of the mutiny were. Investigators at that time pinned the mutiny on John Sullivan and "a deranged army captain" Henry Carbery. The latter had been part of the Eleventh Pennsylvania. According to notes contained in the *James Madison Papers*, both men were able to flee Pennsylvania aboard an English ship. Believing that enough time transpired, Carbery returned in 1784 to Maryland to hopefully be granted a pardon for his earlier behavior. He was promptly arrested and then jailed in Annapolis, Maryland. "Carbery evidently succeeded in extricating himself from the charges against him in Pennsylvania, for he was living in Baltimore by 1789 and launching a vigorous campaign for public employment."

In July 1789, Carbery wrote a letter to then-President Washington. He wrote, "If You can Forgive me, Sir, for one single act of Indiscretion, for which I can never forgive myself, You will make me happy, and I shall ever consider myself as under the most particular, and Sensible Obligations."[74] Carbery asked the president for an appointment to a position within the new government. "I should enjoy the Delightful Idea of being Restored to the Bosom, and Confidence of my Country—and ranking once more, with Those who have fought, and Suffered for America." Washington did not give him the appointment. Carbery asked again for an appointment about a year later. In 1791 Carbery was successful in securing a commission in the United States Army as a captain, a rank he retained after the reorganization of the army in 1792 until his resignation in 1794. In March 1813, he was appointed a lieutenant colonel in the military and served until 1815. He died on May 26, 1822.

As for Sullivan, the cantankerous officer from Newburgh who refused to remove his horses from Foster's pasture, he did not make out as well as his coconspirator. Sullivan returned to Pennsylvania by 1785. He was not arrested, as William T. Hutchinson and William M. E. Rachal wrote in their notes in the Madison Papers: "His attempt to procure back pay was frustrated when on 27 June 1786 his military records were closed with the notation that he had quit the continental service without leave. Two years later, he led an abortive movement to drive the Spanish from the lower Mississippi River valley."[75] In 1787 he was arrested again for "incendiary activities along the Spanish-American frontier."[76] His military career was not rehabilitated like Carbery's career. There is no existing record recalling people's reactions to hearing Sullivan's implication in the mutiny in Pennsylvania. He left and was not brought to justice in Newburgh. One of the issues that complicates what became of Sullivan in Newburgh is the fire in the New York State Archives in early 1911. It destroyed so much, including much of the Clinton's original papers. Hastings, who edited the Clinton Papers, had transcribed them before the fire. I have used some of the papers, and they are still charred. When the British burned Washington, D.C., in the War of 1812, still more was lost in terms of records from the American War for Independence.

As far as Elnathan Foster, he continued to live in Newburgh. He was instrumental in the founding the Newburgh Academy in 1795 and donated land and helped raise funds for the construction. Later in life, he helped found the Methodist Episcopal Church in Newburgh. When Foster died on April 17, 1822, at the age of eighty-five, his neighbors forgot about the issues he incurred during the American Revolution.

# Jacob Middaugh and the
# Marbletown Disaffection

*The Conduct of many of these Traitors was so daring and Insolent that a sudden & Severe Example to me seems absolutely necessary to deter others from the Commission of like Crimes...*[77]

GENERAL GEORGE CLINTON

"The Inhabitants are so much irritated by the Conduct of the Prisoners in marching armed in a Body to join the Enemy that I fear they will soon take the Law in their own Hands ag't them & the wounding of Major Strang, his Brother & Lieut. Terwilliger greatly adds to their Resentment."[78] These words were written by General George Clinton from Fort Montgomery to the Provincial Convention meeting in Kingston, New York, on May 2, 1777. The future first governor of New York State was talking about the fate of what was seen in April 1777 as "a large and dangerous body of Loyalists"[79] that greatly alarmed New York State. One such group of Loyalists was forming in Northwestern Ulster County in and around Marbletown.

In 1777, British Colonel Edmund Fanning traveled to Ulster County to meet with Jacob Rosa, a private in Captain Fuge's company and a member of an established family in the area. Fuge, like Rosa, was a member of the King's American Regiment. Rosa also had meetings with Lieutenant Daniel McGuinn, who lived near Newboro [Newburgh], Ulster County, New York. Newburgh, during this time, was still part of Ulster County.

The King's American Regiment was being implemented by Fanning, who was a good friend of the last Royal Governor of New York, Lord William Tryon. The King's American Regiment, according to

Philip Heslip, of the manuscripts division, William L. Clements Library, University of Michigan was "formed at Flat Bush, New York, under the command of Colonel Edmund Fanning, on December 11, 1776. The regiment was comprised of Loyalists from New York, Connecticut, and Rhode Island, and was stationed at Kingsbridge for much of 1777."[80] Colonel Fanning had been born on Long Island and harbored animosity toward the rebellion. The "rebels" had confiscated his property and driven him from his home, forcing him to find shelter aboard a British battleship in New York Harbor.

Likewise, Lieutenant McGuinn had reason to hold animosity toward the rebels. McGuinn decided to become a recruiter for the British always on the lookout for Americans who wished, or could be persuaded to, join the king's forces in crushing the rebellion. McGuinn at one point, because of his allegiance to the Crown, was captured by the Americans and sentenced to death. While under arrest, his livestock were taken, his property sold, and his shop along with its goods were plundered by the rebels. Before his execution was carried out, he escaped from prison fleeing to New York. Angry at his mistreatment by the Rebels, McGuinn enlisted in the King's American Regiment and he was commissioned a lieutenant.

Together Rosa and McGuinn traveled from Marbletown to New York City. Once there, they made their way to Fanning's headquarters. Rosa explained that where he resided in Ulster County, there was a considerable number of disaffected people who could be coaxed to join the British. Fanning instructed the two men to return to Ulster County and seek out those individuals who would participate in the fight against the Americans. In this process, Rosa and McGuinn found willing participants within the Middaugh family of Marbletown. It would become the job of Abraham Middaugh and his cousin Jacob Middaugh to find and recruit Loyalists in and around Marbletown.

On April 23, 1777, Abraham arrived at the dwelling of Jacobus S. Davis, in Marbletown. This area was still considered part of the frontier at this time, and the English were riding high from their success in routing the Americans in the Battle of Long Island in 1776. They controlled from New York City to the lower Hudson River, and they retained control of this strategically important area until the Treaty of Paris in 1783 ended the American War for Independence. In 1777, the British still wanted to increase their control of the Hudson River to include from New York City to Albany. If the British controlled the entire Hudson River, they could divide the New England Colonies from the rest of the colonies in rebellion. Once the Mohawk River was under control of the British, the Mohawks would be able to move more freely into the frontier.

British strategists believed that if Loyalists could also be enlisted to help in that effort, it had more chances of success due to their knowledge of the land. Loyalists could be used to supplement troops as well as to secure the countryside when the new campaign was launched. The King's American Regiment would be part of the attack and eventual surrender of Forts Montgomery and Clinton in the Hudson Highlands.

Abraham Middaugh was a member of the local militia and a Patriot early in the struggle with England. His name is recorded on the Articles of Association for Marbletown in 1775, a document swearing his allegiance to the American cause. Abraham would serve in the Third Regiment of the Ulster County Militia under Colonels Levi Pauling and John Cantine. He enlisted as a private. Why he defected to the British side is not known for sure, perhaps it was due to promises made by the British of monetary bonuses, made by way of his cousin Jacob Middaugh or possibly family loyalty.

During this time, Patriots watched for any suspicious activities by citizens. Armed citizens patrolled the countryside looking for Loyalists traveling or forming to aid the British. They were especially on alert because they were told to be on the lookout for such activities. It is because of more vigilance on behalf of the Americans that communication and movement by Tories took place after sunset when most people were sleeping. Once Abraham Middaugh arrived at the home of Jacobus S. Davis, he explained to Davis that his cousin Jacob traveled with him and wanted to meet with Jacobus. Jacob was waiting down the road. Jacob wanted Abraham Middaugh to convince Jacobus S. Davis to go with him to the other home to discuss with Jacob switching sides in the war to the British. After patiently listening to persuasive arguments by Abraham, Jacobus S. agreed to travel with Abraham to the home where Jacob was waiting.

When Abraham and Davis arrived, Jacob greeted his neighbor warmly. Jacob explained to Davis that not only were the British going to win the war, but when they did the British authorities would remember who was loyal to King George III and who was not dependable. The lands of those who were not loyal would be confiscated and given to the king's loyal subjects. When Davis asked how he knew so much information, Jacob explained that he had recently come from British-held New York City. The British had asked Jacob to recruit Loyalists for the British army.

He explained to Davis that he was instructed to enlist as many men as he could manage to fight the rebels in an upcoming campaign. If they agreed, the bounty, "would make gentlemen of all those who would go down with him; that the party who had previously gone with him to New York City were encamped at Jamaica, on Long Island" (present-day Queens County). Jacob continued that these men were in want of nothing. The land taken from the rebels would be paid to all enlisting men. It entitled them to "one hundred acres of land himself, fifty acres for his wife, and fifty acres for every son."[81] Whether they fought or not, they would also need to swear allegiance to England.

Davis listened patiently to what the Middaughs proposed to him. After much talk and cajoling, he decided not to go. Jacob lost his patience with Davis and threatened him. He explained again, telling Davis that if he didn't pledge his allegiance to the Crown that when the British won he would be in a bad way and there would be nothing he, Jacob, could do to protect him. When Davis remained resolute in his decision, Jacob threatened that if he breathed a word to anyone about what had been said to him, he would make sure that Davis paid with his life. His response again was that he was not interested. Before they left, they told Davis they were heading to his father's home in order to try to recruit his brother Jacob Davis.

The two Middaughs knocked on the door of Davis's father on the evening of October 23, 1777. When the father answered, they requested to speak with Jacob Davis. They gave him the same information they had given Jacobus. Because the British were going to launch a broad offensive to take the Hudson River from the north, west, and south, they needed local Loyalists with knowledge of the terrain to secure the countryside. Lucky for the Middaughs, Jacob took less convincing. His father outfitted him with all the provisions he would need for the long trek. Jacob disappeared into the night with the other men on their rounds to enlist more help. When they had a suitable number, they would start their journey.

While recruiting members of the Davis family, Jacob Middaugh had dispatched Christian Winne to Little Shandaken to enlist more individuals to join the march to New York City. Two people he was successful in recruiting were Wilhelmus Mericle and Jacobus Bush. The same day, April 23, 1777, the group of men left "Shocan" at night, joining with the Middaughs. The next day, April 24, they all made their way to the Jagh Cripplebush. According to a history of Marbletown, *Yeaugh Kripple-Bush* is a corruption of the Dutch word *jag* (hunting) and *creupelbosch* (thicket). Once at the Jagh Cripplebush, they rested at the farm of Abraham Middaugh.

What later became known as the Marbletown Disaffection came to light by way of the copious amounts of testimony taken by Cornelius Schoonmaker for the Shawangunk Committee of Safety and Observation. Henrick Crispell would plea bargain to save himself by fully dislcoing to the committee all that he knew.

Henrick Crispell later told the committee that he had been recruited by both Jacob and Abraham Middaugh who arrived at his home on the evening of April 23, 1777, along with Jacob Davis. The Middaughs explained to Henrick that "Colonel Fanning had sent them to bring in such persons as were willing to go to New York. That there was a Proclamation from the King that such as were his friends should come in and those who did not when the Regulars got Possession of America should find no mercy. . . ."[82] Crispell continued that it was explained to him that the king viewed them all as rebels and could execute them as rebels.

Motivated by fear, Henrick agreed to join only if his brother Thomas joined him. Thomas attempted to reason with Henrick that it all sounded ridiculous to him. He felt they could not be punished if they were not part of the fighting and were just going about their lives. Still, because of Henrick's urging, Thomas decided to join the Middaughs, though he told his brother, "he thought it was hard to be hanged for what they could not help." The brothers told Jacob to come back the next day.

Jacob Middaugh again met with the Crispell brothers on April 24, 1777. He told them if they swore loyalty and made their way to New York City, the king would reward them. They would also be paid. Their best option, as he saw it, was to take up arms, which, he stressed, while it was their choice, was well worth their while. "Each man should have two Pair of Stockings, a Pair of Shoes, a Pair of Breeches and two shirts and a coat or red jacket . . . and a Waistcoat and the arms they brought with them should be laid in the stores and those that were willing might sell them and if they enlisted they should Draw arms."[83] A bounty of forty shillings was promised in hard money.

Once he was assured they were joining, Middaugh told the Crispells that they had made a wise decision because the British were going to launch an attack on New York around May 5 or 6. They intended to take control of the Hudson River and all of New York. In May the campaign would be ready and the Native Americans allies of the British would join the the campaign. One could only imagine how the Crispells must have felt listening to Jacob Middaugh going on and on about all they would face.

Jacob Davis's home was appointed the initial place of rendezvous. The men assembled included Jacob Middaugh, Jacob Davis, James Merkel, Petrus Bush, Jacob Furler, Coenraadt Missner, Cornelius Furher, Jacob Longyear Jr., and Andries Longyear, among others. They were joined by Hendrick and Thomas Crispell. Hendrick remembered that all the men were armed except Jacob Middaugh. Before the men left, they were told to make sure they had provisions for three to five days.

Traveling at night for safety, Jacob Middaugh led the men to Abraham Middaugh's home. Although Abraham had helped in the early recruitment of the company of Loyalists, he had refused to do anything else. What changed his mind is not known. Not only would Abraham not join the company, but Abraham's brother George refused as well. Disappointed, instead of remaining at Abraham's place for the night as was the original plan, Middaugh and the others departed hastily, walking through a large field to the home of a Marbletown schoolmaster named Daniel Irvin.

It was at the home of Irvin that they found his family fast asleep. Luckily, Irvin was still awake. Henrick Crispell remembers it was about eight in the evening. They knocked on the door, and he greeted the men. Here they were joined by Lieutenant Jacob Rosa, another cousin of Jacob Middaugh. Rosa had another group of men whom he had recruited. Probably because Irvin could write, the schoolmaster inscribed the name of all the men present in a book as officially enlisted in the King's Army. What grabbed Henrick's attention about Rosa is he found it curious that while all the other men were armed, the officer had only a "cudgel in his hand." A cudgel is a type of club.

Once having their names inscribed in the book, the company of Loyalists left Irvin's home, crossed a public road, and went across the Rondout Creek. "Some in canoes and some wading over and stopped at a House."[84] Here they went into a large barn and met "Jack the Negro man of Gysbert Roper, John VanVliet and William Teets." Henrick thinks that Silvester Vandermark and John Rapalje were also present. The group of men now numbered almost fifty, and from there continued to Richard Oakley's where they arrived at about nine o'clock on April 24. After resting again, they traveled, still by night, to William's Woods in the Coxing Clove.

When they reached the Coxing Cove, they met three more individuals, Samuel Freleigh, James Jones, and an unnamed British officer who some believe was Colonel William Edmeston. Jay Gould, in his *History of Delaware County*, described the man as blind in his left eye, where he wore a patch, sporting a "speckled jacket, and old brown surtout coat and blue stockings, with strings in his shoes. He carried with him a bundle of letters in his possession, and he told the men he came from the Mohawk River and passed through Albany disguised as a shoemaker"[85] with all the trappings a shoemaker would carry. The British officer explained that he and the other men would guide the Tories safely to New York City. After traveling most of the night, the company bedded down for the night in William Woods's barn.

On April 25, 1777, the company of Loyalists, Freleigh, Jones, and the British officer crossed the Shawangunk Mountains arriving near the home of Widow Bevier in the Precinct of New Paltz. Lieutenant Jacob Rosa approached the house with Jacob Middaugh. Bevier was sympathetic to the men and seemed to be expecting them. The door opened, and the two men went inside the widow's home to talk with her. She helped them secure a guide as well as canoes to traverse the Wallkill River, which ran near the widow's dwelling. The guide was sent for while the men waited.

When Rosa and Middaugh emerged from the home, they were met by Wouter Sluyter, who would lead the company of Loyalists to a crossing of the Paltz (Wallkill) River near the home of Cornelius DuBois. This ford is today located behind the old Josiah DuBois land, which is known as the Blake House on the way to the current fairgrounds on Libertyville Road. It was known to be a post for American sentries.

Sergeant Joseph Freer of Captain Hardenbergh's Company of Militia in New Paltz, was stationed by the crossing. Rosa and company surprised the sergeant and took him prisoner. Rosa took the soldier's musket, bayonet, cartridge box, tomahawk, and powder horn with a half-pound of powder. At the same time Freer was being interrogated, Lieutenant Jonathan Terwilliger of the same company was heading to join the guard at the river to prevent the Tories from crossing it if they came that way. When Terwilliger saw Rosa and his followers with Freer, one of the Americans, with Terwilliger, yelled out, inquiring if the men with Freer were friend or foe? Rosa responded friend. When the American patrol approached, Jacob Davis grabbed Terwilliger's horse's bridle. A struggle ensued and when Davis jumped up to pull Terwilliger off his horse, his "fuzee" went off, shooting Terwilliger through his arm. The horses threw both riders and galloped off into the woods. In the ensuing confusion, Terwilliger and the other American scouts disappeared into the woods. After some discussion, it was decided to let Freer go but not before his musket was confiscated. Rosa threatened Freer, forcing him to swear on his life not to utter a word about what he saw or who he saw.

The company continued its mission to New York, making it safely across the Wallkill River to the barn of Arthur McKinney. There, exhausted, the company remained from April 25 to 27, 1777. Meanwhile, Freleigh, Jones, and the still-unnamed British officer continued to Major Cadwallader Colden's residence.

Cadwallader Colden II was the son of New York Lieutenant Governor (1762–1776) Cadwallader Colden. "He lived in the precinct of

Hanover, Ulster County, New York. [Montgomery, New York] In addition to farming, surveying and mercantile interests, he held a number of positions including major during the French and Indian War; judge with the Ulster County Court of Common Pleas, 1769–1775; and justice of the peace, 1769–1775. His life changed dramatically with the coming of the American Revolution." He was arrested in early 1776 for Loyalist sympathies and "confined in the Kingston Jail and on a prison ship, and later held as a parolee at homes and country inns, before being banished behind the British lines in New York City in August 1778."[86]

When the three men arrived at Colden's mansion, Colden explained to them that it would be near impossible for the Loyalist company to get through the rebel guard to New York City. After discussing different possibilities with Colden, the three men became convinced that his advice was worth heeding, and they decided it best to abandon Jacob Middaugh and Jacob Rosa.

It is not certain if Middaugh and Rosa were sent a message or if the three men simply did not return. Although they could not have known it at the time, this was the beginning of the unraveling of their expedition. In a short amount of time, they would be apprehended by a militia already out looking for them and probably tipped off by Terwilliger and Freer. The Loyalists decided to continue to make their way to New York City on April 29, 1777.

Somewhere not far from New Paltz, on April 29, 1777, the men started to cross a large hill. An American militia appeared and a short battle ensued in which five of Middaugh's party were killed. Some of the others escaped into the woods and were later found hiding. Still others would be apprehended as accessories to the crime of aiding the raising of the company. Between April 30 and May 5, 1777, trials were held for some thirty men. Men who were not rounded up by the militia were arrested by the Shawangunk Committee of Safety on April 30, 1777, and examined by its chairman Cornelius Schoonmaker. According to a letter sent by Brigadier General James Clinton at Fort Montgomery on April 29, 1777, "Colonel Woodhull had caught up with the Loyalists somewhere near New Paltz. After a few shots were fired the Loyalists were entirely captured or dispersed."[87]

Those caught by the militia were sent to Fort Montgomery on April 30, 1777. The court-martials were held until May 1 at Fort Montgomery. The men were charged with "levying war against the State of New York within the same, and of being enlisted soldiers in the service of the King of Great Britain, when owing allegiance to the State of New York." In a letter dated May 2, General George Clinton wrote, "The Conduct of many of these Traitors was so daring and Insolent that a sudden & Severe Example to me seems absolutely necessary to deter others from the Commission of like Crimes...."[88]

On May 3, 1777, in his public papers, General Clinton reported to the State Convention that all the individuals captured were sentenced "to be hanged by the neck until they be dead."[89] Jack, William Teets, Daniel Reynolds, and Peter Aldridge were acquitted. Hendrick Crispell helped in the convictions of the others with his testimony, including selling out his brother Thomas who did not want to go to begin with. He agreed to become a witness for the State of New York in exchange for a pardon. He was formally pardoned on May 3, in exchange for his testimony. In the end to save his own hide, he sold out his brother Thomas.

Jacob Rosa and Jacob Middaugh were brought before the court-martial. On Wednesday, April 30, 1777, they were charged with levying war against the state, taking orders from the king, enlisting men for England, and being enlisted in the British army. Both men pled guilty to all the charges except enlisting soldiers. Middaugh told the assembled officers that he joined the company because he was so poor that all the promises made to him would benefit him. He did a toast to the king and swore loyalty to the king it was true. He pointed out that the promises made to him were not honored.

Rosa made sure that the assembled officers knew it was not he who shot Terwilliger, and that the shooting took place when he was on the other side of the Wallkill River. He admitted to telling the soldiers to arm themselves and defend themselves if need be. He said to the court that the real recruiters were Fanning and McGuinn. Like Middaugh he cited that the bounties paid were too good to pass up for him. He also stressed that he brought men to New York City, but he did not enlist them. It was Fanning who recruited and enlisted them.

In addition to the men who were tried on April 30, 1777, there were also accomplices who were hunted down and put on trial. Those accomplices were Alexander Campbell, Arthur McKinney, Isaac Lockwood, Silas Gardner, Daniel Reynolds, and Peter Aldridge. Campbell, McKinney, and Lockwood were, "sentenced to Imprism't during Warr."[90] The other men put on trial were acquitted. Others were taken but not tried and spent an extended amount of time waiting in prison.

The Convention at Kingston, on a review of the sentences of those convicted, confirmed all but John Stokes, Lodwyck Seely, and Alexander Campbell. Their convictions were reversed. The men who were convicted and ordered to be executed were sent to the Kingston Jail because there was not enough room at Fort Montgomery. General George Clinton also expected the fort to be attacked any day. Abraham Middaugh was also acquitted.

On May 10, 1777, the Convention pardoned those who were convicted and sentenced to die. There was a stipulation that those pardoned were not to be told until the noose was around their necks. Only Rosa and Middaugh's sentences were not to be overturned. "Resolved, that the above named persons be pardoned, except Rose and Middagh; but that the said pardons be withheld from them. . . ."[91] Rosa and Middaugh would be hanged on May 13, 1777. They petitioned the Convention asking for a reprieve of a few days to prepare for their death and seek last rites. It was rejected.

*To the Honorable the Convention of the State of New York*
*The Humble Petition of Jacobus Rose and Jacob Midah, two unhappy*
*Prisoners, was by order of your House under sentence to be Hanged*
*this Day Most Humbly Showeth,*
    *That altho their Consciences doth not in the least accuse them*
*of being Guilty of any sin against God or their Country, by doing*
*what they are condemned to suffer Death for, yet your Petitioners are*

*heartily sorry for having incurr'd the Displeasure of your House in so*
*sensible a manner. That as sinfull men it is an awfull and Dreadfull*
*thought to be so suddenly sent to Eternity without any time to Repent*
*of the Sins of our past Lives, and to make our peace with that God who*
*must finally judge us all for the Deeds done in the flesh, that therefore*
*to prepare for this great and awfull trial your Petitioners most Hum-*
*bly beg they may have a Repsite of a few Days, and your Petitioners as*
*in Duty bound shall in the mean while earnestly pray.*
*Jacobus Rose*
*Jacob (his mark) Midagh*
*Kingston, May 13, 1777*
*Petition Rejected*[92]

According to Judge Hasbrouck, although a young boy at the time, he believed that the two men were executed "on the first hill from the landing . . . it appears that these unfortunate men expected to be reprieved; when they drew near the gallows and saw the preparations for their execution they became overwhelmed with a sense of their awful situation and exclaimed: '*Oh, Heer! vergeeveen onze sonde!*' (Oh, Lord! forgive our sin!)."[93] Some sources state that their bodies were hanged from a pine tree and left there for several days for all to see. Where they were buried is still a mystery.

Jacob Middaugh's cousin Abraham was able to save his own life by enlisting in the local militia. He served for the duration of the war and continued to live, outwardly anyway, as loyal to the United States as well as the State of New York. Some of Jacob's immediate family members remained loyal to the King of England and were angered that a relative had been executed.

Stephen and John Middaugh were bent on continuing the fight. Stephen had been committed to the Kingston Jail and had even been one of those pardoned, but like others, he was never told and languished in jail. According to family sources, John was never caught and hid in the woods for the winter of 1777, obtaining help from those sympathetic to his cause. When Stephen was finally released from jail, he joined other Loyalists in creating mischief on the frontier of New York State.

As late as 1778, Jacob Middaugh's brother was creating mischief in "Papaconck and Down the River Delaware." This is where Colonel Cantine in his Regimental Orders for August 12, 1778, reported the Middaghs to live and he gave the simple orders to "apprehend all those upon said River who have taken an active part against the United States of America." He especially wanted the detachment to move against "John Middagh, Stephen Middagh, Hendrick Bush, Jun'r. & Nathan Parks."[94] The Middaugh brothers were also suspected of supplying grain to the British. A fifteen-pound reward for each of the men was offered.

In September 1778, Colonel John Cantine wrote to George Clinton, "I have only to add that I have great Reason to believe the greatest mischief arise thro' the agency of the two Middaghs & Parks, & you have, therefore, my consent to Offer a Reward of 100 Dollars for apprehend'g of them or either of them. . . ."[95] When the war ended, Stephen fled to Canada where he petitioned for losses incurred during the war.

Jacob Middaugh's brothers Stephen and John as United American Royalists, asked for compensation for what they lost early on in the war. All three men lost land on the Head of the Delaware River and as well as anything on the property. Jan Middaugh, in his testimony, claimed that from the beginning of the rebellion he was on the side of the English. All his brothers took the side of the Crown, including a brother who was executed by the Americans. John stated that he joined Sir John's Second Battalion Prior to joining the battalion, he was "obliged to sculk in the woods for almost a whole winter."[96] When he fled to Niagara, he served in Sir John's until the end of the war.

Stephen Middaugh joined Sir John's First Battalion after his lands were confiscated by the Americans. He had joined Butler's Rangers in 1776 but was dismissed because of illness. When he was significantly recovered, because he was part of his brother Jacob's mission, he was sent to Kingston Jail in Ulster County. Stephen also stated that from the beginning of the war, he pledged to King George III and that his brother Jacob was executed for recruiting for the English.

Another family member, Martin Middaugh resettled in the Eastern District of Upper Canada, according to the 1779 Canadian Bureau

Archive Records. He was a Grenadier Batallion No. 1 in the Kings Royal Regiment New York, enlisting February 1, 1780, until the end of the war. Martin was a sergeant in the Continental Army before he deserted on May 1, 1778.

What is often overlooked in the history of the American Revolution is that after Jacob Middaugh's hanging, New York State was not done with his family. A law passed in 1779 allowing New York State to confiscate the estates of suspected Loyalists. This list was published in 1781, and it shows that whatever Jacob Middaugh owned at the time of his death was taken by the state.

# The Mutiny on Temple Hill in 1783

*The army is a dangerous instrument to play with.*[97]

GEORGE WASHINGTON

The Newburgh Conspiracy is a little-known event that occurred in the last year of the American War for Independence. Even though it is one of the least-known developments, it's perhaps one of the most crucial events in the early founding of the republic. It created a precedent for the military to be subordinate to the civilian government. Many do not appreciate how close the United States came to overturning the central tenets of the American Revolution that had been hard won through eight years of warfare.

How fitting that at the surrender of Yorktown in October 1781, which turned out to be the last major military engagement of the war, the British band struck up the tune, "A World Turned Upside Down." One of the strongest militaries at the time was handed a humiliating defeat by its colonies. Second, it was a harbinger of events that would transpire in New Windsor at the last cantonment of the war, between 1782 and 1783 when the army was near mutiny.

Most students today learn that the Revolutionary War ended after the Siege of Yorktown, with the British, fighting on multiple fronts, realizing America would have its independence. However, after Yorktown, the Northern Wing of the Continental Army made its way to "Verplanck's Point on the Hudson River where they met and celebrated with French Troops returning from Yorktown."[98] Eventually, the Continental Army arrived at New Windsor to set up a cantonment on October 28, 1782. It housed more than six thousand troops and more than seven hundred huts where the soldiers would spend the winter. The war was far from over as the time spent at the cantonment became one of watchful waiting. Washington had every intention of renewing the war in the spring. However, peace negotiations interrupted his plans. While at the cantonment many issues and problems continued to plague the Continental Army. This was especially true when it came to supplies and pay. Soldiers always griped about rough conditions and what they earned. The next crisis was unusual, however, because senior officers became involved.

George Washington / National Portrait Gallery, Washington, DC

A constant problem throughout the war was Congress trying to provide the troops with supplies. They found many obstacles when providing for the forces, including the need to ask the states for money. States gave less money to Congress as the war looked to be ending. With no money for supplies, many times soldiers were at the mercy of local citizens for their food and clothing. As a result, toward the end of the war numerous mutinies occurred. In June 1781, thirty-one soldiers from the First New York abandoned their post, and according to Dave Richards in *Swords in Their Hands*, these soldiers intended on marching home and taking supplies by force. Other mutinies included the Pennsylvania and New Jersey Line which were part of the Continental Army. As Washington pointed out, many of these soldiers and officers served so long in the war that they had nothing to return home to and faced financial ruin.

The problems lie with the nation's first constitution known as the Articles of Confederation. After the colonies declared their independence from England, they needed to draw up a means to govern the United States. A draft of the Articles was submitted to delegates assembled in Pennsylvania in 1777. Although all the states did not ratify the Articles until 1781, the country operated under the constitution. As most students of history know, it created a weak central government without a president and one house of Congress. In this form of government, the federal government was subservient to the states. What laid the groundwork were problems with not only the Continental Army but creditors. Under the Articles of Confederation, Congress lacked the power to tax the states. Congress could request money from the thirteen states, but for various reasons, they were less than giving to the government. During the war, this created a difficult situation, leaving the government unable to procure supplies or pay the military. And without viable credit, money printed by the government was considered worthless.

Politicians, General Washington included, understood all too well that not paying the troops brought the possibility of the war coming to a disastrous close. Many officers resigned their commissions because they couldn't afford to remain in the army. Their anger hardly contained, they spoke of families at home; in many cases wives going without necessities because their husbands had not been paid in years. Many officers tapped out their savings. Some complained they made significant sacrifices for the country without proper compensation, while profiteers reaped large sums off the war effort. All were equally concerned about life after the war. Considering the hardships they endured, officers felt they were entitled to half pensions for life, back pay, and land bounties. Although Congress made numerous attempts to grant them pensions, the states were not so moved.

Reasons were numerous. Some governors worried that standing armies created a threat to the rights of citizens. Also, allowances legitimized a professional standing army, which many did not believe the United States needed. The governors also abhorred the idea of the states being taxed in order to pay for such an army.

Taxes were very unpopular with constituents, especially when imposed by a distant government in Philadelphia. Did the colonists throw off one yoke in place of another? Would this be another Stamp Act? With the Stamp Act of 1765, colonists were expected to dig deeper into their pockets to help pay off the large debt incurred by Britain in protecting its colonies in North America. This tax gave rise to the popular slogan, "No taxation without Representation!" With the war coming to a close, addressing soldier's needs became less urgent to states. However, Washington warned Congress if his army's pay was not forthcoming, perhaps the next uprising might not be stopped. If this new nation were to survive, Congress needed to act immediately.

Nationalists, being a minority party in Congress, offered up a solution. Prominent members included Alexander Hamilton (representing New York), Superintendent of Finance Robert Morris; his assistant Gouverneur Morris (no relation); and James Madison. They understood the Articles of Confederation weakened Congress and believed that the states should be subordinate to Congress, especially when it came to matters of taxation. As a result, they created the Impost Plan of 1781, which, if passed, allowed Congress to impose a 5 percent tax on the state's imports. Although it probably would not bring in enough money, it gave power to Congress to levy taxes and the means to raise money for the government. Nationalists such as Hamilton reasoned that European powers such as France and Holland wouldn't bestow unlimited funds. Creditworthiness had to be earned and proven. The purpose of the Impost Plan of 1781 was to start attacking the massive war debt of the new government, allow Congress to purchase supplies, and, most importantly, address pay for the army.

However, for the amendment to the Articles to pass, all thirteen states needed to consent. Rhode Island, and still later Virginia refused to comply. The amendment to the Articles of Confederation did not become law. Only a crisis would bring home the need for a more centralized taxing authority by the central government.

After the American victory at Yorktown, Washington spent a short amount of time at Mount Vernon, his plantation in Virginia. Gradually he made his way to the Hudson Highlands to take up his military headquarters at the home of Tryntje Hasbrouck, the widow of Colonel Jonathan Hasbrouck. Widow Hasbrouck was less than thrilled to have the commander-in-chief taking over her home for his headquarters. She vacated the premises months in advance so her house could be prepared for the general. Tryntje had no idea at the time that she wouldn't move back into her home for two years.

The Hasbrouck House was described by Newburgh City Historian A. Elwood Corning, "as not being wholly confined to any central point the more closely populated section, however, lay along King's Street." Contemporaries described the home "as being quite out of town." [99] Many saw it as a good choice for Washington because it not only overlooked the Hudson River but was close enough to West Point and the depots at Fishkill and Newburgh. Finally, the Hasbrouck House was located a short distance from Washington's troops in New Windsor. This home became Washington's most extended military headquarters of the war. Katie Benz, an historian associated with Mount Vernon in Virginia wrote, "although Washington stayed longer at his headquarters in Newburgh than any other location during the war, it was not his favorite. In an account of his first winter in the home, Washington described the home as, 'this dreary mansion in which we are fast locked by frost and Snow.'"[100]

With the possibility of renewed hostilities in the spring, Washington harbored dreams of retaking New York City some sixty miles to the south where the British had held firm since 1776.

If General Washington did not know how dangerous the situation was with his soldiers and officers, Colonel Lewis Nicola confirmed it for him in a document known as the Newburgh Letter. Some historians have incorrectly referred to it as the "Crown Letter" because some believe Nicola offered George Washington the crown to become king of the new nation.

Nicola was colonel of the Invalid Corp since "Congress authorized his command on June 16, 1777."[101] Writing from Fishkill, across the Hudson River from Newburgh, on May 22, 1782, Nicola wrote to General Washington regarding the desperate situation in the Continental Army. He mentioned that Congress provided no supplies, money, pensions, or other provisions to the troops, resulting in a disgruntled and demoralized army. He further insisted that a better form of government must surely exist. Was Nicola hinting that a constitutional monarchy might be a better solution?

Washington's response was swift and ferocious. The commander-in-chief wrote in part, "It is of great surprise & astonishment I have read with attention the Sentiments you have submitted to my perusal . . . no occurrence in the course of the War, has given me more painful sensations. . . ." The general continued that he was "at a loss to conceive what part of my conduct could have given encouragement to an address which to me seems big with the greatest mischief that can befall my Country."[102] At the bottom of the letter are the signatures of two of Washington's aides, Lieutenant Colonel David Humphrey and Jonathan Trumbull. Washington had the contents of the message certified by the two aides in case of any further mischief. Perhaps he was nervous that Nicola was articulating a commonly held belief in the Continental Army.

In October 1782 soldiers began to arrive at their winter encampment in New Windsor. This location was chosen because of its proximity to essential roads for supplies, the Hudson River, and the safety of the Hudson Highlands with the chain and boom at West Point. When all was done, the cantonment at New Windsor encompassed some "700 buildings and 6,000 to 8,000 people."[103] High-ranking officers such as Major General Horatio Gates and Chief of the Artillery Major General Henry Knox were also accommodated here.

After huts and other buildings were constructed, the Reverend Dr. Israel Evan, on December 25, 1782, proposed to Washington that a "public building be built at the Cantonment." It was completed early in the

Horatio Gates / National Portrait Gallery, Washington, DC

following year. According to archaeologist Charles L. Fisher, "by documentary and archaeological evidence, it appears this structure was built of wood on a stone pier foundation and plastered on the interior."[104] The building went by numerous names, the Temple Building, the Temple of Virtue, and finally the New Building. Sometimes the army used the building for religious services, levees, court-martials, and market days. Located on one end of the building was an office for issuing general orders for the day, and for storage of supplies. Washington believed the use of this building for religious services was a way to keep the men occupied with "correct behavior."

Even before construction of the Temple of Virtue started, rumors began to circulate that peace talks had opened up between England and the United States. In November 1782, the two countries signed a preliminary peace treaty. England, for the first time, recognized the independence of the United States. A cause for celebration created anxiety for soldiers and officers at the cantonment. They became concerned that they would be furloughed home with promises of back pay and pensions for their military service but nothing to fill their empty pockets.

Officers, too, believed if they left before securing their pensions and back pay, they'd never get them. "Washington often left Newburgh to visit Congress, where he dealt with issues such as the economy and the right of the central government to tax. To avoid falling further into debt, Congress began looking for ways to cut costs and targeted the Continental Army as the nation's largest expense. Congress initially planned to disband the army with the officers receiving half-pay for life (enlisted men were not to receive pensions)."[105] General Washington sympathized with his troops. In his letters to Congress, he worked to ensure Congress respected his officers. He wrote to James McHenry in October 1782,

> *These are matters worthy of serious consideration. The patience, the fortitude, the long, & great sufferings of this Army is unexampled in history; but there is an end to all things, & I fear we are very near one to this. Which, more than probably, will oblige me to stick very close to my flock this Winter, & try like a careful physician, to prevent, if possible, the disorder's getting to an incurable height.*[106]

As it became apparent that furloughs were to be issued by Washington, talk of mutiny grew louder and louder.

A few miles from the cantonment is the Ellison House, built by Colonel Thomas Ellison for his son John in 1754. John Ellison operated a mill nearby and provided the army with flour and firewood. He also traded with New York City and the West Indies by way of the Hudson River.

Henry Knox / National Portrait Gallery, Washington, DC

Major General Henry Knox occupied this home from 1779 until 1782 when he took command of West Point. With Knox down the river, Horatio Gates, second-in-command and commander of the cantonment took up his headquarters in the home. By November 1782, several senior officers, including Gates, Knox, and Alexander McDougall as well as others, discussed "the great distress under which we labor."[107] Henry Knox wrote "The Address and Petition of the Officers of the Army of the United States to Congress," laying it on the line to Congress. The petition was delivered and read to the chamber toward the latter part of January 1783. It started with,

> *At this period of the war it is with peculiar pain we find ourselves constrained to address your august body, on matters of a pecuniary nature. We have struggled with our difficulties, year after year, under the hopes that each would be the last; but we have been disappointed. We find our embarrassments thicken so fast, and have become so complex, that many of us are unable to go further. In this exigence, we apply to Congress for relief as our head and sovereign.*
>
> *To prove that our hardships are exceedingly disproportionate to those of any other citizens of America, let a recurrence be had to the paymaster's accompts, for four years past. If to this it should be objected, that the respective states have made settlements, and given securities for the pay due, for part of that time, let the present value of those nominal obligations be ascertained by the monied men, and they will be found to be worth little indeed; and yet, trifling as they are, many have been under the sad necessity of parting with them, to prevent their families from actually starving.*
>
> *Our distresses are now brought to a point. We have borne all that men can bear—our property is expended—our private resources are at an end, and our friends are wearied out and disgusted with our incessant applications. We, therefore, most seriously and earnestly beg, that a supply of money may be forwarded to the army as soon as possible. The uneasiness of the soldiers, for want of pay, is great and dangerous; any further experiments on their patience may have fatal effects.*[108]

The petition cited that soldiers who had already retired under half-pay promised them in 1780 were now destitute and starving. It asked Congress to pay the army pensions for service with the option of commuting it for a lump sum. Major General Alexander McDougall, Colonel John Brooks, and Colonel Matthias Ogden delivered the petition.

The Nationalists in Congress realized they needed to figure out a way to not only pay the substantial debt to its army, but also to its foreign creditors and domestic contractors. Simply stated, the government needed the power to tax. Increasing the power of the federal government made the states uneasy. The states could not be convinced to pay their share of taxes or even to grant more substantial taxing powers to the Congress under the Articles of Confederation. Could the army be used to attain those goals? Some historians believe that is what happened.

Historians find themselves split as to what happened at the New Windsor cantonment. One historian, Richard H. Kohn, illustrates three different theories about what happened at Newburgh. First, was the genuine threat of a coup d'etat, which Washington successfully defused; second, was "contrived" to help Washington attain a higher moral stature; and third, was the issue of the Nationalists using the army for its ends.

Most historians believe "the army's discontent had been used to pressure first Congress, then the individual states, into accepting an amendment to the Articles of Confederation giving the national government power to tax imports." This was the only way Hamilton saw for the government to meet its obligations. Also, in order to continue to secure loans, the government had to show a revenue stream. The money coming from the states was erratic and irregular at best. According to this theory, the Nationalists sought cooperation from officers such as Henry Knox to stage, if needed, a small mutiny to scare not only states but Congress as well into action regarding funding. When Knox proved unwilling to use the army as a pawn in this game, Nationalists recruited an adversary of Washington's, Major General Horatio Gates. His motivation has also continued to be a source of debate. Some have written that Gates did wish to replace Washington and even stage a coup that placed him in power. Hamilton in a letter to Washington, warned that the situation in New Windsor might unfold into something worse.

On March 10, 1783, an anonymous letter circulated among officers at the cantonment. Historians generally agree that the author of the letter was Major John Armstrong Jr., an aide-de-camp to General Horatio Gates. Armstrong wrote the letter at his headquarters in the Falls House a short distance away from Gates's headquarters. The message stated, "A fellow soldier, whose interest and affections bind him strongly to you, whose past sufferings have been as great, and whose future may be as desperate as yours."[109] It touched upon many injustices and humiliations that had befallen the army. The writer continued that "faith has its limits as well as temper, and there are points beyond which neither can be stretched. . . ."[110] The general belief was that if the country cared about the plight of its army, it would redress its wrongs. Instead, the anonymous writer wrote that he believed the country trampled on the soldier's rights. Even Washington was included, but not by name, "and suspect the man who would advise to more moderation and longer forbearance."[111] The solution was to make the soldiers' anger known. If Congress continued to ignore them, they could retire from the field refusing to take up arms for the new nation or march on the Congress. If the soldiers left the field of battle, the British could take over the colonies without much of a fight.

The meeting called for at the Temple Building was to listen to the response of Congress to the grievances that the officers had sent to Congress earlier in the year. The news coming out of Congress was not positive. One of the issues was that Congress was broke and could not compel the states to give them money. The officers who sent the petition to Congress met to consider the next step. They decided to call a meeting of officers at the Temple Building. A meeting was called to discuss what to do about the inaction of Congress. Calling for a meeting without first consulting General Washington was highly irregular.

When a call for a meeting without permission landed on Washington's desk, he was not happy about it. One can imagine him sitting in his office, once the Hasbrouck family's kitchen. Just outside Washington's office, his aide's de camp office bustled with correspondence arriving from all over the states.

The Armstrong letter asked all disgruntled officers to attend a meeting at the Temple Building at the New Windsor cantonment on the morning of March 11, 1783. Should Washington forbid the meeting? Should he allow the meeting? What should he do next? General Washington issued his General Orders from Newburgh on March 11. "The Commander-in-Chief having heard that a general meeting of the officers of the army was proposed to be held this day at the New Building, in an anonymous letter which was circulated yesterday by some unknown person, . . ."[112] Washington acknowledged how irregular the invitation. Washington made it

seem as though he had no intention of attending the meeting of the officers. Instead he would allow the senior officer (Gates) to report back to
Washington after the meeting, which Washington had changed "to be
held at twelve o'clock on Saturday next." It would convene at the Temple
Building. Washington knew that one of the issues to be discussed was, "to
hear the report of the Committee of the Army to Congress."[113]

Since the Battle of Saratoga in 1777, Gates had tried to capitalize on
his success there in hopes of replacing Washington as commander-in-
chief of the Continental Army. His effort became known as the Conway
Cabal, named after Brigadier General Thomas Conway. A group of senior
officers in the Continental Army as well as certain congressmen worked
with Gates in his efforts. A letter exposing the designs of Conway and
others eventually found its way to General Washington.

Conway realized he had underestimated Washington's popularity as
allies rallied in support of him. Gates admitted his role in the whole affair
to replace the popular general, and issued an apology. However, Washington would never trust him again. General Washington liked that Gates
was near the cantonment where he could keep an eye on him.

On the morning of March 12, 1783, a second anonymous letter
announcing that the meeting to be held earlier was now on March 15,
1783, circulated, stating that all were welcome to discuss their grievances.
Officers believed Washington endorsed the meeting because he had
allowed it to proceed. They would learn soon that they were indeed wrong.

The meeting on Saturday, March 15, started promptly at noon, with
Gates chairing the discussion. Soon after deliberations commenced
Washington "slipped through a side door unnoticed."[114] While Gates
spoke, he realized his commander was in the building listening to him.
He stopped midsentence. General Washington motioned for the meeting
to continue, requesting a moment to address the assembled men when
Gates was finished. This whole turn of events took Gates, who was hardly
in a position to deny the commander-in-chief his wish, by surprise.

When Washington stepped up to the dais, he started, "by anonymous summons, an attempt has been made to convene you together—
how inconsistent with the rules of propriety! How unmilitary! And how
subversive of all order and discipline—let the good sense of the Army

decide." Washington continued, saying the person who wrote the address had "insidious purposes" and "intended to take advantage of the passions, while they were warmed by the recollection of past distresses, without giving time for cool, deliberative thinking, & that composure of Mind which is so necessary to give dignity & stability. . . ."[115] Washington told the men he sympathized with them. He argued against taking up their swords against the civil government or even leaving the nation defenseless against its enemy. As historian Thomas Flemming wrote in *The Perils of Peace: America's Struggle for Survivial after Yorktown*, Washington looked out at the assembled men, and they did not appear very moved by his presence. Washington started to read a letter from Joseph Jones, a Congressman from Virginia, explaining how Congress was addressing their complaint.

Washington looked all of his fifty-one years of age. The war had taken a toll on him physically, emotionally, and, since he paid for all his expenses out of his own pocket, financially. Only those close to him knew that over the past few years he had struggled with his eyesight. He refused to bow to the weakness of wearing glasses, and instead frequently borrowed colleagues' glasses so he could read the mountain of correspondence on his desk. He finally had no choice but to order his own pair of glasses. A month before the crisis currently engulfing Washington's attention, he wrote a letter to David Rittenhouse thanking him for reading glasses. Rittenhouse was an optical expert who lived in Philadelphia. When Washington was headquartered in Newburgh, he was still struggling with the prescription as his eyes strained to adjust to them. In a February 16, 1783, letter to Rittenhouse, Washington referenced his new glasses that Rittenhouse had made for the general. "My sincere thanks for the favor conferred on me in the Glasses—which are very fine. . . ." The general continued that he still struggled with the spectacles because of their newness. "I find some difficulty in coming at the proper Focus—but when I do obtain it, they magnify perfectly."[116]

These glasses proved to be magical glasses. As Washington started to read Joseph Jones's letter he grew quiet. The officers saw Washington struggling, then hesitating, then growing silent as he squinted and moved his head closer to the letter. What was wrong with Washington? The general's hand disappeared into his great coat, removing something from a pocket. It was the silver frame eyeglasses made by Rittenhouse. Maybe the moment was staged or maybe not, but Washington looked into the eyes of those assembled and said, "Gentlemen, I too have grown gray in the service of my country, and I too find myself going blind."[117]

It was at that moment that the assembled officers realized the war had started when Washington was still relatively young, with his health intact. They noticed their commander-in-chief had aged dramatically since 1775, when he took command of the Continental Army. Officers softened their stance and swore allegiance to Washington. Some remembered that others had tears in their eyes. Horatio Gates was defeated again.

After General Washington left the meeting, the officers continued the agenda, but not before a resolution was passed reaffirming the military's allegiance to Congress. The same month, March 20, 1783, the Commutation Act of 1783 passed in Congress. It recommended, "five years full pay to all officers entitled to half-pay."[118] In April 1783, the impost amendment was approved but did not pass. For the Articles of Confederation to be amended, all thirteen states had to ratify the proposed amendment. In 1781, when it was first introduced, Rhode Island and Virginia voted against it. When it was recommended again in 1783, Hamilton could not vote for it in its present form, so New York did not ratify the amendment, and it was defeated again.

There was the possibility that if the army at New Windsor had not had its needs addressed, they might have marched on Philadelphia where the Confederation Congress met. A military dictatorship might have been established or even a tradition of the military becoming involved in politics instead of being subordinate to the government. General Washington quelled the crisis, "with an eloquent plea to his officers to remain loyal to Congress...."[119] Washington wrote to his friend Joseph Jones on March 18, 1783, "The storm which seemed to gather with unfavourable prognostics—when I wrote you last—is dispersed; and we are again in a state of tranquility to relax your endeavours to bring the requests of the Army to a conclusion."

"In April, the provisional peace treaty was announced, prompting Congress to release its Proclamation of the Cessation of Hostilities" and enabling Washington to issue cease-fire orders. He ordered a copy of Congress's proclamation be posted on the door of the Temple Building. "The Commander in Chief, orders the cessation of Hostilities between the United States of America, and the King of Great Britain, to be publickly proclaimed, to morrow at the Newbuilding and that the proclamation, which will be communicated therewith, be read tomorrow evening at the Head of every Regiment and Corps of the Army . . . ,"[120] and in June 1783, the troops were furloughed home. The Treaty of Paris was signed in September 1783.

When the war came to an end, it must have come as a relief to General Washington. By November 25, 1783, he was supervising the evacuation of New York City. He'd been chased from the city in 1776 and hoped to return triumphantly. In the long room in Fraunces Tavern, located in the southern end of New York City, Washington bade farewell to his officers on December 4, 1783. Afterward, he traveled to Annapolis, Maryland, arriving on December 19, 1783, to return his military commission to Congress.

After returning to civilian life, he headed to his beloved Mount Vernon. It must have been a welcoming sight as his home came into view, a place at which he wished to pass the rest of his life. George Washington finally was home on December 25, 1783. Instead, a tradition was created that stood with Washington's principles that the military should be subordinate to a civilian government.

# Cornelius Hasbrouck

Cornelius Hasbrouck was born in Newburgh in 1755. He was the son of noted patriot Colonel Jonathan Hasbrouck and his wife Tryntje DuBois. He had two sisters, Mary and Rachel, as well as four brothers: Joseph, Abraham, Isaac, and Jonathan Jr. In 1772, "nervous fever" took the lives of both Joseph and Abraham. A nervous fever is one that caused a person to be delirious or affected mentally. We cannot be sure what these individuals had because eighteenth century medicine dealt with symptoms not causes.

After the battles of Lexington and Concord, the Hasbrouck Household became energized. Cornelius's father, a leading, wealthy member of the community, was an early leader of the Committee of Safety for Newburgh. Both Cornelius and his father signed the Committee of Safety Pledge. Cornelius became the clerk for the committee. Still later, his father was commissioned a colonel in the Fourth Ulster County Regiment of Militia of Foot. Cornelius was commissioned an ensign and later recommended as an officer. His military career came to an end about the time his father became ill and resigned his commission. In 1778 and 1779 Cornelius was listed as exempt from military service. His father had resigned his commission permanently by May 1778.

By 1777, Newburgh had become an important place for military supplies. An additional ferry known as the Continental Ferry was near enough to the Hasbrouck's home for the family to benefit. Their mills supplied flour to the army, as evidenced in Jonathan's account ledger. It was about this time that Cornelius was helping his father with the day-to-day merchant activities, as his father was not healthy. The Hasbroucks' mills were also used in 1779 for the Continental Army to make clothing. Newburgh only increased in importance as time went on and along with that came friction with the quartermaster's department.

According to depositions in the Ulster County Archives in Kingston, New York, as well as housed in the New York States Archives (NYSA) in Albany, New York, in 1779, Continental livestock was being kept at the pastures of Colonel Jonathan Hasbrouck. His pastures were considered some of the best in the area. A Continental drover periodically moved the animals between different pastures, frequently staying at the home of the person who owned the pasture.

John Stillwell, a Newburgh innkeeper and butcher for the Continental Army, was approached in November 1779 by Cornelius Hasbrouck about an ox in his meadow. Cornelius asked Stillwell for his help because the animal had gotten out many times. It was wrecking his fences and he was tired of repairing them. He requested that Stillwell kill the ox, for which he offered part of the ox or pay." Stillwell came to one of Hasbrouck's pasture to investigate and seeing that the ox's horns bore the mark of the Continental Army declined Cornelius's request. Stillwell told a neighbor he would butcher the ox only if, "Cornelius got an order for that Purpose."

Stillwell recounted afterward that Cornelius came to his house mid-November in 1780 and informed him that there was a drover of cattle in his pasture. If Stillwell meant to make any money for himself, the time to move was now for the "cattle might easily be got out of the Pasture." Cornelius also told him the reason behind this was that "the Public had done much damage to him in his meadow and Pasture and was indebted to him and had not half paid him, and that he thought it would not be any harm to take cattle for it." All he was asking was that Stillwell go to Hasbrouck's pasture where the animals were kept and turn out two or three "yoke of cattle." Cornelius explained that he had spoken to another neighbor named John Simpson who would gather the cattle and take them back to his home. Stillwell refused.

One night in November 1780, the Continental drover lodged at the home of Cornelius Hasbrouck or Henry Smith. Stillwell refused to help Hasbrouck. Hasbrouck sent "a Negro man of the said Cornelius Hasbrouck came to Stillwell's house."[121] It is possible, because of depositions that were taken after Hasbrouck and his cohort were arrested that list the time that Cornelius was going to take the cattle as of November 1779, that Stillwell meant to say last November and not the last month, which would have kept it in 1780. The New York State Archives fire of 1911 badly damaged some of the evidence collected in this case, so there are some holes.

Still refusing to take no for an answer, Cornelius sent a slave to discuss the specifics of the plan with Stillwell. He asked Stillwell to contact John Simpson and have him let the cattle out of Hasbrouck's pasture. After Cornelius's slave left, he returned to Hasbrouck's home. Stillwell remembered that he went to bed shortly afterward. Then came a knock on the door. It was Cornelius.

He wanted Simpson to come to his house and wanted Stillwell to fetch him. Cornelius further instructed Stillwell that when he brought Simpson back to his home, if there were no lights on in the Hasbrouck home, then not to wake him. Instead, simply tell Simpson of the plan, which is what happened. After Stillwell explained the plan to Simpson, Simpson said, "he did not like it that Cornelius Hasbrouck was gone away, and that he feared if any Blame arose, Cornelius meant to throw the whole on him." After more discussion Simpson decided to do the deed requested of him. For some unknown reason, Stillwell decided to become involved after repeatedly telling Cornelius no.

The two men "proceeded to the field."[122] They threw down the fence with the intention of letting six oxen out of the enclosure, but six more managed to escape. They drove all the cattle to Stillwell's house. Once there Stillwell and Simpson decided to tether two oxen to a tree and turned the remaining cattle loose.

The next morning, Cornelius made his way to Simpson's house with Stillwell. All three men made their way to Hasbrouck's upper meadow. When people, probably the drover and others, started looking for the cattle that were missing, they quickly stumbled upon the three that were allowed to roam, which were grazing in the pasture of John Griggs. They also found the other seven returned to Hasbrouck's upper meadow where they contently grazed.

Perhaps fearing that they could be apprehended for their crime, Stillwell and Hasbrouck agreed they should let the two oxen tied to the tree go. The oxen had the initials N.H. on their horns. While in the woods

Hasbrouck provided Simpson with a tool to remove the letters from the animal's horns, but Simpson refused. Hasbrouck stated if the two oxen were not claimed he would give them to Simpson for drawing logs and other tasks he had completed for him. The five, which included the untethered oxen, made their way into the field of John Dolson.

Simpson must have been frantic when he found out the cattle that he untethered from the tree were now in Dolson's field with three other animals. He had to talk to Hasbrouck. Simpson searched for him and finally "found him in the Place called Newborough Town." Cornelius listened to Simpson and his solution was to leave the oxen there. He would simply give Simpson another pair of oxen from his, meaning Hasbrouck's, field. When Hasbrouck showed him the oxen that were to replace the ones in Dolson's field, Simpson objected. He went to Silas Gardner, later labeled a Tory, from whom he was able to secure a more suitable pair of oxen. Oxen there were not obviously stolen.

Both men retired for the night. The next morning, Cornelius came by to see Stillwell. The latter told him that Simpson, as of last night, was still not sure about the whole scheme and was still very nervous. The plan seemed to be rapidly unraveling. Hasbrouck told Stillwell and Simpson if they wished to back out of the plan, they should not be involved. Once the men decided they wanted to back out, Cornelius, an expert manipulator, seemed to accept this and asked the men how much he owed them for their trouble. They exclaimed nothing. Pretending not to know what to do with the cattle, Hasbrouck told Simpson to take two unmarked animals from his field and work them. If an owner came, he should just let the owner take them and pretend he did not know. If after a certain amount of time passed and no one claimed the animals, Hasbrouck said that "he might keep them work them or sell them."[123]

Hasbrouck appeared again to look over the animals in Dolson's field, Stillwell related to the court in his deposition. He found two animals that he claimed did not have army marks or brands and asked Stillwell if he wanted to buy them. Stillwell again declined payment for his help or the animals in question. Shrugging his shoulders, Cornelius took the animals, telling the men that he decided to keep the animals without the marks in order to work them or if no one claimed them, sell them.

Only a fool would believe that the army was not going to look for the missing animals.

Cornelius met Simpson the next day "at a horse race or some other public event." Simpson resided on land he had purchased earlier from Hasbrouck. During the conversation Cornelius informed Simpson that he had a pair of oxen that he wanted Simpson to take to his house and work. He told him this privately, having taken Simpson aside so others could not hear. A day or two after the race Simpson went to Hasbrouck's dwelling and looked at the oxen. Cornelius offered to sell the pair, which he claimed to have purchased from the Continental drover, to Simpson. Simpson remembered that the oxen were still marked with the initials N.H. When he inquired about it, Hasbrouck stated that the brand could easily be removed with a rasp. His asking price for the pair of oxen was $2,000 from the drover, but seeing the mark, the drover stated that he need not say anything about it. The drover lowered the price to $950. Simpson, impressed and actually believing Hasbrouck's rouse, paid Cornelius $2,000. This was a blatant lie by Hasbrouck. He needed to come up with a reason to satisfy Simpson that they were not stolen cattle.

Simpson recounted that he then drove the oxen to Benjamin Knap's property where he kept them for nine to ten days. He then exchanged the animals with Stillwell for a mare. The oxen he traded were between four and five years old. Hasbrouck, after the purchase, told Simpson that he had more cattle, which he (Simpson) understood to mean that they were public or Continental Army cattle. As Hasbrouck told Stillwell, he also explained to Simpson that since the army owed him money, "he had a Right to the Ox."[124]

Hasbrouck had other plans once the issue of the oxen was settled. He explained to Simpson that there was a milch cow at what was known locally as Jonathan Hasbrouck's Mill. The cow had been there for some time. Hasbrouck told Simpson he could purchase it for $700 with the stipulation that the cow be taken in the night and killed at Simpson's home. Simpson believed this cow did not belong to the military so he went along with the plan.

Simpson procured the help of his neighbors, Martin Weygant Jr. and Benjamin Knap, to retrieve the milch cow. When they arrived at the pasture, however, Weygant and Knap both balked, refusing to have anything to do with the killing of the animal. When Simpson asked why, the men pointed to the bell around the animal's neck. It was their belief that it indicated that it might be some poor old man's only milch cow. When Simpson assured them that it belonged to Hasbrouck, and he approved it, they refused to believe it. When Simpson returned to Hasbrouck's to tell him that the cow remained in the meadow, he was told to keep an ox instead. They "proceeded a mile farther to the meadow" where an ox was being kept. They drove the ox a distance of about two miles along a foot path and tied it in the woods where it would not easily be discovered.

When it was safe, the animal was taken to Stillwell's where he, Knap, and Weygant butchered it. Each man was given a quarter of the ox. Only Simpson seemed to notice that on the rump of the ox was "C.M." It clearly was an army ox. He had been duped! After the animal was slaughtered and no one had yet inquired about it, Hasbrouck approached Simpson yet again. He told him out at his mill that he had more cattle in his field. He asked Simpson to take them.

Many individuals would have quit at this point. Especially when the Continental Army's drover started looking for missing animals. Cornelius explained that he expected more cattle to come across the Hudson River soon. When they were about to arrive, he would tell Simpson by way of his slave so he could come down and take some away. When the cattle arrived, if it was not a good time for Hasbrouck, he would send his slave with "two half Johannes's to Simpson and that on receipt of such Token Simpson must immediately come down and take some of them away." A Johannes was a gold coin with a likeness of King Johannes V of Portugal, according to Ron Michener in his article on money in the American colonies.

A few nights later Hasbrouck's slave, whose name has been lost to history, came to Simpson's house and "brought him two half Johannes's."[125] When Simpson and Stillwell went to Hasbrouck's to discuss the cattle recently delivered, they were told that Cornelius had gone home because he was fearful that if the drover saw him out late, when the animals disappeared, he would be implicated. As indicated in Stillwell's testimony, Simpson became nervous that the two of them were being set up to take a fall for Hasbrouck.

Soon after this last interaction Hasbrouck, Stillwell, and Simpson were arrested. The harshest punishment was reserved for Cornelius because he was the acknowledged ringleader who not only received the stolen animals, but advised others to take them. Cornelius confessed, and was "indicted, tried and convicted of being an accessory both before and after the fact in grand larceny of sundry oxen of the goods and chattels of the United States of America."

Judge Robert Yates, in a letter dated January 13, 1781, to Governor George Clinton included the sworn examinations of John Stillwell, and John Simpson. He alerted the governor that Cornelius Hasbrouck had been tried and convicted in the theft of Continental Army Cattle. Governor Clinton no doubt was also made aware of the examinations of Benjamin Knap and Martin Weygant Jr. Judge Yates continued, "that Congress may upon your Excellency's representation, appoint pursuant to a law of this State a procurator or attorney, for the purpose of commencing suits ags't him"[126] in order to recover damages from Hasbrouck.

Two letters were penned the next day by the secretary of the New York Assembly, John McKesson, to the Congress, in which McKesson recounted the court case and his belief that an example needed to be made of Cornelius under a law enacted by the New York State Legislature in 1779, which "enabled the recovery of Continental Demands and punishing the misbehavior of persons in Continental employ."[127] He advised that the case for damages be pursued with great haste because Hasbrouck's jail sentence expired in less than two months. Since Hasbrouck appeared to be a man of financial means, it would be easy to recoup the damages. Although Cornelius Hasbrouck was not the first individual to steal from the Continental Army, it appears he was one of the more high profile individuals to be made an example of by use of this law.

Cornelius was released from jail on March 4, 1781. He returned to his home in Newburgh, New York, disgraced. It appears that almost eight months to the day he finished his sentence for stealing cattle, Cornelius was in trouble again for journeying to British-occupied New York City without permission. He sought to save his own skin by turning over other local enemies of the Patriot cause. He wrote in part to Governor George Clinton,

*Sr.*

*Conscious of Guilt for Past Offences leaves me Heart sick. But if a Confession of my Crimes Or the Sorrow I Conceive at the Sence Thereof, Could Raise Any Compassion in Your Breast for One Who Ever was his Countrys and Has Acted his Addressors Friend, But His own Greatest Enemy, is Buoyed up with Hopes he may be Forgiven & Admited to Return to his Once Peasfull Home. Not But Shame Forbids there Being A Stain left which will Remain and Cannot be Removed.*

He further assured Governor Clinton that he would create no more disturbances. Hasbrouck continued that his going to New York City "was without Any ill Intention, to the American Arms, But was Fully Actuated from Sinister Motives which I have communicated to Maj'r. Brush and shall leave the Relation to Him."[128] He concluded asking for a pardon from the governor and included a list of known Tories in the employment of the British.

Cornelius was correct in assuming that his name and reputation were ruined. This is made evident in the fact that no one remembered when he left Newburgh. All anyone could remember is that he went to Canada. Where in Canada? Everyone assumed he went where all Tories went, Nova Scotia. This too was wrong. Why did Cornelius stick around after his humiliations, including being branded? The answer lay with his late father Colonel Jonathan Hasbrouck.

In July 1780, Cornelius's father, passed away due to ill health. In his Last Will and Testament, Colonel Hasbrouck instructed that his lands be held in common by his surviving sons. His daughters were given a one-time monetary payment. Cornelius continued to work and live on his family's properties and focused his energies on managing the mills. During the same year, his grandfather on his mother's side, Cornelius DuBois Sr., made Cornelius an executor of his will along with other grandchildren. In 1785, Cornelius and his mother "both of the Precinct of Newburgh bound themselves to a Samuel Fowler Jun. for £2,040."[129]

Probably, Hasbrouck was waiting for his father's will to take effect, which occurred in 1786, when Jonathan Jr. turned twenty-one. Cornelius, who described himself as a miller, sold a good portion of his real estate interests to his brother Isaac for nine hundred pounds and a smaller portion to his brother Jonathan Jr. At this point, Cornelius all but disappears from the public records.

Whether Cornelius actually left Newburgh, at this time, is not known for certain. Most likely, his departure occurred between 1792 and 1800. He is listed in the 1792 estate inventory of Joseph Coleman, a yeoman living in Newburgh, as are his brother Isaac and his mother Tryntje. He is not listed in the First Federal Census in 1790; Isaac, however, is listed. The household at this time numbered ten individuals. In the category of "Free White Males over 16 including Heads of Families," there are four individuals. One of these individuals might be Cornelius, because Isaac's children were not old enough to be included in this category. Jonathan Hasbrouck III was born in 1785, Sarah Hasbrouck in 1788, and Israel in 1789. Four slaves are also listed.

There is no doubt that by 1800 Cornelius had left Newburgh. There is a transfer of property dated May 1800, for land he owned on the east side of what was known as the "Jacobus Kipp and Company Patent." He sold it to his brother Isaac for "500 dollars."[130] In this land transaction, he is described as Cornelius "late of Newburgh in Orange County."

It is quite possible that Cornelius Hasbrouck speculated in lands in western New York in the Military Tract, as is evidenced in the Hoffman purchase. Hasbrouck purchased soldier land bounties given to them for service in the American Revolution. Soldiers needed the money so sold the vouchers at lower prices for cash. It was a good investment for wealthy individuals like Hasbrouck. He could sell the lands later and make a large profit. There is no compelling evidence that he settled in that area.

In 1803, a notice was published in various newspapers by order of the Court of Chancery, a court that dealt with cases involving equity, compelling Cornelius Hasbrouck to appear. Cornelius, it is believed, was "either residing out of the state or concealing himself in the same."[131] The public notice lists Cornelius as a defendant in an action initiated by George Gardner and Richard Trimble, both of the Town Newburgh. There is no indication they ever located Cornelius. Isaac Hasbrouck still lived in Newburgh, and no light could be shed by him on his brother's whereabouts.

He was either protecting him or simply did not know. However, the death of Cornelius DuBois Jr., Cornelius's mother Tryntje's brother, again set off a flurry of public notices to find his whereabouts. When Cornelius DuBois Sr. drew up his Last Will and Testament, it stated in part:

> *Unto my son Cornelius during his natural lifetime All my whole Real*
> *Estate in New Paltz excepting such parts thereof as I shall hereafter*
> *to be sold by my Executors . . . after his decease unto the Heirs of my*
> *said son Cornelius and to my daughters Tryntje, Jannetie,*
> *Jacominetie, Saraetie, and to my Grand Children Nathaniel Dubois,*
> *Wilhelmus Dubois and Polly Dubois the Children of my Daughter*
> *Rachel deceased to my Grand children Direck Wynkoop and Lea*
> *Wynkoop the children of my daughter Lea deceased.*[132]

The nature of the will itself set off controversy. As instructed by Cornelius DuBois Sr., the lion's share of land he owned in New Paltz was vested in Cornelius DuBois Jr. The will stipulated that upon the death of the son, lands were to be divided among his surviving siblings.

Cornelius DuBois Jr. died in the spring of 1816. A complication arose, as most of the late Cornelius DuBois Jr.'s siblings predeceased him. A surviving sibling, as well as the children of the deceased siblings (and in some cases, grandchildren), believed the lands rightfully belonged to them, and filed claims for the parcels they felt were owed to them. Their share amounted to one-seventh for each person. Their intentions appeared in the papers of the day as public notices in 1816. Kingston Attorney John Sudam represented the petitioners before the Court of Common Pleas of Ulster County, New York. One of these was:

> *Tryntje, a daughter of the original testator and mentioned in his will*
> *who intermarried with one Jonathan Hasbrouck, of Orange County,*
> *before the termination of the life estate the said Jonathan*
> *Hasbrouck and Tryntje his wife, died leaving the following to wit;*
> *Cornelius Hasbrouck, Rachel now the wife of Daniel Hasbrouck,*
> *Mary*
> *the wife of Israel Smith, and Isaac Hasbrouck. . . .*[133]

A problem arose regarding the whereabouts of Cornelius Hasbrouck. In the public notice, it stated that the petitioners believed Cornelius Hasbrouck resided "out of this state, in what place is unknown to your petitioners."[134] Daniel Hasbrouck and Rachel, his wife, were known to reside in Orange County, New York. Finally, the notice concluded that both Isaac Hasbrouck and his wife were dead and "that before the termination of the life estate of Cornelius that both Mary and Israel died."[135] The petitioners listed Isaac's children as the rightful heirs to their parent's inheritance. It is, in part, because Cornelius Hasbrouck could not be served the papers that a copy was published in two newspapers, one in New York City and one in Albany, in order to satisfy the court. The public notices were published for three months. The division of the lands initiated a new round of legal problems.

During this time, Cornelius either saw the flurry of public notices or someone located him. The place where Cornelius was located was "the Town and County of Sandwich in Upper Canada," which today is just west of the Ambassador Bridge that links the United States with Canada. Both the town and county no longer exist, as they were absorbed into Windsor, Ontario, in Essex County.

Two years later, in 1818, the lands that Cornelius inherited with his sister, nieces, and nephews appeared in a local newspaper as an advertisement for foreclosure. The reason given for the foreclosure on the lands was that all members of the family, according to Rachel Hasbrouck, did not or could not reimburse the petitioners for the court costs related to the partitions. Thus, the original petitioners sued Cornelius and others to recover these costs. A judgment against Cornelius and his family in the Court of Common Pleas in Kingston, New York, was handed down. However, at the last minute, Cornelius's brother-in-law, Daniel Hasbrouck, and another family member, Rueben Rudd, saved the properties from foreclosure.

Cornelius Hasbrouck, realizing the legal problems caused by his absence, divested himself of all lands and interests. He accepted a payment of "1,350 dollars"[136] from John Sudam, the attorney and land speculator. The $1,350 Sudam paid was for those lands that Hasbrouck inherited from the partition of Cornelius DuBois Jr.'s lands. Cornelius

Hasbrouck also, for the sum of "one hundred dollars," granted Sudam all his lands in the "town of Newburgh in the County of Orange and elsewhere within the counties of Ulster or Orange."[137] Finally, Cornelius gave Sudam full power-of-attorney to conduct any business in his name in the future. Once those legal papers were completed, Cornelius Hasbrouck again drifted back into obscurity.

Speculation that Cornelius settled in the military tract in New York State does need further investigation in order to narrow down where Cornelius was between the time he left Newburgh and appeared in Upper Canada. Two questions remain unanswered—how and why did he disappear? In the earliest public notices of 1803, it is speculated that he purposely wanted to remain unfound for whatever reasons. He clearly disappeared from Sandwich after 1818. Perhaps one local historian in Canada can shed some light on this aspect of Cornelius's history.

Because that part of the province (our modern-day Windsor area) has changed hands a few times over the years, the reason someone may seem to disappear is because they technically no longer live there . . . even though they are still there . . . because the area has become known by another name (e.g., Upper Canada before it became the province of Ontario). As well, a person—for whatever reasons—may change the spelling of his family name, or change the name entirely.[138]

Cornelius Hasbrouck of Newburgh probably was not a Tory. There is no doubt that his neighbors, who in some cases suffered more than the Hasbrouck family, saw his actions as that of a crown sympathizer; a reason he might have been remembered as a Tory. His subsequent trip to occupied New York City probably cemented, in some minds, any doubt. A constant reminder to his neighbors was the visible brand he wore that proclaimed he could not be trusted.

# The Tory Ettrick

*Power always thinks . . . that it is doing God's service when it is vio-
lating all his laws.*[139]

JOHN ADAMS

Students are taught that the turning point in the American War for Independence was the surrender of the British at Saratoga. The Americans
openly courted France's direct involvement as an ally against the British.
King Louis XVI of France proved reluctant at first because the United
States had yet to win a significant encounter with the British army. When
the battle was won, the king was finally convinced to give the United
States not only money and weapons, but actual troops as well as France's
powerful navy. The French navy directly aided the United States in a deci-
sive win that turned out to be the deciding battle of the war.

The Siege of Yorktown lasted from September 28 to October 19,
1781. It started when Lord Charles Cornwallis, the British commander
in the southern colonies, retreated to the peninsula at Yorktown, Virginia.
One of the reasons was to keep his supply lines open with New York City.
General George Washington, who was in the Hudson Valley, planned on
attacking New York City in an effort to reclaim the city he had lost in
1776. He would be helped by the French navy and Count Rochambeau.

Washington's plan was abandoned when it was found out that Cornwallis was in an extremely vulnerable position in Virginia. When it was
discovered where the British were located, it was decided that the attack
on New York City would be abandoned. Instead, thirty-four French battle ships were sent from the West Indies to Virginia under the command
of Count Rochambeau. The French also had a large infantry. All of the
Continental Army's available resources were now focused on Yorktown.

With the Chesapeake and the Atlantic to his back, Cornwallis felt reasonably secure that the invincible British navy, if necessary, could supply his troops or evacuate him. He placed his faith in Sir Henry Clinton. However, both American and French officers realized quickly that they had almost ten thousand British soldiers bottled up in a trap. They moved quickly. General George Washington moved his troops from New York toward Virginia, while the French navy, under the command of the Count Rochambeau, joined General Washington's troops in order to lay siege to the British. The French navy sealed their escape route with a blockade, not allowing the British to be supplied or evacuated.

After some three weeks, the British army surrendered in October 1781. The Siege of Yorktown marked the end of major military engagements between the United States and Great Britain. However, almost three years passed before a treaty signed with England formally ended the war. Those three years, for the Continental army, became a time of watchful waiting.

As early as November 1781, scouts descended on the towns and villages near the cantonment in order to find suitable quarters for General Washington, who picked the Hudson Valley as the region to house his troops. General Washington was not distracted by the victory at Yorktown. Instead, he saw the opportunity to seize the momentum of the success in order to build more momentum to realize his desire for an eventual invasion of New York City. Washington was unconvinced that the British government intended to give up America that easily.

Since winter was upon them, the campaign season ended, and eventually, in 1782, the northern wing of the Continental army relocated into winter quarters in the safety of New York's Hudson Valley above the chain and boom located at West Point. The soldiers made the long journey from Verplanck's Point over present-day Storm King Mountain to New Windsor. Once at New Windsor, the Continental army constructed a cantonment, a semipermanent military encampment, that stretched for miles. This became the winter quarters for thousands of Continental troops. General Washington did not winter with the troops in the Hudson Valley, but rejoined his troops in the spring of 1782.

Prior to Washington's arrival, the quartermaster general's office scoured the countryside, looking not only for comfort for the commander in chief, but also for a home capable of accommodating his large military household. Many homes were considered but ultimately rejected. Thomas Ellison's house, the site of an earlier headquarters in the 1770s, was not available; nor was the home of Governor George Clinton, as scouts were met with vigorous opposition from his tenant. The exhaustive search by the quartermaster's department continued.

Timothy Pickering, quartermaster general, sent Hugh Hughes, assistant quartermaster, to the home of a widow named Tryntje Hasbrouck living in the village of Newburgh. Pickering knew the home well, as his family had rented quarters from the Hasbrouck family. The dwelling sat facing the King's Road, close enough to the Continental Ferry, Newburgh's supply depot, and finally a short distance from Washington's troops, who started arriving in October 1782. The home was deemed adequate by Washington's staff, however Hughes wrote on November 18, 1781, about the home and some of its possible "inconveniences."

> On the left hand, as you enter, is a Room about 12 by 14 with a Fire Place. Opposite to it is a narrow Room formerly a Shop, without a Fire Place. East of the two first mentioned, is a large Parlour, about 20 feet square, With a Dutch fire place or hanging Mantlepiece, North of which are Two small bed rooms & no Fire place in either. Upstairs, is one Bed Room Without a chimney—South of the Parlour, is a large Room with a chimney, Adjoining to which, on the West, is the Family's Kitchen—Supposing a Billet to be obtained for the two Rooms on each side of the Entry, that is, the Shop & the Room that Mrs. Pickering has, with the Parlour & the two Bed rooms North of it, I don't see where the General's Lady can be accommodated with a Room & Fire place, without incommoding the General, which I mention for your Consideration, Sir.[140]

What became an issue was Widow Hasbrouck's reluctance to leave. She was used to accommodating "guests" in her house, but these prior guests did not result in her having to leave. It was documented in a letter by Major John Tyson to Hugh Hughes:

> *On hearing that his Excellency was to Quarter in her home, [she] sat sometime in sullen silence. . . .All that I recollect she said was that General Washington & her could not both live in the house. . . . Indeed the whole Family seem as averse to his Excellency's quartering there as it is possible for people to be.*[141]

Tryntje Hasbrouck would have to endure months of inconvenience and displacement. New barns, privies (bathrooms), and other outbuildings needed to be constructed to accommodate the swell of people, animals, and stores. Accompanying General Washington were his slaves, aides-de-camp, cooking staff, and an almost constant array of visitors.

Hugh Hughes explained that Timothy Pickering's office and the kitchen he had built needed changes to "accommodate Mrs. Thompson and her Culinary Corps—An entire New stable needed to be built, as Mr. Hasbrouck has a large Stock & no more room than is requisite for them."[142] A stable also had to be built for the influx of horses that accompanied the officers staying at the Hasbrouck home. Also, accommodations for the Commander-in-Chief's Guard needed to be constructed.

Artisans from the Fishkill Barracks worked to ready the home for General Washington. There were numerous alterations to the dwelling, and even the Hasbrouck's storehouse on the Hudson River needed to be used by the army. Various writings convey that artisans completed the required work hours before the general arrived on March 31, 1782.

When General Washington arrived in Newburgh, his Life Guard not only accompanied him but camped near the corner of present-day Liberty and Ann Streets.

On June 15, 1775, George Washington was made commander-in-chief of the Continental army by Congress. The day after he accepted the position with a speech to the Continental Congress. Washington took command in Cambridge, Massachusetts. Roughly a year later, in his General Orders for March 11, 1776, he created the Commander-in-Chief's

Guard also known as the Life Guards. He chose four men from each of the regiments of the Continental army. He asked the officers of these regiments to,

> *for good Men, such as they can recommend for their sobriety, honesty and good behavior; he wishes them to be from five feet eight Inches high, to five feet ten Inches; handsomely and well made, and as there is nothing in his eyes more desirable than Cleanliness in a Soldier, he desires that particular attention be made in the choice of such men as are clean and spruce.*[143]

The commander of the guards was Major Caleb Gibbs. One of his staff officers was General Washington's nephew, Lieutenant George Lewis.

These soldiers were primarily charged with protecting General Washington, his baggage, staff, papers, as well as serving as a guard detail for headquarters. Their uniform became distinctive of their position of importance,

> *Gibbs was successful in securing blue and buff uniforms, but contrary to General Washington's expressed orders, Gibbs, for some unknown reason, probably the lack of an alternative, chose red waistcoats [vests]. These waistcoats became symbolic of the C-in-C Guard for the duration of the war. He also procured leather helmets with a bear skin crest, in lieu of the traditional tricorn hats. These apparently were captured by a privateer and were bound for the British 17th Dragoons. He had the red cloth binding removed and replaced with medium blue, and a white plume, tipped in blue placed on the left side. This unique headgear was to add to the distinctive appearance of the Guard.*[144]

Their buttons would have a first, USA on the face instead of their native state.

They became indispensable early on during Washington's stay at the Hasbrouck House when they helped prevent his kidnapping by a Tory who lived a short distance away.

There is a story that appears in E. M. Ruttenber's *History of Newburgh* about an individual identified only as Tory Ettrick or sometimes as Colonel Ettrick. The story has been reported as far back as 1837, appearing in various books and magazines. Where the sources came from or even the origin of the first name of Ettrick is lost to time.

According to Carlos E. Godfrey, who wrote about the commander-in-chief's guard, "There was no road along the river to the south for some distance, for in front of head-quarters the bank was a hundred feet high, and went sheer down to the water." He continued that the road went on for about a mile. Beyond where the Quassaick Creek "emerges from a chasm," into the Hudson, it created a "beautiful little valley, known afterward as the Vale of Avoca."[145] It is where Colonel Ettrick lived with his daughter Margaret. "His house lay almost in a straight line south of Washington's head-quarters and within cannon range." Ettrick's home is alleged to have later been owned by a Richard Trimble. Still later, it was, "mainly occupied by the Branch Railroad and the Pennsylvania Coal Company."[146]

When Ettrick found out that General George Washington was quartered in the Hasbrouck House, he decided to invite the commander-in-chief for supper at his home. Ettrick sent an invitation to the general that he wished to have the pleasure of his company. Prior to sending the invite, Ettrick prepared a boat for an escape from the house. Because the tide of the Hudson came so close to the home, the boat would be readily accessible to ferry himself or the general to a waiting British ship for the trip to New York City. He also planned to have additional Loyalists in the woods to surround his home while Washington ate. Once the signal was given, Ettrick would proclaim that Washington was his prisoner. The plot thickened when Margaret Ettrick found out about the plot.

Tory Ettrick's daughter was a Patriot. For many days, she listened to her father planning the abduction of General Washington. When she had enough information, she made her way to the Hasbrouck's home. She expressed to the guard at the door that she had very useful information for the general. After telling one of his aides the information, she was brought before the general himself sitting in the former Hasbrouck kitchen, now being utilized as his office.

She recounted to Washington the plan she overheard her father talking about with other Loyalists. She explained to the commander-in-chief of the Continental army that her father intended to have the meal last late into the night. Once captured, Washington would be brought to the ferry and strong rowers would easily reach the English vessels below West Point before Washington would be missed. It was not uncommon for Washington to arrive back at headquarters late. So, by the time something seemed amiss, Washington would be safely in British hands.

Washington's aides advised him not to keep the engagement, but Washington insisted. He called for his Life Guard. General Washington, "ordered a detachment of the Life Guard, dressed in the English uniform, to be on the ground before the arrival of the Tories."[147]

Washington made his way to Ettrick's home. The actual date has never been stated and has probably, again, been lost to time. While eating, Ettrick heard the shuffling of men gathering around the house. He became excited as he assumed his plan was nicely unfolding. Legend has it that Colonel Ettrick got up from his seat, walked over to Washington, placed one hand on the general's shoulder, and said, "I believe, General you are my prisoner." Washington removed the man's hand from his shoulder stating to his host with absolute confidence, "I believe not, sir, but you are mine."[148] A bewildered Ettrick looked out the window at soldiers now entering the dwelling. He realized he had been tricked and that the men who were taking him into custody before the general were his Life Guards.

Colonel Ettrick's daughter asked Washington what would become of her father. Most likely Ettrick would have been executed on the spot or soon after. His daughter became hysterical and dropping to her knees begged General Washington not to execute her father. When the general asked why he should spare his life, Margaret explained that if she knew he would kill her father, she would never have told him. She saved the general's life and she was asking him to have mercy on her father's. Without her father what would become of her? She had no means of support or a husband or any other family. The general, according to the story, spared Ettrick's life at the behest of his daughter under the condition that the two leave the area. Some authors write that they left immediately for New York City aboard the same ship meant for Washington as a prisoner. Still others believe that they eventually made their way to Nova Scotia in Canada.

General Washington officially departed Newburgh on August 18, 1783. "I shall set off for Princeton tomorrow. . . . I carry my baggage with me, it being the desire of Congress that I should remain till the arrival of Definitive Treaty which is everyday expected."[149] General Washington told George A. Washington, a nephew of General Washington, on August 18, 1783, that he did not expect to be back to Newburgh. The general took up his last military headquarters outside Princeton, being unable to secure accommodations within Princeton. The Ettricks were never heard from again nor can the story of Colonel Ettrick's betrayal be substantiated in any meaningful way because the sources where the story was written have since been lost. General Washington's papers and other notables from that period are silent about this kidnapping.

# Tories from Newburgh

*Elnathan Foster is a person notoriously disaffected to the liberties of America.*[150]

ABEL BELKNAP

Today Newburgh, in Orange County, New York, is a bustling city. Some two and a half centuries ago it was mainly a farming community that utilized its placement on the Hudson River to trade with New York City and Albany. Late Newburgh City Historian A. Elwood Corning described Newburgh, during the American Revolution, as not being "wholly confined to any one central point. The more closely populated section, however, lay along King's Street [Liberty]." A contemporary account recollected that the village "was limited in growth because of a great swamp."[151] The swamp ran for a considerable distance along the Hudson. Newburgh, because of its location and excellent bay, played an essential role in the American Revolution as a military depot and convenient Hudson River crossing, as well as hosting numerous high-ranking Continental Army officers, including General George Washington.

When you think of Newburgh during the American Revolution, it is generally not thought of as a hot bed of Loyalists. After New York City fell to the British in 1776, it is believed that some Patriots removed from downstate to Newburgh. On April 29, 1777, Colonel Jonathan Hasbrouck reported that there were fifty known Tory families living in this small precinct. Some remained in Newburgh and others fled to New York City. Some of the individuals, however, proved to be quite dangerous to the survival of the American cause. Elnathan Foster was one of thirteen Tories captured in April 1777. Captured with him were James Flewelling, who went on to join Claudius Smith's murderous Ramapo Loyalists, and another family member, John Flewelling, who defiantly refused to sign the Committee of Safety Pledge in 1775. This was a document that proved you were loyal to the Patriot cause.

Once the American Revolution commenced, many of Elnathan Foster's neighbors eyed him with suspicion and openly questioned his loyalty to the Patriot cause. Even though he signed the Committee of Safety Pledge proclaiming his loyalty to the Patriot cause in 1775, Foster still managed to run afoul of his neighbors, especially his regimental commander who ultimately had him arrested and sent to Kingston Jail in New York. Abel Belknap, a local justice, categorized Foster as "a person notoriously disaffected to the liberties of America."[152]

Foster's troubles commenced in July 1776 when orders arrived instructing him to attend a drill with Captain Samuel Clark, an officer in the Fourth Ulster County Militia. This militia company was mainly drawn from the village of Newburgh and was nicknamed "Newburgh's Own." According to Albert Gedney Barratt's multipart series, *The Fourth New York Regiment in the American Revolution*, published in the New York Genealogical and Biographical Society Record, during the first two weeks of July, the militia boarded the Sloop *Speedwell* to Fort Montgomery, which was under construction south of Newburgh on the Hudson River. The appointed place the militia would assemble was Weigand's Tavern.

Elnathan Foster did not appear at the scheduled time. His officer recorded that he refused to "stand his draft, class or to give money to raise the men required for that purpose."[153] The offense came with a steep fine that Foster easily paid as a somewhat affluent citizen. A short time later, Captain Clark issued orders again ordering Foster to join the troops because the British landed about two miles below Peekskill and the Fourth was ordered to Fort Constitution. Once again, Foster refused to muster.

He agreed to pay the fine again for refusing to assemble with the local militia. According to sworn a letter from Abel Belknap, Chairman of the Committee of Safety of Newburgh to the President of the Council of Safety in New York City, Belknap asserted that Foster made his way to the site where the men were assembling. Accounts relate that instead of participating he "mocked the parade under arms."[154] Foster later denied this accusation and claimed he could not join the militia because of ill health. He does not describe the illness. Another time, he was ordered to report for duty, this time to Ramapo, probably to guard the passes in the eventuality the British invaded. Once again, he ignored the order. He expected again to just pay a token fine and go about his life. Captain Clark decided to escalate the confrontation with the citizen who flaunted disobeying direct orders.

Captain Clark ordered the soldiers, the same ones with whom he was supposed to have reported, to place Foster in custody for insubordination. Surprised at this most recent turn of events, Foster insisted to the captain that he paid someone $16 to stand in for him. It was not his fault that the person he paid never showed up. He pleaded that the replacement should be in chains not him.

Foster seemed to have convinced the officer of his sincerity. After payment of yet another fine, authorities granted Foster parole until March 1777. While out on bond, the militia captain ordered Foster to march to an alarm at Fort Montgomery. "Foster neglected to march with the rest of the company, and he found himself arrested, put under guard, and a court-martial ordered by Colonel Jonathan Hasbrouck."[155] While awaiting the court-martial, which was delayed by seven days, Foster paid a twenty-pound bond to ensure his good behavior. While on parole he was arrested for a more serious offense. The complaint filed against Foster recounted that about "2 days before the court-martial sat, Foster deserted his country, to go to the enemy, and with several other of our neighbors, was taken by Major Wisner, and carried to Kingston."[156]

Major Henry Wisner of the Fourth Orange County Militia, was from Warwick in Orange County. He informed the Committee of Safety in Kingston, the first week of April 1777, that he "gained intelligence of a Party of Tories going down to join the Enemy upon which he raised a party of Men and went in quest of them."[157]

Wisner testified on April 9, 1777, that

*On Wednesday morning heard of two men going thro' a pass—called two Capts—proceeded by a Highway—overtook one—& afterwards*

*the others—overtook IV men & next day sent them to Goshen Goal—*
*That they were going to the Enemy—that they had procured a pilot—*
*That one says he was to be a Lieut'—That they acknowledged they*
*were going away—That he has bro't thirteen prisoners here—chiefly*
*from Newbury—acknowledged that they were going off.*[158]

Wisner overtook John Flewelling and his son James, "a little North of Stoten Berg"[159] and they stopped to talk for a bit. Wisner pretended he was leading men to New York City. In his later affidavit before the Committee of Safety in Kingston, Wisner recounted that both Flewellings told him they were going to New York City as well and would accompany him. Wisner believed it was with the intention of enlisting in the British army. Once the two men believed that Wisner could be trusted, they described their plan in great detail.

John Flewelling, told Major Wisner that the place of rendezvous was located in the Warwick Mountains. He was given the date and time to assemble. When they all met at the assigned place, Major Wisner's men seized the said "Fluining & twelve others belonging to this State,' viz' James Fluining, Elnathan Foster, David Wiot, Solomon Combs, Benjamin Smith, Stephen Wood, John Moffit, Benjamin Derby, Timothy Wood, Robert Denton, James Causman and Amos Ireland; and also four others belonging to the State of New Jersey viz' Micajah Waggoner, Coonrod Sly, Ebenezer Ellis & —Van Anden."[160] They would be placed on trial as enemies of the State of New York in Kingston, New York after spending some time in the jail in Goshen, New York.

The first testimony before the committee in Kingston came from Samuel Smith who was a private in Wisner's militia. He helped capture the Tories. Smith testified that Robert Denton told him he was going to leave Newburgh and go to the enemy in New York City. Earlier attempts had failed including an attempt last winter. This time he explained to Smith getting there would not be a problem because he was determined. Denton hoped to join the Light Horse if his horse was deemed good enough for the task at hand. Smith swore under oath that Denton told him he was a loyal subject of King George III.

William Wisner, a relative but not his brother, and a private in the Fourth Orange Militia, testified that John Flewelling approached Major Wisner asking him if he was going to New York City to join the British. Major Wisner told him yes.[161] When Flewelling felt he could trust Major Wisner, he told him a pilot had already been procured. In addition, Flewelling explained he already met with a Colonel Beardley who wanted to leave as soon as possible because he felt local citizens were beginning to suspect them as Tories and it was becoming too dangerous. It is important to point out that John Flewelling did not sign the Association Pledge ordered by the local Committee of Safety, so this already made him a suspect in the minds of his neighbors.

The longest of the testimony came from William Benedict also of Wisner's company. Benedict confirmed what had already been stated and added that he remembered Flewelling stating that if he could go home to Newburgh, for just three days, he could recruit between one hundred and one hundred fifty men to join the King's troops.[162] This was in addition to the twelve men already marching south with him. This was an impressive number because 238 citizens of Newburgh are listed on the Association Pledge rolls, 174 signed it and 54 refused to sign it. This would indicate that most in Newburgh were sympathetic to the king, which was probably not true.

Elnathan Foster, was the first Tory testimony heard before the Committee of Safety. He testified under oath that he was not an enemy of his country, nor did he desert his militia to enlist with the British. Quite the contrary, he stated he had paid an individual $16 to stand in for him with the regiment. For the last alarm, which ended up in his arrest, he could not find anyone to hire for his place. Foster explained that he was ill and contacted the lieutenant of the regiment to request permission to stay back. He continued, "That the Lieut desired him to meet him next Day at the wharfe which he did but the Lieut had not yet rec.d the orders. That he returned home and next morn.g about 9 oClock a guard was sent for him."[163] Colonel Jonathan Hasbrouck paroled Elnathan and ordered him to appear the next day for his court-martial.

He returned the next day as he promised his commanding officer, Hasbrouck, but was told that the court-martial had not been assembled.

Hasbrouck and the other officers present insisted on a bond of twenty pounds to assure he would show up a week later for his trial. If he did not have the money or refused, he would be placed in jail.

Between the time of his arrest by Colonel Hasbrouck for failing to assemble with his militia company and the bond that Foster posted to ensure he would show up for his courtmartial, Foster had decided to go to South Hampton on Long Island in New York. He told the court it was where he had been born. He does not explain the reason behind it or how he would get back in time for his trial. He intended to go down with a few neighbors and had contacted a man named Waggoner who ran a piloting company. This is where Foster was introduced to Robert Denton, who believed he was promised a lieutenant commission if he could get to New York City. Foster denied he knew of the ulterior motive of Denton.

Amos Ireland also testified he wanted to visit family on Long Island. He explained that he was a solider in the local militia. "That he was discharged by his officer because he was a cripple having had a tree fall across his Leggs."[164] He could not care for himself and had family on Long Island. This family was his uncle. When asked by the committee where his uncle lived, he told them he did not know. He never visited his uncle in Long Island prior to this, but his uncle was willing to take care of him.

Robert Denton swore, "That Flewelling set on to go & went into New Jersey and he the Examinant set out to go to New York. That he went about seven miles farther than Flewelling and was returning home when he was apprehended." The only reason he had for going to New York City was because others, most notably his brother who was a private in Captain Campbell's Company, persuaded him. In addition, a James Leonard, also of Newburgh and refusing to sign the Association Pledge, had already been to New York. Leonard told Denton that if he came in by May 1, he would be safe. Leonard and Morris Flewelling both had been to New York City and came back to Newburgh. Leonard explained that those who did not come to New York would suffer, "as they would put all to the sword."[165] Finally, Denton said he was told by Leonard that Campbell had sent for him. If he arrived before the stated date "he should have an Ensign or a Lieut Commission." Leonard directed him to one Van Orden who was a pilot and could safely guide him to New York.

Benjamin Smith, also caught by Wisner, had been a lieutenant in Jonathan Hasbrouck's regiment. Two months before being caught, he resigned his commission to Colonel Hasbrouck. He denied he was an enemy of New York State. When apprehended by Wisner, he said he had come up from New York City to buy horses in Wallkill. He did buy the horses and was going to head back to New York City when he was caught and charged.

The most dangerous of the men caught by Wisner's troops no doubt was John Flewelling and his son James. There is no doubt they both were avowed enemies of the American cause and New York State. They steadfastly maintained they had no intention of leading men to New York City to enlist in the British army. Both men felt, in fact, that they had been tricked by Wisner into something they clearly were not doing. John stated he was looking for employment in the Charlottenburg Furnace when he met Wisner. He decided to go to New York City only when Wisner asked him, but he went for employment, not to enlist with the British.

All the men seized by Major Wisner were confined to the Kingston Jail until it could be decided what to do with them. Roughly a week later the men were still in limbo. They created a series of petitions to the committee asking to be relieved from their deplorable conditions in the jail. The accused Tories asked if they could be allowed to return home to their families because while they were in jail their families could not provide for themselves. Their petitions were also sent to the Congress and they told the legislative body they would join the Continental army for three years as a way to prove their loyalty.

They allowed Elnathan to secure a bond to ensure his good behavior by May 26, 1777. Elnathan had to pay the treasurer of the State of New York one hundred pounds. He was also ordered to take an oath of loyalty to the State of New York.

*The condition of this obligation is such that if the said Elnathan Foster shall and do forthwith proceed to his usual place of Abode and there continue to reside & not to depart from the Bounds of his Farm untill he shall receive Permission from the Council of Safety or future executive Power of this State for so doing and also that in the mean time he*

*shall not say or do any thing inimical to the Liberties of America then*
*this obligation to be void else to remain in full force.*[166]

Foster claimed that from being in jail he was in a poor state of health
and that his wife was near death. He promised to be a loyal subject of the
State of New York. Foster was eventually allowed to go back to Newburgh shortly after Denton and another alleged Tory named Solomon
Comes were discharged from jail. Elnathan's freedom did not last.

When word reached Colonel Jonathan Hasbrouck that Elnathan
arrived back in Newburgh, he responded to the wishes of the Committee
of Safety in Newburgh to have him marched back to the jail in Kingston.
Hasbrouck ordered Captain Stephen Case to take him. In the event Case
was unavailable, he needed to appoint someone else to take Foster back to
Kingston. The job fell on Sheriff Egbert Dumond because Captain Case
was unavailable. It is important to point out that Newburgh was part of
Ulster County during this time period.

When Foster arrived, the committee in Kingston, which had freed
him, demanded to know why Newburgh disregarded their decision. They
demanded an answer especially from Hasbrouck, writing in a letter that
his actions were against an, "express Resolution of the Council of Safety &
unaccompanied by any reasons which might excuse that proceeding...."[167]
They issued an order that Colonel Hasbrouck "attend the Board to answer
for a measure so derogatory to their authority."[168] Instead of Hasbrouck
attending the meeting a letter arrived from Committee Chairman Abel
Belknap asking that Foster be kept in jail because the committee believed
him to be a threat to Newburgh as well as to New York State.

Abel Belknap wrote on May 29, 1777,

*Sr.—In pursuance of a resolve of the Honourable the Convention of the*
*State of New-York, dated the fifth of May last, for electing committees*
*in the different precincts of the counties within this State, for expedit-*
*ing the measures necessary for the general weal: we, in consequence*
*thereof, being elected for the aforesaid purpose of committee for the*
*precinct of New Burgh, think ourselves in duty bound to remonstrate*
*the evil consequences that we apprehend must arise from enlargement*

*of Elnathan Foster, an inhabitant of this precinct, whose conduct has*
*rendered him notorious to the liberties of America, which we presume*
*the Convention was ignorant of at the time of his enlargement: and*
*whereas the good people of this precinct are extremely unhappy to find*
*a character thus marked by his base conduct, to exist among them, as he*
*would have it in his power, on the approach of an enemy, to do infinite*
*mischief, have sent him back to Kingston; and we, therefore beg leave to*
*transmit to you the several charges against said Foster, which we pre-*
*sume will be proved on his trial, and which charges are as follows. . . .*[169]

Elnathan refused to obey orders from his officers in the Fourth Ulster County Militia to march or train. He pointed out that many of the militia men refused to march with him because they felt he was a Tory. Belknap stated that Foster made treasonous statements that the men who started the war could fight it. Finally, he was charged with desertion two days before he was going to be court-martialed. Proof that this was his motive was when he was apprehended by Major Wisner. The committee of New-burgh felt that in the event the British sailed up the river or invaded, the men apprehended, including Foster, would be the worst enemies in the area. Additionally, they felt for the accused Tories, remaing in Newburgh their personal safety could not be guaranteed because "Sundry persons have sworn they would not live in the neighborhood with them."[170]

The committee moved ahead with granting Foster until June 1 to pay the bond in full. By June 13, 1777, he again sent a petition to the commit-tee explaining he could not raise the money they requested. He requested their permission to travel to New Paltz to his sister's house. He did even-tually raise the money and was able to secure his freedom.

On April 17, 1777, Robert Denton and Solomon Combs were allowed to "enlist in Col. Van Schaick's or Gansevoort's regiments, pro-vided no more than one enlists in same Company."[171] They allowed these two men to join the service because they believed that Combs was simply heading toward Kingsbridge because he had a brother in Washington's Army. He was bringing his brother clothing and hoping to secure some salt for his family back home. Combs also told the committee that Ste-phen Pine and a man named Nathan Pine advised him to go to New

York City. He decided against continuing on to New York City. As far as Robert Denton, he also had a brother near Kingsbridge and was told by Leonard that if he did not come to New York before May 1, he would suffer the consequences as previously stated. They also believed that he was on his way back to Newburgh having realized what he was about to do was wrong.

The most notorious of the group caught by Wisner, as previously stated, was James Flewelling and John Flewelling. Many probably saw the letting of them go free as a mistake. After the two men were freed from the Kingston Jail, James Flewelling joined Claudius Smith's band of guerrillas in the Hudson Highlands. Smith's band lived in caves attacking those not loyal to the king. The partisans stole valuables as well as supplies to hand over to the British. Some papers reported that they also kept some for themselves. Their robbing and later killing of innocents became such a problem that Governor Clinton offered a $500 reward for the capture of Smith. He was brought to justice on January 22, 1779, and executed.

When James Flewelling and Richard Smith came to the house of John Clark they knocked on his door, and after being admitted "one pulled out a watch." He looked up at Clark and said, "it is about 12 O'clock & by one Clark, 'you shall be a dead man.'"[172] When Clark asked why they were going to kill him, he was told it was to avenge the death of two Tories he killed and a third he wounded. It occurred when Clark was soldier and, as he saw it, was done during wartime. After killing Clark, they handed a paper to his widow,

*A Warning to the Rebels: "You are hereby forbid at your peril to hang no more Friends to Government as you did Claudius Smith. You are warned likewise to use James Smith, James Flawelling & Wm. Cole well and ease them of their Irons, for we are determined to hang six for one, for the Blood of the innocent cries aloud for vengeance; your noted Friend, Capt. Williams & his Crew of Bobbers & Murderers we have got in our Provoe, & the Blood of Claudius shall be repaid; there is particular Companies of us that belongs to Col. Butler's army, Indians as well as white men . . . this is the first & we are determined to pursue*

*it on your Heads & Leaders to the last till the whole of you is Mas-*
*sacred. . . ." Eventually they sought sanctuary in the mountains.*[173]

Alarmed at the murder of Clark, Orange County Sheriff Isaac Nicoll
wrote Governor George Clinton on February 25, 1779, that he was worried if these men were not caught, when the weather became warmer
there would be more murders committed. James Flewelling was arrested
in February 1779 for the murder of Clark. He was executed in June 1779,
as was James Smith one of the killers of Clark. There would be other
Tories, such as the Tory Ettrick, from Newburgh in the coming years,
including one who would make an attempt to abduct General George
Washington, and even an attempt to abduct Governor George Clinton
that caught the attention of George Washington. General Washington
sent a letter warning Clinton of the potential plot.

One of the oldest cemeteries in New York State is the Old Town
Cemetery in the present-day city of Newburgh. Like so many cemeteries in large cities, it has become a refuge from city life with its grass and
large trees, a place of nature where, in an urban environment, there tends
to be little nature. If you walk across the burial ground, which was once
part of a five hundred-acre glebe for the Lutherans who first settled the
area, you pass among more than 1,300 gravestones that still survive today.
Historians believe more existed at one time.

As you continue to make your way across the uneven grounds from
Grand Street toward Liberty Street, in the direction of where the rem-
nants of Weigand's Tavern are today, you find the final resting place of
Elnathan Foster interred by his family on April 17, 1822. In the general
vicinity you will also find the unmarked grave of Robert Denton who
died twenty-one years before. Unfortunately, like so many stones, they
no longer stand. The anonymity Elnathan and Robert enjoy today eluded
them during their long lives. John Flewelling also returned to Newburgh
where he died in 1801.

# THE LOWER HUDSON

# Enoch Crosby

*I hasten this express to request you to order Captain Townsend's company of Rangers to repair immediately to the barn, situated on the west side of Butter-Hill.* [174]

ENOCH CROSBY

On October 15, 1832, an eighty-two-year-old man walked into the court of Oyer & Terminer and General Jail Delivery in Putnam County in New York State. Congress had passed an act in June 7, 1832, that entitled the elderly Revolutionary War Veteran to a pension. Looking at Enoch Crosby one would not know he was employed as one of America's earliest spies during the American Revolution. He took a seat and a clerk took down his story, which spanned almost six years. Some knew of him as Harvey Birch, a character based on Crosby's life in James Fenimore Cooper's novel, *The Spy*.

Most of what we know about Crosby comes from very few documents that are often quoted and reused. It makes sense that since he was involved in the war as a spy, there really was no paper trail, which might compromise his life or the lives of others he associated with when employed by John Jay. Perhaps three of the best sources in researching his life as a spy are his pension records, his biography, and the *Minutes of the Committee and the First Commission for Detecting and Defeating Conspiracies in the State of New York*, published between 1924 and 1925.

One problem with his pension records and his biography is that these two documents were created many years after the events they describe. Crosby's pension was recorded almost sixty years later and his biography, cowritten, was almost fifty years later. Other than the large events surrounding what is said, many facts really can't be corroborated.

Enoch Crosby / National Portrait Gallery, Washington, DC

Unfortunately, by the time there was great interest in this individual, most of the earlier pension applications and other files pertaining to the American Revolution burned when the British attacked Washington, D.C. during the War of 1812.

One thing is for sure, this shoemaker, born in New England, lived a life of excitement and intrigue, which is many times subsumed by more well-known spy rings such as the Culper Ring or more notorious individuals such as Benedict Arnold. When Enoch Crosby was starting out as a spy, it was also the early years of Washington's creating an intelligence network occurring between the Siege of Boston and the Battle of White Plains. Nothing in his early life would have indicated that Crosby was destined to be anything other than a farmer or a cordwainer.

Crosby was born in Harwich, Massachusetts, located in Barnstable County. Where he lived on Cape Cod was mainly a fishing and farming town much as it had been when founded in the late 1600s. He was born on January 4, 1750, the son of Thomas and Elizabeth Crosby, who had several other children. Thomas made his living primarily as a subsistence farmer. Because of New England's rocky soil, short growing season, and long winters, most farmers were only able to grow just enough for their families. If the harvest was a good one, they might have a little left over for trade.

When Enoch was about three years old, his father packed up the family and left Harwich for reasons unknown. He left Massachusetts and moved to Putnam County located in New York's Lower Hudson Valley. According to his biography, the farm was purchased in the township of Southeast, then part of Dutchess County, but today is considered part of Putnam County.

The family seemed to struggle financially from the onset, and eventually they lost their farm. Thomas was forced to move the family a short distance away to Brewster, also in New York. Enoch decided, probably due to better economic opportunity, to leave Brewster for what was then called Phillipstown and later Kent, New York. In Kent he became an apprentice to a cordwainer or shoemaker and shoe repairer. He spent the next five years as an apprentice until he completed his required service in 1771 at the age of twenty-one. The same year, he left Kent, New York, for nearby Danbury, Connecticut, to begin working his trade.

As a cordwainer, Crosby was more of a peddler than a shop owner. He had his wares in his knapsack, and traveled throughout the area looking for work. People would seek out his services to have shoes repaired or new shoes made. So, early on in life, Crosby was able to move and work among people of different classes and backgrounds unnoticed. Since most people still could not read, Crosby became a walking newspaper bringing news and gossip from town to town.

A turning point, according to Crosby in his pension and memoir, occurred after the Battles of Lexington and Concord. When word reached Danbury about the opening of the conflict with England, Crosby enlisted in his local militia as a minuteman. Two regiments were created for the relief of Massachusetts. They were commanded by Colonel David Wooster and Colonel David Waterbury. Crosby's direct officer was Captain Noble Benedict, who was part of Colonel Waterbury's regiment. According to Crosby's pension application, his enlistment was for eight months.

The Continental Congress decided to send an expedition against Quebec in August 1775, Enoch's regiment met in Greenwich in Connecticut where they camped for two or three weeks. From Greenwich they continued under General Wooster on to New York City, where again they remained for a few weeks, and finally left New York, carried to Albany aboard sloops. They "went directly to Half moon was there a few days went then to Ticonderoga staid there a few days to have the batteaus finished which were to convey them further."[175] Crosby remembered that General Philip Schuyler had the command of the invasion force all the way to the Isle aux Noix, at which time General Schuyler became ill and General Richard Montgomery assumed command.

According to historian Nathan Wuertenberg, the invasion began on August 25, "when General Montgomery ordered approximately 1,200 men mustered at the recently captured Fort Ticonderoga to march into Quebecois territory." Crosby was on this route embarking for Isle aux Noix in the Richelieu River. Wuertenberg writes, for Mount Vernon, that when they reached the Isle La Motte, they were rejoined by General Schuyler. It was from Isle aux Noix on September 17, 1775, that Montgomery laid siege to Fort St. John, "which commanded the entrance to Quebec at the northern end of Lake Champlain."[176] The soldiers came into full view of the garrison at St. John, which started firing cannons at the advancing Americans. As they continued their advance toward the fort, they were attacked by Native Americans. A retreat was sounded after the officers held an informal council.

Once they returned to the Isle aux Noix the soldiers started constructing breastworks under almost constant shelling. After finishing the defensive works, that night they left and marched upriver, where they remained for two weeks waiting for reinforcements. Finally, more soldiers arrived and the Americans moved back into position before Fort St. John.

On September 17, 1775, another problem was encountered, a shortage of ammunition. A detachment took Fort Chamblee six miles away with enough powder captured to continue the assault on Fort St. John. During this time Crosby became ill with a fever that forced him to be hospitalized. Against the doctor's wishes, as soon as he felt a little better, he rejoined his comrades in time for Fort St. John to fall on November 3, 1775. Crosby claims they entered the fort to the tune of *Yankee Doodle*. His enlistment expired on November 12, 1775, and Crosby, with Colonel Waterbury's regiment, marched toward home. They reached Albany and from there continued home to Fredericksburgh in the County of Putnam.

While at home and probably recuperating from the march to Quebec, the British and American armies battled over Long Island and New York Island. There is no doubt that Enoch Crosby heard about the loss inflicted on General George Washington. Maybe because of this or a simple desire for adventure or patriotism, in late August he went to visit friends in Kent, New York, where he re-enlisted in the Continental Army as a private in Colonel Jacobus Swarthout's regiment in Fredericksburgh now Carmel in the county of Putnam. Enoch signed on for nine months. The company left before Private Crosby could leave, forcing him to catch up to the troops. Their destination was White Plains in Westchester County, New York.

Shortly after they left, Crosby set out alone to catch up to the men. His ultimate destination was the American Camp at Kingsbridge. He set out traveling in early September after the Americans had already lost the Battle of Long Island. Washington was encamped at White Plains. Westchester has been claimed by many writers to be a neutral ground at this point. There was a lot of recruiting in Westchester for both sides of the war as well as a lot of violence originating from both sides.

While heading to White Plains, Crosby fell into the company of a man he referred to initially as a stranger. He met this stranger about two miles from "Pine's Bridge."[177] The stranger asked Enoch if he was "going down," which meant going down to New York City to meet up with the British. When Crosby answered in the affirmative, the stranger he identified later as Bunker, told Crosby that it was not safe to go alone. He explained, once he trusted Crosby, that he was in the process of raising a company to help the British defeat the Americans. He asked Crosby to wait a few more days because the raising of the company was nearly complete. Once it was complete they would "be ready to go down." Bunker also told Enoch that a gentleman by the name of Fowler was to be the captain of the company that was being raised and another individual named Kipp the lieutenant. Crosby's career as a spy for the Continental army was in full gear.

Crosby allowed Bunker to tell him what he knew about the plans to assist the English in New York City and even who was involved in heading to the British lines. All the time Crosby played along, pretending he, too, was a Loyalist. Enoch asked for as many details as Bunker would furnish to him, and he insisted on meeting the other men who had enlisted. The following morning, Bunker introduced Crosby to the neighbors who were going to be part of this Loyalist company. Crosby recollected that he spent three days in all at Bunker's home gathering as much intelligence as he could, before he informed Bunker that he could no longer wait because he was anxious to get going.

According to Crosby, he started on the road to New York in case he was followed by any of the men he just met. "He took advantage of an abrupt angle in the road, to change his course. . . . . ."[178] He bushwhacked through thick forest and brush. His ultimate destination was about eight miles outside White Plains. Historian John Bakeless writes that Enoch "made for the house of 'Esquire' Young, whom he knew to be a member of the Committee of Safety."[179] It was probably the home of Joseph Young, a member of the Committee of Safety in Westchester.

When Crosby finally arrived at Young's mansion late at night, the two men spoke for a while until both realized they could trust the other. Crosby informed Young about the information he had obtained from Bunker and how he believed it could be of some use to the right people. He asked Young to put him in touch with those people. In his pension, he recollected that Young asked him the next morning to accompany him to White Plains to the courthouse where the local Committee of Safety was meeting.

When they arrived, Young went in first to be interviewed. After the committee deliberated over the information presented by Young, they sent for Enoch. He relayed to them what Bunker had told him, and they requested his help in capturing the Loyalists. He agreed as long as they communicated to Colonel Swarthout that he did not desert the regiment. It was agreed that this would be communicated to the colonel. The committee explained that in this capacity he would be much more useful to the American cause than as a mere private.

In order to make it more believable that he was not working for the Americans but for the British, Captain Samuel Townsend, who headed up a company of rangers, was instructed to take Crosby as a prisoner. While being held a prisoner, Crosby asked the guard if he could go outside for some reason. It was allowed and once he was near a cornfield, Crosby absconded. A general alarm was raised but it was too late, Crosby was on his way back to Bunker's. He had been allowed to escape.

Once he made his way back to Bunker's home, Crosby explained the ordeal that he endured trying to make it to the British lines. In the end he explained, Bunker was right and he would wait for the safety of numbers. Bunker introduced Crosby to the rest of Loyalists and told him they were about ready to leave. The night he arrived Crosby walked several miles back to Young's home to advise him of what was going on with the company of now thirty Loyalists. Stationed at Young's home awaiting orders was Captain Townsend and his detachment of rangers. When Crosby returned to Bunker's that same night the Loyalist company, along with Crosby, were taken prisoner.

Crosby was taken with them and the group was eventually confined to White Plains where they remained for several days. "A part of the time locked up in a jail with other prisoners."[180] Periodically Crosby was brought before the committee to testify about the information he was able to obtain from the other men currently in jail. According to him, White Plains lacked a proper jail so they were marched after several days and he was housed in, among other places, a hatter's shack, where he remembered being guarded by a company of rangers commanded by Captain Clark. At Fishkill a committee for detecting conspiracies had been created and was composed of John Jay, Zepeniah Platt, Colonel William Duer, and

Nathaniel Sackett. These men deposed Crosby and were impressed by his abilities. He remained in the hatter's shop for about a week before he was bailed out by a man named Jonathan Hopkins. This was according to plan because the committee feared for the safety of their new spy.

During this time, the committee asked Crosby if he would continue to spy for them. They had reason to believe there were many companies being raised just like the one he had busted. Again, Crosby expressed concern that he would be labeled a deserter for not showing up to Colonel Swathout's regiment. The members of the committee told him they would write a letter to his commander telling him that Crosby was working for them. He would continue to receive his pay like he was with the regiment the entire time. If Enoch Crosby accepted the terms of the Fishkill committee, they had another assignment for him. Crosby accepted it. His disguise would be that of a cordwainer with varying aliases, including John Smith, Levi Foster, and John Brown.

When Crosby was sent on his way to root out Loyalists in Westchester, he was posing as a shoe repairman when he entered what he believed to be a Loyalist household. Harry Edward Miller, in his article entitled "The Spy of the Neutral Ground," in *New England Magazine* wrote, "He learned from them that a company of Tories was then being mustered with their headquarters at a farmhouse three miles distant." Crosby told the gentlemen in whose house he was staying that he wished to join the company. The gentleman introduced Enoch to the captain as well as the rest of the Tories. Enoch insisted on seeing the names on the muster roll to make sure no one knew him. He was asked to enlist, but he refused, saying he would sign it once they arrived safely behind British lines. He also found out that their assigned rendezvous was a "hollow haystack standing in an adjacent field."[181]

Enoch set a trap for the Tory company by suggesting that they meet in the haystack on a particular night. Unbeknownst to the Tories, while the men lay sleeping Crosby was able to make his way back to White Plains to alert his handlers to where the company was sleeping and tell them that he would make sure they were there the next day to meet. When morning came it looked as if he never left. The next day while the company made plans in the hollow haystack, they heard the noise of men outside where they were meeting. When they emerged they saw they were surrounded. All of the men, including Crosby, were arrested and marched off to jail in White Plains.

When the company of Tories reached White Plains, they were placed on trial. From White Plains, they were marched to Peekskill and from there to Fort Montgomery, which was still under construction. In an often-told story, Crosby met his old schoolteacher from when he was a child. The Patriot schoolmaster was horrified to find that one of his pupils was a Tory. What hurt the most is that it was sure to get back to Crosby's father, as he and the schoolmaster were friends, that his son become a Loyalist. Even though it was not true, Crosby was not able to tell anyone to the contrary because it could threaten his safety. Once the group left Fort Montgomery they were marched to Fishkill where they were housed in the Dutch Reformed Church. After meeting with the secret committee, Crosby had to come up with a way to escape. He was able to accomplish this by finding a window that he was able to force open. A tree close by allowed him to scamper down where a short distance later he mistakenly alerted a sentry. Crosby was able to escape into the night while soldiers fired at his escaping form.

Becoming increasingly concerned about his safety and the meeting of the schoolmaster, Crosby asked Jay that if anything happened to him could Jay tell his family that he was never a Loyalist. He wanted his family to know that he had in fact been working for the Patriot cause. Jay agreed and told Crosby that things were becoming unsafe for him in Fishkill. He was told that his next mission was across the Hudson River. Crosby gathered equipment for his journey, including tools, a knapsack, and other materials to make his identity as a cordwainer more believable.

Once ready, he was instructed to go to the house of Nicholas Brawer near the mouth of Wappingers Creek. Brawer would ferry him across the Hudson River. He was then to proceed to the house of John Russell, which was about ten miles from the Hudson River. Once at the home, he hired himself out to Russell "to work for him but for definite time."[182] Where Russell lived was known to be a neighborhood of Loyalists. Crosby tells us that the area he was working in was the town of Marlborough in Ulster County. He would remain employed by Russell for a total of ten days in

Dutch Reformed Church Fishkill, NY / HABS/HAER Library of Congress, Washington, DC

late October 1776. While at Russell's, he confirmed what John Jay feared, that a company of Loyalists were being formed with the hope of joining the British.

Crosby on a fairly regular basis was expected to cross the Hudson River to update someone from the secret committee about his progress. On one occasion he met with Zepeniah Platt to inform him that the

John Jay / National Portrait Gallery, Washington, DC

company was not yet ready to depart. Crosby was directed to cross the Hudson River back to the home of the Loyalist. Shortly after arriving, he was introduced to

> *Capt Robinson said to be an English officer & who was to command the company then raising. Capt. Robinson occupied a cave in the mountains & deponent having agreed to go with the company was invited & accepted of the invitation to lodge with Robinson in the cave they slept together nearly a week in the cave & the time for the company to start having been fixed & the rout designated to pass Severns, to Bush Carricks where they were to stop the first night.*[183]

Soon after meeting and staying with the captain, a time was set for them to depart. Unfortunately, it was also a time that Crosby was due to cross the Hudson and report to a member of the secret committee. He simply did not have the time to get across the river and back, so Crosby decided to trust the information to Silas Purdy. The Tories, he remembered, "called him a wicked rebel & said that he ought to die."[184] Crosby gave Purdy the information to take to the committee, a task Purdy swore to complete. Crosby returned to Russell's home.

The following evening the company assembled and left Russell's house, eventually arriving at Bush Carricks', where they spent the night in a barn. Purdy did his job well for Crosby. Before morning, the barn was surrounded by American troops. The whole company, including Captain Robinson, was taken prisoner. The place of meeting for the company the next day was Butter-Hill near Cornwall near New Windsor, New York. They never made it because Colonel William Duer of the Committee of Safety approached the hiding place with a detachment of Townsend's Rangers, commanded by Captain Melancthon Smith. Once again, all the men were arrested, including Crosby. As Bakeless writes, there is no doubt that Duer knew the identity of Crosby but did not tell it to the arresting officer. Robinson and the other Loyalists, including Crosby, were marched to Fishkill and placed in prison. Once back in Fishkill, Townsend recognized Crosby as the man who escaped from him and was determined to make sure it did not happen again. He was placed in the home of John Jay, which was the Van Wyck House.

If they thought this would hold him, they were surely mistaken. A servant working for Jay was employed to help Crosby escape. She served Townsend and his guard some French Brandy that was spiked with a drug to make the men fall asleep. She had received the drugs from a local doctor. While the men slept, she stole the keys from the guard's pocket and let Crosby out. He was able to escape and free himself of his irons with tools supplied to him.

John Jay felt it was becoming increasingly unsafe for the spy in and around Fishkill. He felt that some Loyalists were beginning to catch on that every time Enoch was around, they were caught and somehow, he always escaped. Jay wanted Crosby to lay low for a bit until he heard from the secret committee. Crosby made his way to a Dutchman's house who was a farmer.

The Dutchman, Crosby could not remember his name anymore, was located about five miles from the village of Fishkill. Enoch went to work making shoes while patiently waiting to be contacted again by a committee member. A short while after he arrived at the Dutchman's home, Crosby was contacted and told to go to Doctor Osborn's home about a mile from Fishkill. When he arrived at Osborn's house, he found that the doctor was not home, so he sat and waited. Eventually, John Jay showed up on horseback, dismounted, and walked into the doctor's home, making his way into his apothecary apparently looking for some medicine. He spent a considerable amount of time doing this until pretending to not find what he wanted, he emerged. Jay made his way over to his horse where Crosby stood holding it for him. Jay told Crosby to go back to his work with shoes because there were too many people around to see, as well as hear, their conversation. He informed his spy that he would return in a day or two.

When Jay returned, Crosby was notified that he should go to Bennington, Vermont, and from there, historian James Pickering writes in his article "Enoch Crosby, Secret Agent of the Neutral Ground: His Own Story"[185] in the journal *New York History*, to Walloomsac near North Hoosick in Vermont. Once in Walloomsac, Crosby was to locate a notorious Tory named Hazard Wilcox. John Jay wanted his spy to find out what Wilcox was doing to help the British. Apparently, Wilcox gave Crosby a list of people to the south that were friendly to the British. He found this to be true in Pawling, New York. Once in Pawling, according to Enoch's memoirs, he found the recruiting officer. He was able to gain his confidence and add his name to the muster rolls.

"In the centre of this town was extensive valley, boarded by high hills on the east and west; and in the midst of the valley is a great swamp, where the Croton river, Fishkill creek and some other streams, take their rise." It is here that there is a hill called Quaker Hill, so called because of the predominance of Quakers as well as a meeting house high on the hill. Near this meeting house the Tories held their meetings. Crosby called upon a "Doctor, whose name he thinks was Presser, & informed him that he wished to go below, but was fearful of some trouble."[186] Presser informed Enoch that there was a company being raised in the vicinity to go to New York to join the British army. The captain of the company was Joseph Sheldon. There was also a Lieutenant Chase who Presser was doctoring. Crosby was informed that the company was being formed for the campaign of 1777.

Crosby believed the last week in February 1777, the company of Tories were scheduled to meet at Quaker Hill, which was about three miles from the home of Colonel Andrew Morehouse, who commanded the Third Regiment of Dutchess County militia. Things were unfolding quickly and meeting with Nathaniel Sackett of the secret committee was not convenient. There simply was no way Crosby had the time to go to Fishkill. Instead he arranged to meet at the home of Colonel Henry Ludington, who Pickering writes, was also a member of the Dutchess County Militia. Ludington, he notes, was frequently involved in the apprehension of Loyalists. Crosby explained later in his pension paper that the time of leaving and the time it would take to get to Fishkill would not work, and because of this he traveled to Colonel Morehouse's and explained to him the need for his services. Morehouse agreed and started to raise the militia, which did not escape the notice of Tory surveillance.

Two Tories arrived at the meetinghouse on Quaker Hill. While heading over there, they saw Morehouse's militia assembling. They wondered if they were assembling to arrest them and if there was an informant among them. Some Tories were sent by Sheldon to gather intelligence on what was happening at the Morehouse home. While they were doing this, Morehouse sprang his trap and arrested all the Tories including, again, Crosby. In his affidavit, Enoch stated that he was at the home of Enoch Hoag when it was surrounded by Morehouse and the company taken as prisoners. It was around February 28, 1777, that the men were arrested.

Already planning an escape, Crosby approached Colonel Morehouse to tell him that while trying to escape he had injured a leg and could not walk. Pretending to show him no preference, Morehouse stated that he would be tied to a *crupper*. A *crupper* is "a strap buckled to the back of a saddle and looped under the horse's tail to prevent the saddle or harness from slipping forward."[187] Eventually, Crosby was allowed to escape. It was "ordered, That Ten Dollars be paid to Enoch Crosby for secret services."[188]

Crosby, it was clear was still a very valuable asset for John Jay and the American cause. Some, like Jay, however, were afraid that Crosby's luck was beginning to run out. Crosby did not share that apprehension and left Pawling for the nearby town of Patterson, New York. He could find no evidence of Tories planning any organizing. Quite possibly the Loyalist recruiters were becoming wise to infiltrators from the Americans. Crosby made his way back to his home base of Fishkill where he received orders to go to Doctor Cornelius Osborn (Miller in the Committee minutes). The cost was three pounds, two shillings for a smallpox inoculation because he was to head to Albany where there had just been an outbreak of the dreaded disease. He also would be sent to the town of Claverack.

During Crosby's absence, the Committee of Safety was disbanded. Crosby, while at Claverack, "acted as an agent, in transferring the property, which had been left by those Tories who had joined the enemy."[189] Bakeless writes that Crosby's success ended his career as a spy. Westchester Tories, especially, started to make the connection that everywhere Crosby was, they were arrested and he always seemed to find an escape under the most impossible conditions. "He became a marked man."[190] He was told by John Jay at the Van Wyck House that his services were no longer needed because it was too dangerous. Once he was no longer a spy, he was told he could tell his family about what his real role was during the conflict, that he was not an enemy of liberty, but a great asset.

Enoch Crosby decided to go in the Highlands of New York's Hudson Valley where his brother lived. Word had spread about his missions that resulted in many Tories being imprisoned. Local Loyalists made several attempts on his life. One attack almost cost him his life. When he was at the home of his brother-in-law Solomon Hopkin, "Tories burst into the house. There was an exchange of shots. Then the leader yelled, 'Let us pound him to death.'"[191] They beat Crosby unconscious leaving him for dead. It took a long time to recover from the beating. During an earlier stay at his brother's house a shot came through the window, grazing Crosby and lodging in the wall of the house. When he was able to, he decided to reenlist in the Continental army as a regular soldier.

This time he signed on for six months as a sergeant in Captain Jonah Hallett's company in May 1779 in Westchester County, New York. He continued to spy on Tories and assisted in capturing twelve British sailors who ventured ashore from a British vessel. His enlistment expired in six months and he enlisted again in May 1780 in Fredericksburgh, New York. He was again mustered in as a sergeant and enlisted for six months in a company commanded by Captain Gilbert I. Livingston in Major Elias Van Benschoten's first regiment of New York.

The regiment assembled at Fishkill, marched to West Point, and was stationed there for ten to fifteen days. "A call was made for troops to fill up the Brigade or Brigades under the command of Gen De La Fayettes, and they were to be raised by drafts or volunteers." Crosby volunteered for a company commanded by Captain Daniel Delavan. The company crossed the river and "marched to Peekskill where they remained one night. The next day marched to Verplanks point & crossed over to Stony point & from thence made the best of their way to New Jersey where they remained until late in the fall," probably October 1780. When Crosby's six-month enlistment expired, he was discharged. He remembered that during his six months, Major John Andre, the noted English spy who almost gained possession of West Point with the help of Benedict Arnold, was arrested. Andre was later "condemned & executed, several of the soldiers of Capt. Delavan's company went to see him executed."[192] Enoch was on guard duty and regretted that he could not attend the execution.

With his enlistment expired, Crosby's military career came to an end. He looked to put the war behind him and settle down. As an interesting note, it must have felt just that he was able to buy property seized from Tories that he spent his career rooting out. Enoch, along with his brother Benjamin, bought almost three hundred acres of land from Samuel Dodge and John Hathhorne, Commissioners of Forfeiture, in October 1781. It had been confiscated by New York State after the Forfeiture Act of 1779 was passed. Its full name was *An Act for the Forfeiture and Sale of the Estates of Persons who have adhered to the Enemies of this State, and for declaring the Sovereignty of the People of this State, in respect to all Property within the same.*" Those who remained loyal to the King during the war or had left for England were effectively banished from New York State and also gave up their rights to lands within the states. The land was confiscated from Colonel Roger Morris and his wife Mary Phillipse. It had been part of a fifty-thousand-acre land grant as part of the Upper Phillipse Manor. It would become the subject of a lawsuit by John Jacob Astor who claimed rights to the land because he had purchased it from Morris.

Sometime around 1785, Enoch Crosby married Sarah Kniffen, widow of Ephraim Nickerson. She was a close family friend when he was growing up. Why he married so late could be because his job as a spy was a dangerous one. Perhaps he did not want to have a family harmed or held hostage because of his life's choices.

He would have several children with Sarah. Enoch also was elected deacon of the Presbyterian Church two years after his father died and left a vacancy. Enoch served as a deacon from 1804 until his death. Sarah died in 1811 and was buried in the Gilead Burial Ground. In 1812 he was elected Town Supervisor of Southeast. He would also become a justice of the peace and associate judge for the court of common pleas.

In 1814 he married Margaret Green the widow of Colonel Benjamin Green of Somers, New York. He continued living on the land she had purchased, which also included a house. Margaret died in 1824. She was buried next to her first husband in Somers, New York.

If John Jay did not meet James Fenimore Cooper, we might never have known the story of Enoch Crosby. After conversations between Cooper and Jay, Cooper became enthralled with the exploits of Crosby, whom he claims he never met and never knew his true identity. Jay maintained to have never betrayed the true identity of the spy he discussed. Cooper's first successful novel was entitled *The Spy*. It featured the exploits of a spy named Harvey Birch. It is obvious when reading it that it is Enoch Crosby. It not only created instant fame for Cooper, but also for Crosby. In 1828, Crosby collaborated with H. L. Barnum and wrote his life's story entitled *The Spy Unmasked*. It was very successful and people wanted to know more about this man.

Listed as an invalid on his application in 1832, Enoch Crosby applied for a pension not only for being a spy from August 1776 to May 1777, but also a soldier in the Continental army from 1775 to 1780. He applied under the Benefits of the Act of Congress passed on June 7, 1832. In his affidavit he recounted, under oath, his exploits, with many of the names listed that he was able to remember. He must have felt that in his eight decades of life, he had little worry about individuals still looking to exact vengeance. His pension application was allowed on October 15, 1832. Enoch Crosby was granted a $100 pension.

According to an obituary in a local newspaper Enoch Crosby,
*On Friday evening, 26 instant, at his residence in the town of South-east, Putnam county, after a lingering illness, which he bore with pious resignation in the 88ᵗʰ year of his age. . . . He has fallen, like a shock of corn, fully ripe for the harvest of heaven.*[193]

Enoch Crosby passed away on June 26, 1835, in his home. As he requested, he was buried next to his first wife Sarah in the Gilead Burying Grounds.

Over the years as his popularity grew, people gathered at his grave to not only see it, but also to chip off a piece of his headstone as a souvenir. This took such a toll on the headstone that by May 15, 1914, a fourth and final headstone was erected over his grave. It was sponsored by his great nephew Ferdinand Travis Hopkins. The new marker was of Vermont granite and brought to the grave from Barre, Vermont. It measures ten feet, eleven inches high and weighed some seventeen tons.

If you travel around Carmel and Brewster, New York, reminders of Enoch Crosby are all around you. Although most of the lands he purchased are now submerged under the Croton Reservoir, his grave and the plaque placed there as a memorial over a century ago still exist. His home is also still standing and looks much as it did during Crosby's lifetime. It sits on four of the original acres. It stands as a testament to the humble origins of a shoemaker who turned spy for Washington's army.

# Ann Bates

*I had the opportunity of going through their whole army remarking at the same time the strength and situation of each brigade, and the number of cannon, with their situation and weight of ball each cannon was charged with.*[194]

ANN BATES

When Lieutenant General Burgoyne started his campaign in 1777, he was under the impression that General William Howe would come from the south in order to destroy the chain across the Hudson River and take the twin forts guarding it, rendering the Hudson River impassable. Instead of joining the force to ensure success, Howe left General Sir Henry Clinton in charge of a small force to both protect New York City and distract troops away from General Horatio Gates.

On July 16, 1777, General Howe loaded British warships under the command of his brother Vice Admiral Lord Viscount Richard Howe. According to Martha K. Robinson, an Associate Professor of History at Clarion University of Pennsylvania writes, Howe's move on Philadelphia surprised his superiors. "He sailed South along the coast and then headed up the Chesapeake Bay toward Philadelphia. He landed with 15,000 English and Hessians at the Head of Elk in August 1777."[195] Howe decided to attack Philadelphia to inflict psychological distress on the Americans. After all, Philadelphia was the seat of the new nation and where the Continental Congress met. Some have suggested that he had doubts about Burgoyne's chances at success or that he might be able to quickly defeat Washington and move into place for the 1777 Campaign. Finally, Howe overestimated the number of Loyalists who lived in the largest city in the British Colonies in North America.

General Washington and his roughly eleven thousand troops attempted to stop Howe but were defeated at the Battle of Brandywine Creek on September 1, 1777. General Howe entered Philadelphia on September 26, 1777. General Washington would be unsuccessful in defeating the British and forcing them from Philadelphia, in the Battle of Germantown on October 4, 1777.

Joseph Bates and his new wife Ann lived in Philadelphia when the British army entered the city. Some sources have listed Bates as already being a soldier, having met Ann when Howe occupied the city. Still others have recorded that he enlisted later, when the British were evacuating the city back to New York. The records about both of them are sparse. Much of what we know about them both comes from Ann Bates memorials located in the archives in London. Most of what we know about Ann comes from her deposition requesting a pension promised her by the British government for "Services performed during the late War in America September 14, 1785." It was presented before His Majesty's Justices of the Peace in the County of Warwick.

Her husband is listed as an "armourer"[196] in the Royal Train of Artillery, which means he would have been in charge of maintaining the cannons and making sure they were in good working order. However, he does not appear in any of the muster rolls in the archives in London, because, as one London historian explained to me, "the rank of armourer is never shown in the pay and muster books of the companies present in the 4 Battalions of the Royal Artillery shown to have been in New York and Philadelphia from 1775–1780."[197] We know more about Ann than we do about her husband.

At the time General Howe was getting ready to conquer the capital city, it is generally accepted that Ann was earning a living partly as a schoolteacher. She worked in a "Philadelphia school earning £ 30 a year." Ann supplemented her scanty income by "keeping bees, running a little store, and raising a few sheep."[198] In 1777, she was twenty-nine years old, having been born around 1748.

General Howe was the commander-in-chief of the British army in North America since 1776. However, in 1777, the tide had turned against him. Increasingly it was seen partly as his fault that General John

Burgoyne failed at Saratoga. The occupation of the rebel's capital city had been seen by some of his critics as a complete failure. His epic defeat of the Americans in the Battle of Long Island in 1776 was not enough to save him. Howe tendered his resignation in October 1777. It was accepted in April 1778.

Howe was replaced by General Sir Henry Clinton who decided it was best to evacuate Philadelphia because the British could not completely control the Delaware River that was vital for supplies. Also with the American-French alliance after Saratoga, New York City could be threatened by the French navy. The British left Philadelphia in June 1778. Having been recently married, Ann wished to join her husband, who was ordered to proceed with the evacuation to New York City. If her intelligence and fortitude had not been recognized, she might have just been one of many camp followers who followed the British army.

Prior to the evacuation, in May 1778, Ann met an American Loyalist whose job it was to recruit spies for the British network. His name was John Cregge (Craig) who, in the words of one historian, urged her to work as a spy for the British. Why or how she decided to start working as a spy is largely not addressed. It could have been because she knew artillery so well because of her husband or, as a schoolteacher, she was literate. Finally, because she was a "businesswoman" she could move among different circles of people without raising suspicion. Some have hinted that her personality hinted at success in this endeavor. Using the alias Ann Barnes, she would become employed by the "Different Commanders in America during the late war in bringing and conveying Intelligence from the Rebel Camps in America under the Command of General Washington."[199]

When the order came for the evacuation of the city by General Henry Clinton, Ann approached Major General Benedict Arnold, who had been appointed the military commander for Philadelphia when the British left. She requested a pass from him to leave Philadelphia to sell her wares in New York City. It is ironic that Bates was receiving a pass from one of the most notorious spies in American history. Once she had the pass in her hand, she was able to go from New York City toward General Washington's Camp under the assumption she was visiting some British prisoners. While on her journey she met some paroled British prisoners and they agreed to let her accompany them to New York. In late June, she arrived on New York Island where she was brought before Lieutenant Colonel Nesbit Belfour.

Balfour was a veteran of Bunker Hill where he had been grievously wounded, although he recovered sufficiently enough to participate in the battles in and around New York City in 1776. Once he was promoted to major, he began working closely with General William Howe, and was part of the campaign to conquer Philadelphia. Still later, he was placed in command of the Twenty-Third Regiment of Foot. After meeting Ann Bates, he introduced her to Major Duncan Drummond who was headquartered on Wall Street in Lower New York Island. Ann accompanied him to John Cregge's lodgings a short distance away. Drummond was one of General Clinton's aide-de-camps; he was also a Commissary of Accounts for Clinton, and handled Clinton's spy network, which shortly would include Ann.

It was at Cregge's that they spoke about how Ann could be of service to the British as a spy. When the meeting adjourned with Drummond, Ann was told to wait for her assignment. She was called for on June 27, 1778, by Drummond. When she went to Drummond's headquarters, Cregge and Belfour were also in the room. Drummond asked Ann to "go to General Washington's camp then at the White Plains."[168] During the conversation she was told in exchange for her service she would be granted "an annuity of ten pounds per annum for life." The major also asked her for a total sum of money that she believed would cover her losses in Philadelphia. Ann responded that her losses were thirty-two pounds consisting of "sheep, bees and clothing."[200] She was promised that she would be compensated for her losses. The conversation continued as to the logistics of this dangerous mission: what was expected of her and who she would be meeting and what information the men wanted from her.

Colonel Belfour presented Ann with a token. This would indicate to the person she would meet at Washington's camp, another fellow spy, that she was employed by British intelligence. She was to meet an individual in the Eighth Pennsylvania Regiment. Ann's disguise would be one familiar to her. She would be a *sutler* selling "thread, needles, combs and knives," which she would in turn be peddling to the men in the rebel camp. The four individuals disbanded until the morning of June 28, 1778.

After General Sir Henry Clinton approved the plan involving Ann, the new spy met again with Mr. Cregge. He gave her five guineas to buy the "necessaires" she needed to stock her moving store. Cregge told her she would begin her journey the next day on June 29, 1778. Ann told the Justices of the Peace in 1785, that she began her journey to White Plains, "having proceeded to Kings Bridge I was detained by a British Officer till evening then at my request was guarded to Colonel Simcoe's Camp, where the Colonel took care of me till the next morning when I received a pass to go through the out posts."[201]

She proceeded in the direction of the Rebel Camp, wading through the Crosswick's River because the bridge over the river was down. Ann remembered being in the water up to her armpits. John Bakeless wrote, "Her mention of this stream, near Trenton, [New Jersey] shows that the shrewd woman took a roundabout way to White Plains, passing through New Jersey to conceal the fact, that, though carrying a pass from the American commandant in Philadelphia, she was really coming from New York."[202] Bates finally arrived at the Rebel Camp on July 2, 1778. Once there she encountered an unforeseen problem. Ann, as she remembered in 1785, was supposed to meet a disloyal American officer. When she looked for him she was dismayed to find he had resigned from the American army for a reason unknown to her.

While in the camp her eyes went to work. She took in the position and strength of the Rebel army herself without the help of the officer with whom she was supposed to make contact. Until she found this person or received counter orders, she unpacked her wares to sell to the soldiers. While soldiers flocked around her goods, Ann took in all the information around her, especially ordinance.

Since she spent a lot of time with her husband as he worked on the ordinance for artillery, Ann Bates became quite familiar with the different types of cannons. While she walked about the Rebel camp she scouted out where the cannons were located, their size, type, and finally their condition. This expertise proved vital to the British. Since she was also a sutler, Ann could make small talk without arousing suspicion. After all, since she was traveling much of the time, many people relied on their news from her as well as gossip. Ann, in the process of small talk, was able to pick up bits of information in addition to just keeping her ears peeled for information she could use. This included listening to officers who sometimes had loose lips.

While making her way around the camp, either someone recognized Ann or she recognized them. How she knew this person she does not elaborate in her pension. Ann obviously trusted him enough to reveal her real reason for being in the camp. This soldier told her that he would be a good replacement for the officer she was supposed to have met but who had earlier resigned. He could not tell her why or where this officer went. All we know about this new contact is he was a freemason. Always thinking, Bates stated, "being a freemason [I] gave him what money I made of my goods that he might attend the Lodge and get acquainted with the commissaries clerk who was also a freemason . . . who would be likely to know the state of affairs."[203] In addition, this new contact told Ann that there was a potential deserter in Captain James's company. He told her the whole company was going on a mission to intercept English scouting parties nearby.

Once her wares were all sold, there was no reason for Ann to remain in the Rebel camp. She had downloaded into her memory a lot of useful information to report back to her handlers. Ann decided it was time to return to New York City. It was a dangerous mission going back to the British Headquarters as she found out. When she was in route to New York City, she was captured by a Rebel scouting party about four miles from White Plains. The experience must have been a harrowing one. If she was found out as a spy she could have been executed. Ann immediately found herself under suspicion by the American scouting party.

Ann described where she had come from and what her purpose was in going to the camp. She explained that she was a sutler simply selling her wares in General Washington's camp in White Plains and she was returning to gather more supplies. The interrogation went on for a long time. Finally, the officer in charge called for a woman to be brought to him. The woman arrived and after talking to the officer in charge, she ordered Ann to strip. They suspected she was a Loyalist and looked for papers or anything that might reveal she was spying. It must have been a humiliating experience. After she was allowed to get dressed, Bates found the Rebel woman "stole a pair of silver shoe buckles which cost two Guineas. A silver thimble, a silk Barcelona handkerchief and three dollars in cash."[204] After a short while longer the Americans decided to let her go. Ann continued her journey to New York City to report to Major Drummond all she was able to find out.

In his book *Turncoats, Traitors, and Heroes,* John Bakeless writes that Ann's information was reported to General Henry Clinton. To make sure she was not feeding them lies or, worse, acting as a double agent, Ann's information was collaborated by John Mason and John Romers, two other British spies on a similar mission. These two spies also reported hearing camp gossip that a combined French and American force was going to attack New York City. We know looking back from today that this did not happen

After resting for a day, Ann Bates was approved by Clinton to go again to the Rebel camp. She was given another five guineas to restock her stores of wares to sell at the camp. Ann was back in the camp at White Plains by the end of July 1778. This time she was told she would make contact with a disloyal American soldier named Chambers. Luck did not seem to be on Ann's side. According to an entry in Major Drummond's diary:

> She [Ann] went into camp Thursday 29 July unfortunately found that the Regt. Chambers belonged to, had been detached from Belly Forge against the Indians under the comd. of Coll. Butler. . . . And that he fell amongst the rest.[205]

Drummond was discussing the Wyoming Massacre of July 3, 1778. During this massacre 360 men, women, and children in the Wyoming Valley on the Pennsylvania Frontier were massacred by a force of Loyalists and Iroquois under the command of Colonel John Butler. American troops were sent in pursuit of the raiders and during a skirmish Chambers was killed.

Even though her contact was confirmed dead, she decided it best to do what she did last time. Ann Bates decided to again display her wares and make her way slowly around the camp to see if she could find any information. What she found out on this trip was that four brigades under four generals, including General John Patterson and Brigadier General Enoch Poor, were on a secret mission to Rhode Island. In addition, Ann also made her way into the Purdy house on August 12, 1777, which served as General Washington's headquarters, where two aides-de-camp were discussing additional information. Bates believed that one of the officers had just returned and was being brought up to speed on the latest plans by the other aid.

Bates was astonished that these men so freely talked in front of her, a stranger, about such sensitive matters. She took it all in, and even after the men noticed her, they continued to talk. They spoke of some four hundred boats that would be ready in fourteen days to carry troops to Huntington located on Long Island Sound, and from there the troops would attack and destroy Long Island. The information she heard was alarming and she felt that her handlers needed to know it as soon as possible. She waited until her wares were sold or mostly sold and once again made her way back to New York Island.

When she finally arrived back to New York City she gave the information to Drummond, who in turn presented it to Clinton. Ann also found out that Major General Horatio Gates and Colonel Daniel Morgan had 3,800 light infantry near Dobbs Ferry. General Marquis de Lafayette, with three thousand Continentals and two thousand militia, had left for Rhode Island. As previously stated, part of England's grand strategy to end the American Revolution was to isolate the New England Colonies from the rest of the colonies. Included as part of that strategy was a plan to blockade crucial American ports such as the one at Newport, Rhode Island. It was felt that once the Hudson River was secured, then Rhode Island could be used as a base of operations against the rest of New England. Prior to Ann Bates's information, December 7, 1776, the British under Lord Richard Howe sailed into Newport Harbor with some six thousand British and Hessian soldiers. Newport was quickly taken by the combined forces. Although prior attempts were made to rid Newport of the English, concentrated efforts occurred in the summer of 1777.

What Ann Bates was overhearing was the talk of Washington's army at White Plains attempting to cooperate with the French fleet and soldiers under the command of Charles Henri Hector.

This would be their first attempt at a joint operation since France and America became allies. General Washington hoped to dislodge the British from Rhode Island.

The French fleet arrived in American waters by July 11, 1778. While preparing for an attack on New York City, Washington also prepared Major General John Sullivan for an assault on the British at Newport. The planned attack against New York City was abandoned with "d'Estaing reporting that he refused ships to enter the New York Harbor"[206] because his ships would be vulnerable to British fire. Meanwhile, the British set their sights on Newport, Rhode Island, using Ann Bates's valuable intelligence.

Lord Richard Howe sent reinforcements to Newport on August 10 to match the French navy head on. Howe appeared at the mouth of the Narragansett Bay and the French sailed out to confront them, but a massive storm that lasted for days damaged many ships on both sides. D'Estaing, the French commander, made the decision to sail to Boston for needed repairs. Without the French navy, the American position in Rhode Island could not be defended. The expedition led by General Sullivan to take back Newport failed miserably. The Americans were forced to withdraw to the mainland on August 30, 1778. The British finally left Newport in October 1779 to protect the more important New York City from the French. While General Henry Clinton was in Rhode Island, Ann Bates remained in New York City until she was needed again.

In addition to the information about Rhode Island, word came back that the Continental army was on the move yet again, but where were they heading? Toward the end of September 1778, Bates packed her wares again and headed toward enemy lines. She found that fourteen thousand troops had been ordered to either Fishkill or Pigskill (Peekskill) the first couple of weeks in September 1778. Troops were placed under arms and divided into three divisions. The right was commanded by Major General Horatio Gates who marched for Danbury, the left was commanded by

General Israel Putnam who marched for King's Ferry, and the center was commanded by General George Washington who was headed to North Castle Mills.

Ann Bates decided she should follow Washington for the best intelligence. Taking the route she knew through New Jersey on her way back to New York City, she was met by Cregge who ordered her back to the center troops to find out their ultimate destination. It was during this time, September 1778, that Ann's spying in Washington's camp came to an end. She bumped into a British deserter named Smith who knew her and her purpose for being in the camp. Ann feared this deserter might turn her in to the Americans and she decided it was best to leave the camp. This, according to Bakeless, was September 25, 1778.

While returning to the safety of the British lines "she unexpectedly plunged into, instead, another American column—five thousand troops under General Charles Scott."[207] She was arrested for the second time on suspicion of being a spy and was interrogated by Scott. This was an extremely unlucky turn of events for Bates because Scott had been an intelligence officer near New York. Ann must have been quite nervous of being found out. What got her out of the predicament, she told the justices in 1785, was that she told Scott she was a soldier's wife and that her husband was a soldier in the center division under Washington. She claimed she was close to the American camp because she had forgotten something in the camp. She asked Scott for a pass to continue, which, surprisingly, he gave. She must have felt very lucky and not wanting to tempt fate anymore.

Once she was let go, she set out traveling again and eventually came into contact with British troops under the command of General James Grant. This was on September 28, 1778. She was sent by Grant to the rear of the column where she sat down with one of the general's aide-de-camps. This aide, with pencil and paper in hand, sat on a tree stump and copied down the information on the enemy that Ann told him. In an effort to prove who she was, Ann also showed the general the token that had been given to her in case of an extreme emergency.

Much to her relief, Ann Bates made it back to the safety of New York City on September 30, 1778. Once again, she met with Drummond.

While with him, she explained that she could no longer spy in that area for the British army. In her words, it was just too dangerous for her. She believed that her identity had possibly been compromised. If she was caught, she would be executed for sure.

Drummond listened to Ann and finally looked at her and said that he did not know what they should do. Drummond still wanted to use this quite awesome spy and asked her to accompany him to Long Island to meet a man he knew who was also working for him. Bates accompanied Drummond to the destination on Long Island. When they called on this individual, however, they learned they had missed him by a couple of hours.

Ann in 1785, again in her pension affidavit, explained to the justices that the next time she met Drummond, he directed her to go "about Forty Seven miles from Philadelphia," Bakeless writes that "this might have been Easton, Allentown or Bethlehem."[208] She was to meet with a representative of General Benedict Arnold. According to Bakeless, it was a woman she met. Nothing else is known about this spy. Bates continued her journey to Philadelphia by way of Middletown and Bordentown and finally reached her destination of Philadelphia. She had come full circle as she waited to meet with Arnold, would Arnold remember her as a woman who asked him for a pass?

What is frustrating, and echoes in other works about Ann Bates, is she does not use names very often, especially of fellow spies. Quite possibly this was purposeful because she did not want to endanger their lives. She feared for their safety as many of them returned to their prior lives.

When she arrived at Philadelphia the nameless woman spy became suspicious of Ann Bates because she did not have the special token that identified her as a spy from Drummond. Eventually, Ann convinced the woman that she was not a double agent. Ann gave her the directions she needed to meet with Arnold and left to head back to New York City. When she Middletown, New Jersey, the nameless woman spy caught up with Ann but decided it would be safer to split up again, and they each continued on to New York City.

Drummond had returned to England "after a quarrel with Sir Henry Clinton."[209] She records that without Drummond to look after her she was forced to shift for herself. It appeared to her that her days of espionage were over until she was called on again by Cregge in August 1779. He asked if she would meet with Major John Andre. When she arrived, Andre asked her to go back to Philadelphia to bring the lady spy she met earlier back to New York. Andre paid her ten guineas for her trip. After making the same trip that Drummond had sent her on, Bates returned to New York. By this time Major Drummond had returned from London. Since she assumed that her days of spying were over, Bates asked him about her annuity and how it would be paid to her. He explained much to her astonishment that he had a falling out with General Henry Clinton and was no longer his aide-de-camp so he could do nothing to help her. He assured her that Clinton was a man of honor and was sure he would honor the agreement.

In early May 1780, Bates was with her husband on board the ship *Earl of Darby* with reinforcements to join Clinton at the Siege of South Carolina. During the siege, "the magazines were blown up the armourer's Barracks being near were destroyed with Several men." She remarked that she had no quarters for shelter. When Major Andre found out about it, on June 3, 1780, she explained, "Major Andre knowing my distress was pleased to give me a few lines addressed to Major [George] Benson." She secured quarters by way of Benson. She obtained the quarters after being given a license to sell liquor, wine, and more by Major Money. Shortly after, she was contacted by Colonel Nesbit Belfour who was now the "Commandant of Charles Town."[210] He told Ann that her services were needed again. Ann was going to be sent with a letter of recommendation from Belfour to Major Money who would introduce her to the Lord Charles Cornwallis. This is where her services would be needed. When she was about to leave, Major Money was killed and the plan fell through. Belfour gave her a guinea for being so ready to go north to Cornwallis.

Ann Bates wrote a letter to Major Benson in March 1781. In the letter she wrote that her "health and Constitution being generally impaired I request Major Benson for Permission for my Husband and myself to return to England." Major Benson agreed and on March 6, 1781, they received permission to sail for England. Shortly after they set sail, a storm separated their ship from the other ships heading to England. Eventually they were able to dock in Ireland and made their way to Dublin where Joseph and Ann hoped to regain their health.

While in Dublin, she petitioned the English government for her annuity that Drummond had promised her now years ago. Ann was told that she would need to petition the Lord Lieutenant of Ireland of whom she wrote sarcastically about the petition, "which he was pleased to reject."[211] So, without her annuity she managed to set sail from Ireland and return to England to continue pursuit of her annuity. "Soon after our landing sickness sometimes on my side and sometimes on my husband. Reduced us to the greatest extremity of poverty."[212] She also told the English government in her petition that to make matters worse, shortly after arriving in England her husband deserted her.

Eventually, Ann Bates, one of the first women spies for the British during the American Revolution, had her promise fulfilled. This was probably due in part to a letter written on her behalf by Drummond. She was successful in gaining her small pension from the army for her services. She lived the rest of her life in England. In one of her last letters she wrote that if she stayed in America, she might have met the same fate as her good friend Major Andre who was executed as a spy helping Benedict Arnold to betray West Point to the English. Ann Bates died in 1801; where she is buried is no longer known.

# New York City and Long Island

# Margaret Corbin

*The preservation of the Passage of the North River is an Object of so much Consequence that I thought no pains or Expence too great for that purpose...*[213]

GENERAL GEORGE WASHINGTON

The opening battles of the American Revolution took place in New England. Most schoolchildren learn early on that on April 19, 1775, the "shot heard around the world" at Lexington ushered in armed conflict between the Americans and the British. Lexington, of course, was followed by Concord. Gage's troops retreated from Lexington and Concord as New England militia poured into Boston surrounding the British. The Patriot militia forces moved to surround Boston to restrict the movements of the British who occupied the town of Boston. It was an almost impossible goal to achieve because the British navy controlled Boston Harbor. With control of the harbor they could move freely as well as reinforce their garrisons.

In order to further entrench their position, the British began fortifying the hills that at one time surrounded Boston. The two most strategic hills were Bunker Hill and nearby Breed's Hill. Initially the thought was to fortify Bunker, but later officers decided to move to a smaller hill known as Breed's. On June 17, 1775, Major General William Howe and Brigadier General Robert Pigot led British forces in an attack on Breed's Hill as the British warship *Lively* shelled the militiamen. While the British defeated the Patriot militia, the determination of the New Englanders surprised them. It gave the Patriots a morale boost because the taking of Breed's Hill cost the British the lives of over a thousand soldiers and officers.

From April 1775 to March 1776, the Patriot army under command of George Washington, as of July 19, 1775, were also able to fortify Dorchester Heights giving the Americans unrestricted shelling of the British. Their siege was enhanced by the capture of ordinance by Colonel Knox from Fort Ticonderoga. It was transported from Ticonderoga by March 1775, on Dorchester Heights. The newly christened Continental army was almost twice the number of the British in Boston at this time. Although superior in number, the Patriots were hesitant to attack the British because of a serious lack of powder and shot. The tide changed once cannons arrived with Colonel Knox, and with the Americans commanding Dorchester Heights, they had the British at a distinct disadvantage.

The military governor since 1774, General Thomas Gage, along with Generals Howe, Henry Clinton, and John Burgoyne, was in Boston since the Battles of Lexington and Concord. Because of the large casualties on the British side, General Gage was replaced in October 1775, by General Sir William Howe. Seeing fortifications peering down on Boston from Dorchester, the new Commander of British Forces in America, General Sir William Howe quickly recognized the hopelessness of the situation. He decided to evacuate Boston on March 17, 1776, and sailed for Nova Scotia. The war would now shift south to New York City.

Washington anticipated General Howe's next move. Even before the British left Boston, he sent his second-in-command, Major General Charles Lee to New York City. Although loyal at this time, General Lee would later commit treason against the American army after he was captured by the British. Lee harbored resentment toward Washington because he was picked by the Continental Congress to be the commander-in-chief of the Continental army. It was Lee's opinion that he was more experienced than Washington and also had held a commission in the British army. However, at the present, General Lee's mission was to begin to set the stage for an attack on New York City.

General Charles Lee would continue south where, on June 28, 1776, he would heroically defend Charleston against a superior force of British regulars under the command of General Sir Henry Clinton. Although Lee was credited with the victory, it was not completely his victory to claim. Accolades rained on Lee when Washington recalled him from the siege of Charlestown to New York City. The commander-in-chief changed the name of Fort Constitution in New Jersey to Fort Lee in honor of Lee's heroic actions in Charleston, South Carolina. However, by this time, Lee was already bad-mouthing General Washington and seeking to undermine his command. This included writing letters to Congress and other generals about how inept Washington was as a commander. Lee hoped to replace Washington. His bad-mouthing of the general continued through the defeat in New York City. What ended his attempt to take Washington's job was Lee's capture.

The 1776 campaign opened with the British, still smarting from the tenacity of the New England militia, deciding that the best way to end the rebellion would be to capture New York City. With its ports and access to the ocean as well as the Hudson River, New York City held a tremendous advantage for transporting troops using the superior British navy. Once New York Island was secured, His Majesty's Navy would then conquer the entire Hudson River. By separating the New England colonies from the rest of the rebellious colonies, the rebellion, it was believed, would be crushed. George Washington was determined to prevent this strategy from becoming a reality for the British and their hated Hessian mercenaries.

On August 27, 1776, The Battle of Long Island (Brooklyn) took place. The Continental army was defeated with the loss of two of Washington's generals, Major General John Sullivan and General William Alexander, Lord Stirling. General Washington was forced to retreat from Long Island to Manhattan Island in the closing days of August 1776. His troops sought the safety of the northern tip of Manhattan.

General William Howe and his brother, Admiral Richard Howe, in an attempt to capitalize on the defeat, sent the prisoner, General Sullivan, to the Continental Congress to propose bringing the rebellion to a close. Congressman John Adams had his reservations about the intentions of the Howe brothers, he knew that William Howe did not have the blessing of Prime Minister Frederick North, or better known as Lord North, to open up talks with the rebels. His ambassador role was limited to granting pardons, not signing treaties or negotiating an end to the war.

Admiral Howe also attempted to open up communication with Washington, who at first refused to accept any letters from him because he found the letters addressed distastefully. Instead of their being addressed to General Washington they were addressed to George Washington, Esq. A clear snub at not recognizing his rank. He eventually agreed to meet with an emissary and quickly realized that Admiral Howe had only limited powers. He believed the peace conference would be a waste of time.

After much debate in the Continental Congress, it was agreed that Congressmen John Adams, Edward Rutledge, and Ben Franklin would meet with Lord Howe, Commander of British Forces in New York on Staten Island at the Billop House (Conference House) on September 11, 1776. "Lord Howe received the Gentlemen on the Beach. Dr. Franklin introduced Mr. Adams and Mr. Rutledge. Lord Howe very politely expressed the Sense he entertained of the Confidence they had placed in him, by thus putting themselves in his hands,"[214] recorded the secretary for the commission, Henry Strachey, who kept minutes. It became clear that Admiral Howe could not recognize the independence of the colonies, nor did he have the power to negotiate with Congress. John Adams recorded it succinctly on September 14, 1776,

*We met L[ord] H[owe] and had about three Hours Conversation with him. The Result of this Interview, will do no disservice to Us. It is now plain that his L[ordshi]p has no Power, but what is given him in the Act of P[arliament]. His Commission authorises him to grant Pardons upon Submission, and to converse, confer, consult and advise with such Persons as he may think proper, upon American Grievances, upon the Instructions to Governors and the Acts of Parliament, and if any Errors should be found to have crept in, his Majesty and the Ministry were willing they should be rectified.*[215]

Anything he agreed to had to be sent back to London. He had no power to enter into a treaty, especially with a government that the king's government did not recognize.

On September 14, 1776, the Second Continental Congress gave General Washington permission to leave New York Island to the British.

The general had been hanging onto Manhattan, believing it was the wishes of Congress. If the Battle of Long Island was a humiliating defeat for Washington, another blow would come on September 15, 1776, at Kips Bay, "where a Connecticut militia unit fled in fear and confusion." Washington was perhaps feeling low himself when he wrote to Congress that the behavior of some Connecticut militia was, "disgraceful and dastardly."[216] A bit of a boost to morale came on September 16, 1776, at Harlem Heights.

By September 16, 1776, Washington withdrew most of his exhausted and demoralized troops to the northern part of Manhattan near Harlem Heights. The general was anxious to know what the British plans were and when he should expect to engage them in battle. He sent Knowlton's Rangers to scout and bring back any useful intelligence.

Knowlton's Rangers was named for Lieutenant Colonel Thomas Knowlton. Thomas had enlisted in Durkee's Connecticut Regiment Twentieth Continental during the French and Indian War. Knowlton also showed himself quite competent at both Bunker Hill and the Siege of Boston. It was decided he would create the rangers after the defeat in New York City, "General George Washington recognized the Continental Army's grave need for an elite group whose sole objective was intelligence and reconnaissance . . . consisting of 130 men and 20 officers, the unit was charged with conducting reconnaissance, carrying out raids against British facilities and other dangerous covert missions."[217]

On September 16, 1776, Knowlton and his rangers were scouting in advance of Washington's army at Harlem Heights, New York. "While reconnoitering the British outposts they were engaged by elements of the light infantry brigade commanded by Major General Alexander Leslie."[218] The rangers were forced to retreat. As the British approached the American camp, they "were playing 'Gone Away,'" the tune sounded when a fox has been killed and the chase was over in a hunt. It is unknown whether the call was meant to mock the retreating rangers or was a direct insult to General Washington, well-known for his many foxhunts at Mount Vernon. Either way, the effect was the same. "I never felt such a sensation before," General Reed later remembered, "It seemed to crown our disgrace."[219] The Rangers were able to pull themselves together and counterattack with support commanded by Major Andrew Leitch. This time the British Light Infantry retreated. Unfortunately, among the American casualties were Knowlton and Leitch. However, Washington won a first battle.

After the Battle of Harlem Heights, George Washington waited for General Howe to make his next move. "On October 12, the British force landed at Throg's neck, a marshy peninsula, which was actually not part of the mainland. Marching westward toward the King's Bridge, Howe's troops were held initially off by a small group (about 25) of American soldiers at a bridge near Westchester Square, before the Patriots moved more troops into position. Today this is the site of Herbert H. Lehman High School, along the Hutchinson River Parkway."[220] They were thwarted by American fighters as they attempted to cross Westchester Creek.

Washington wrote his brother John Augustine:

*Whilst we lay at the upper end of York Island (or the heights of Harlem) How suddenly Landed from the best Accts we cd get, about 16,000 Men above us, on a place called Frogs point on the East River, or Sound, this obliged Us, as his design was evidently to surround us, & cut off our Communication with the Country, thereby stopping all Supplies of Provisions (of which we were very scant) to remove our Camp and out Flank him, which we have done, & by degrees got Strongly posted on advantageous Grounds at this place.*[221]

Friends of Pelham Park, which is an organization committed to the conservation and protection of Pelham Park, explains that General Howe tried again on October 18, coming ashore this time at Pell's Point in modern-day Pelham Bay Park, which was a few miles north of Throg's Neck. "The brigade of nearly 4,000 British and Hessian troops proceeded to an area now part of Split Rock Golf Course."[222] General Sir Henry Clinton and Lord Charles Cornwallis commanded the assault.

A small force under the command of Colonel John Glover used guerrilla-type tactics to thwart General Howe's plans. Glover's men hid behind stone walls to fire at the army, not unlike in the Battle of Concord. Overwhelmed by the oncoming British, they retreated to another wall, suffering losses in the process. Finally, Howe gave up and retreated. Glover's heroic actions allowed General Washington to retreat to the safety of White Plains from Northern Manhattan. "Only a handful of Americans died at The Battle of Pell's Point, while the much larger British force suffered serious casualties, estimated at 800 to 1,000 men killed or wounded."[223]

The Patriot army decided to eventually retreat to White Plains, which left Forts Washington and Lee exposed. Fort Washington was on the New York side of the Hudson River near present-day 183rd Street, while Fort Lee was across the Hudson River in New Jersey. These forts, especially Fort Washington, were seen as important obstacles to the British on the lower part of the Hudson River. From its vantage point, atop the Palisades, Fort Washington could rain cannon fire down on British shipping. However, with New York Island now abandoned, the forts stood isolated and undermanned. This was true especially after the Battle of White Plains, when Washington was unable to send help to Fort Washington.

Washington established his headquarters in White Plains on October 22, 1776, at the home of Elijah Miller. Here he hoped to not only consolidate his troops and supplies, but also avoid being destroyed by the British. Up until this point, by his ability to conduct an orderly retreat and the lack of aggressiveness of the British high command, Washington was able to keep his army intact. He believed that the terrain in and around White Plains would allow his troops to successfully defend themselves against the British. "As the British forces closed in on the Continental Army at White Plains, Washington prepared his Army for the coming battle. He anchored the American right on Purdy Hill near the Bronx River and the left on a large pond. Washington did not initially occupy Chatterton's Hill, which was to the right of the American lines."[224]

The Battle of White Plains commenced on the morning of October 28, 1776. A combined force of the Continental army and accompanying militia met the British advance. Washington sent additional men to Chatterton Hill as an advantage for his troops. Unfortunately, the British saw the importance of this hill and fought hard to secure it. Washington, in turn, sent Colonel Rufus Putnam to reinforce the hill that was under the command of Major General Alexander McDougall. The British knew if the Americans were allowed to take that hill, they could train a withering fire upon the British and their Hessian allies. "Howe dispatched eight regiments (approximately 4,000 soldiers) and 20 British cannons to attack the hill." The Americans were able to repel the first British assault on the hill. Colonel Johann Rahl, "reinforced by British cavalry, struck the militia on the extreme right of the American line and the militia began to retreat in disorder."[225] Washington, again defeated, needed to retreat, this time to North Castle by November 1, 1776.

Prior to the Battle of White Plains, as the Continental Army retreated to White Plains the question came up again among Washington and his advisors about what to do with Forts Washington and Lee. Washington felt the forts should be abandoned. He later wrote to his brother John Augustine in November 1776 that he felt the post was

> *a dangerous one: but being determind on by a full Council of General Officers, & receiving a resolution of Congress strongly expressive of their desires, that the Channel of the River (which we had been labouring to stop a long while at this place) might be obstructed, if possible; & knowing that this could not be done unless there were Batteries to protect the Obstruction I did not care to give an absolute Order for withdrawing the Garrison till I could get round & see the Situation of things & then it became too late as the Fort was Invested. I had given it, upon the passing of the last Ships, as my opinion to Genl Greene under whose care it was, that it would be best to evacuate the place—but—as the order was discretionary, & his opinion differed from mine, it unhappily was delayed too long, to my great grief.*[226]

Major General Nathanael Greene was convinced he could hold onto Fort Washington. He stressed the importance of retaining possession of the fortification. It is important to point out that the garrison lacked a suitable barracks or even a dependable fresh water source. If the British decided to lay siege to the five-pointed earthen fort, it could be a disaster. In addition, it was pointed out, if the redoubts extending outward from the fort failed, it would force the defenders to fall back to the main fort. In the event this did happen, Fort Washington would become very crowded with retreating soldiers.

Instead of crushing Washington's troops at White Plains, General Howe decided to reverse course and move on the Hudson River forts. A token force had been left at Fort Washington. The purpose, according to the Continental Congress, was to stop the British from ascending the Hudson River. There were not only the forts, but also various river obstructions such as *cheval-de-frise*, which looked like log cabins filled with rocks that were sunk to the bottom of the Hudson River. Protruding from the water were cast iron spears meant to rupture the hulls of passing ships. It was thought they would be especially effective because of the tides of the Hudson River.

As previously stated, the commander of the garrison at both Forts Washington and Lee was Nathanael Greene. Although the fort in November 1776, was under the direct command of Colonel Robert Magaw. General Greene, in anticipation of having to defend the forts, continued to increase the garrison at Fort Washington, swelling the troops to three thousand. Included in the troops was the First Artillery Company commanded by Captain Francis Proctor. A member of Proctor's artillery company was Private John Corbin, who enlisted as an assistant gunner. He was stationed on Laurel Hill, which would be later renamed Fort Tryon after the last British governor of New York.

Born in 1741, Private John Corbin was originally from Virginia, but later moved to Pennsylvania where he met Margaret Cochran, whom he married in 1772.

After Lexington and Concord, in April 1775, John Corbin enlisted in the First Company of Pennsylvania Artillery. Margaret accompanied him when he was sent marching. She would have been known as a camp follower. She prepared his meals, kept his uniform clean, and, if needed, she nursed him if he was wounded or sick. During battle she also brought him water for both drinking and cooling the cannon.

Camp followers were common in both armies from all classes of soldiers. They were not prostitutes like in later wars; they came along for many reasons. For some it came down to danger living on a farm without men or militia in the area, and for still others it was because of marauding armies. If they were useful to the army sometimes the women were given half rations. It is written in some sources that because of her gruffness and commitment to the army life, Margaret Corbin earned the moniker, "Captain Molly."

Howe hoped to conquer Fort Washington by launching a three-pronged assault on the fort. Prior to the attack, a British delegation approached under a flag of truce with a message for Colonel Magaw. They gave him the chance to surrender or face an attack in which the advancing troops would show the defenders no mercy. Magaw was given three hours to discuss the situation with his advisors. At the end of three hours the delegation expected an answer. Magaw explained that he did not need to wait the allotted time nor meet with his advisors. His answer was ready and he assured the delegation he would fight to the last man! Why were the British so confident? Perhaps they knew all too well the plans of the fort.

Some historians believe the British were so confident of their ability to take Fort Washington because they had help from the inside. William Demont, Magaw's regimental adjunct, defected from the fort on the night of November 2, 1776. He approached British lines with plans of the fort as well as the placement of cannons. Some historians have written that it simply confirmed what the British already knew about the fortress.

When the attack finally came on November 16, 1776, Washington was across the river at Fort Lee. In a letter to Congressman John Hancock, written the same day, Washington wrote:

*The preservation of the Passage of the North River was an Object of so much Consequence that I thought no pains or Expence too great for that purpose, and therefore after sending off all the valuable Stores except such as were necessary for its Defence, I determined agreeable to the Advice of most of the General Officers, to risque something to defend the Post on the East Side call'd Mount Washington.*[227]

Although he had given Magaw the order to defend the fort to the last man, Washington later instructed General Greene who had the command on the Jersey Shore, "to govern himself by Circumstances, and to retain or evacuate the post as he should think best," revoking the earlier order for an absolute defense of the fort.

Washington, to get a better look at the battle as it unfolded, crossed the Hudson River against concerns for his life. Corbin and his artillery crew were able to repulse two Hessian charges. Eventually the fort was overwhelmed. British General Hugh Percy got through the outer defenses of the fort's south defenses. Followed by Percy's break, British Generals Edward Matthew and Lord Charles Cornwallis broke through the fort's eastern defense.

On Laurel Hill, John Corbin was manning a small cannon almost continuously firing at the Hessians who were storming the outer defenses of the fort. His wife Margaret steadily carried water for the men, as well as to cool the cannon that must have been very hot from constant use. Eventually, a Hessian bullet found one of the gunners and he dropped. Corbin took up the recently killed man's post of loading the cannon. His wife, seeing that the crew was short a person, began helping with keeping the cannon clean of embers as still more men fell. It was an important job because the hot embers could cause the canon to fire prematurely, resulting in serious injury or death of those nearby.

While Margaret and John Corbin continued to fire the canon, a bullet found John. He fell with a mortal wound. Margaret, stunned for a minute, did not have time to think much about what just happened. She was under almost continuous fire from the Hessians advancing toward her. Without thinking, she picked up his tool and made sure with the other surviving crew to keep the cannon active. An enemy cannon found the current range and fired deadly grapeshot at the position. Grapeshot is a small canister filled with iron balls, much like a shotgun blast. Some of the spray from the blast of grapeshot ripped through Margaret's body. She must have felt shearing pain, as her left arm was almost severed and grapeshot shattered her jaw and tore through her chest.

Fort Washington surrendered November 16, 1776, at 3 p.m., about five hours after it had been attacked. In a letter to his brother John Augustine, Washington wrote about the falling of the fort,

*We have no particular Acct of the loss on either side, or of the Circum-
stances attending this matter, the whole Garrison after being drove
from the out lines & retiring within the Fort surrendered themselves
Prisoners of War, and giving me no Acct of the terms. By a Letter wch
I have just receivd from Genl Greene at Fort Lee (wch is opposite to
Fort Washington) I am informd that "one of the Train of Artillery
came across the River last Night on a Raft—by his Acct the Enemy
have suffered greatly on the North side of Fort Washington—Colo.
Rawlings's Regiment (late Hugh Stephenson's) was posted there, and
behaved with great Spirit—Colo. Magaw could not get the Men to
Man the Lines, otherwise he would not have given up the Fort.*[228]

When the battle stopped, British soldiers walked over the field. There
were many wounded and still more dead or dying. As the British were
going over the field looking for those they could possibly evacuate, they
came across Margaret Corbin laying near her husband. She looked dead
from the grievous wounds that were apparent to the soldiers. Upon closer
examination, the field doctor realized the woman was covered in blood
but apparently still clinging to life, just barely.

In a tremendous amount of pain, she was placed in a wagon along
a bumpy road back to the British camp. Arrangements were made to
bring her to a waiting boat to transport her to Fort Lee, which still held
out against the British. Fort Lee would be retained by the Americans
until November 20, 1776. Margaret Corbin was kept at Fort Lee while
she recuperated. It is believed she remained in Fort Lee even after it
surrendered.

When she was strong enough to travel, the British granted Margaret
parole to go back to Pennsylvania for additional care. It appears this is
what she did. Doctors patched her wounds up the best they could, but her
left arm remained lame for the rest of her life. One imagines with a shattered jaw that eating was also a chore. A shattered jaw could not be set as
doctors can do today. There is no doubt that her wounds, even if healed,
were still a source of discomfort.

"Included in the papers of the War Department is a letter book kept
by William Price, Commissary of Military Stores at West Point from

1784 to 1787. In the early years of the 1780s, West Point was home to the Corps of Invalids, a regiment of permanently disabled Revolutionary War veterans that had been established in 1777." It is through these papers that we can piece together a little about Margaret's life after Fort Washington. Once she was able, she made her way to Highland Mills near West Point in the Hudson Valley of New York. Once here, she became one of the first members of the Invalid Corp commanded by Colonel Lewis Nicola, which was located at West Point. "The Corps was disbanded in 1783, at least one of its members remained in the Hudson Valley and appears in Price's letter books: Margaret Cochrane Corbin, also known locally as Captain Molly."[229]

Captain Molly was unable to work due to her injured arm. She also could not support herself because she was in a constant state of pain. It is reported that by 1779, Corbin was destitute. In June 1779, her heroic actions in battle as well as her wounds caught the eyes of people who did not realize her story. Prompted by petitions, the Continental Congress passed the following resolution:

> *Resolved, That Margaret Corbin, who was wounded and disabled in the attack on Fort Washington, whilst she heroically filled the post of her husband who was killed by her side serving a piece of artillery, do receive, during her natural life, or the continuance of the said disability, the one-half of the monthly pay drawn by a soldier in the service of these states; and that she now receive out of the public stores, one complete suit of cloaths, or the value thereof in money.*[230]

This awarded Corbin $30 a month for life. The pension did not appear to help her needs because again, "in 1780 the Board of War reported that Corbin still remains in a deplorable situation in consequence of her wound, by which she is deprived of the use of one arm, and in other respects is much disabled and probably will continue a cripple during her life."[231] Corbin also caused stress to the local officers at West Point because she was almost constantly in trouble.

In 1782, she met another soldier in the Invalid Corp and they married. The marriage lasted a short period of time because he died within a few years. According to a report filed by Captain Samuel Shaw, by 1782 Corbin had married a soldier who was also an invalid. Captain Samuel Shaw wrote that "her present husband is a poor . . . invalid who is no service to her but rather adds to her trouble."[232] Once again, she remained on the roles until she was discharged in 1783, but she remained at West Point because she could not care for herself. She was in need of special care her entire life.

Some years after the war when many people forgot who Margaret Corbin was and the role she played in the American Revolution, Carol Berkin writes, "she became a figure of scorn rather than admiration." For one thing she was an alcoholic, probably drinking excessively because of physical pain and no doubt mental pain. Margaret Corbin continued on this way until she died on January 21, 1800. "Few local citizens realized that the sharp-tongued alcoholic woman known as 'Dirty Kate' had taken a 'soldiers' part in the war for liberty."[233] She was buried in an unmarked grave until the Daughters of the American Revolution took an interest in her life.

The local Daughters of the American Revolution made it their mission to find her remains, which were located "on the property of New York Financier J.P. Morgan." According to one newspaper on March 17, 1926, her remains were dug up and a surgeon and dentist examined the bones found in the grave. The surgeon who examined the bones stated, "that a wound had been inflicted in the left shoulder and that the skeleton was that of a woman."[234] Finally, the remains of Corbin were also identified by what looked like a shattered jaw, and the three pieces of grapeshot still lodged in her body. Her remains were removed from the Morgan estate and brought to the cemetery at West Point where Captain Molly was reinterred behind the chapel where she remains to this day . . . or does she?

Fast forward to 2016. Local newspapers, including the *Army Times* published stories purporting that the individual buried in the West Point cemetery in 1926 is not Margaret Corbin. It has been determined by forensic experts that the remains are not those of Captain Molly Corbin. Once again, as in 1926, the Daughters of the American Revolution have launched a campaign to find her real grave.

According to a military newspaper, excavators building a retaining wall near her monument "accidently disturbed the grave, starting a chain of events that led to high-tech tests on the exhumed remains." According to the Associated Press, the forensic anthropologist who conducted the tests showed that the remains were a man who most likely lived in the late eighteenth to mid-nineteenth century. What is complicating the identification is that the estate where J. P. Morgan lived is long since gone. Where his old estate was once located is now a housing development and sewer plant. "And it would be hard to verify remains through DNA, since Corbin had no known children."[235] So once again, as the newspaper article pointed out, the woman who died in obscurity once again has returned to obscurity. Captain Molly, however, will forever be known as the first woman to receive a pension for military service.

# Nathan Hale

*I wish to be useful, and every kind of service necessary to the public good becomes honorable by being necessary.*[236]

NATHAN HALE

The story of Nathan Hale is one of the most enduring spy stories of the American Revolution. Probably second in notoriety to Benedict Arnold and John Andre. So much has been written about Hale, yet so little is really known about the "patron saint" of the Central Intelligence Agency (CIA). Even today historians debate where he was hanged, the purpose of his mission, if he was even qualified to undertake it, and even if he uttered his most famous words, "I only regret that I have but one life to lose for my country."

Nathan Hale's life began on June 6, 1755, in Coventry, Connecticut. He was the son of Deacon Richard and Elizabeth Hale. They had a large family, including nine sons and three daughters. His mother died early in his life and his father remarried shortly before Nathan left for Yale College in New Haven. He married Mrs. Abigail (Cobb) Adams, widow of Captain Samuel Adams from Canterbury, Connecticut.

Nathan, it appears, was closest to his brother Enoch. The two, when Nathan was fourteen and his brother sixteen, headed off to New Haven to study divinity at Yale College. The brothers graduated in 1773. George D. Seymour, biographer of Hale's life, noted, Nathan strayed from divinity and moved toward a more traditional education.

Lieutenant Elisha Bostwick described him many years later as tall and in good athletic shape and quite agile. Still others commented on his looks, which were just as impressive as his build. He reportedly had fair skin, blue eyes, and flaxen hair. His voice was, Bostwick recalled, "rather sharp or piercing."[237] Finally, Bostwick reminisced that Nathan Hale was above the common person in intelligence.

Upon graduating from Yale, Nathan became a teacher and his first job was in East Haddam, Connecticut, which was located on the Connecticut River. Hale taught there from 1773 until 1774. His stay there was short because it was, in his opinion, isolated. Nathan's next teaching job would be in New London's Union School. A larger town, it was more to his liking. Henry Phelps Johnston wrote, "it was a thriving port of shipbuilders, shipmasters, importers, and whalers, some of them rough-and-ready men."[238] Enoch Hale, who also entered teaching, eventually left teaching and followed in his father's footsteps by becoming a preacher.

If there was a date that catapulted Nathan Hale with fate, it was what Ralph Waldo Emerson called "the shot heard around the world" and the battles of Lexington and Concord, which occurred on April 19, 1775. Three of Hale's brothers joined the battle from Connecticut. Nathan, however, stayed behind. Some believe it is because he was obligated to remain in his teaching position because he was under contract and did not want to break it. When Massachusetts sent out a request for troops

Nathan Hale Schoolhouse / HABS/HAER Library of Congress, Washington, DC

from New England to come to their aid, Connecticut sent troops to help the besieged Bostonians. Among the four thousand men sent by Connecticut were Nathan's two brothers John and Joseph, who marched from Coventry. According to Nathan, in a letter to his brother Enoch, "No liberty-pole is erected or erecting here; but the people seem much more spirited than they were before the alarm."[239] For now he had to sit on the sidelines and watch the excitement.

After Lexington, Patriot militia forces moved to surround Boston to restrict the movements of the British who occupied the town of Boston. In order to entrench their position, the British started to fortify the hills that used to surround Boston. Militia responded by fortifying Bunker Hill and later Breed's Hill. On June 17, 1775, Major General Howe and Brigadier General Robert Pigot led British forces on an attack against the militia on Breed's Hill, a smaller hill located next to Bunker Hill. The British defeated the Patriot militia, who were no match for the highly trained and experienced British forces. It still gave the Patriots a morale boost because the taking of Breed's Hill came at a very high price for the British.

Nathan Hale joined the American cause for what he saw as the defense of liberty on July 6, 1775. He became a first lieutenant appointed by the General Assembly of Connecticut. Eventually, Hale joined the Seventh Regiment of the Continental Army. Another regiment was also formed, the Eighth Regiment. Hale, according to Paul R. Misencik in his book, *The Original American Spies: Seven Covert Agents of the Revolutionary War*, was part of a regiment created "for the special defense of the colony,"[240] since so many troops were called away to Boston. This regiment was commanded by Colonel Charles Webb, who hailed from Stamford, Connecticut. There was little excitement for the young Nathan. He mainly patrolled along the coast and recruited men for the local militia.

He received his marching orders on September 8, "when General Washington made a request for the two new Connecticut regiments."[241] He was told he would be marching toward Cambridge, Massachusetts, in a couple weeks. Referencing Hale's diary, Henry Phelps Johnston, in *Nathan Hale, 1776: Biography and Memorials* writes that he marched from New London, "to Providence and beyond through the Massachusetts towns of Rehoboth, Attleboro, Wrentham, Walpole, Dedham, and Roxbury, to Cambridge,"[242] which was the headquarters of General Washington. Washington had arrived in Cambridge in July of 1775. Hale desired action like his brothers, but instead, his regiment was encamped on Winter Hill miles from the British lines. A map in the Library of Congress shows the extensive fortifications created on the 120-foot-high hill located in Somerville, Massachusetts.

Eventually, Hale's Seventh Connecticut was combined into the Nineteenth Regiment of Foot of the Continental Line. By January 1776, he was commissioned a captain. Cannons also arrived by January 1776, by way of Major General Henry Knox, who had been captured from Forts Ticonderoga and Crown Point. Washington ordered that Dorchester Heights, which overlooked Boston Harbor, be fortified. According to Abigail Adams who lived nearby, canons opened up on March 2, 1776.

*I have been kept in a continual state of anxiety and expectation ever since you left me. of It has been said to morrow and to morrow for this month, but when the dreadfull to morrowwill be I know not—but hark! the House this instant shakes with the roar of Cannon. I have been to the door and find tis a cannonade from our Army, orders I find are come for all the remaining Militia to repair to the Lines a monday night by twelve o clock. No Sleep for me to Night . . .*[243]

What Abigail might have heard was the diversionary tactic employed by Washington to make sure the British could not hear the real fortifications going on atop Dorchester Heights. When the British awoke, they were amazed at what had happened overnight. General Howe remarked, "The rebels did more in one night than my whole army would have done in one month."[244] Major General Howe decided that it would be best to withdraw his troops and navy, which he started on March 8, 1776, after looting Boston first. The British sailed for Nova Scotia by March 17, 1776. Boston was free from the British army for the first time since 1768. When the British occupied the city it housed almost a thousand troops on the Boston Commons.

The war switched south to New York City as the Hudson Valley became the focal point of the war. It was decided that the only way to beat the rebellion was to destroy New England, specifically Massachusetts, which the British believed was at the heart of the rebellion. This could be accomplished by taking New York City with its harbor and access to the Hudson River, which, if controlled, split the colonies in two, isolating Massachusetts and New England.

Hale's regiment was one of the first to leave Massachusetts to go to New York City. He headed to New York City under Major General William Heath. They left shortly after the British evacuated Boston. The troops marched to New London and from there took transports to the East River in New York. Captain Hale disembarked from the transport at Turtle Bay (50th Street near 1st Avenue) on March 30, 1776. Johnston writes that the first structure that would have greeted Hale's sight would have been the Beekman Mansion, where in a short period of time his death sentence would be passed. The Beekman Mansion became the residence of General Sir William Howe, who had recently replaced General Thomas Gage as the commander of the British forces in America. Hale marched to what is believed to be modern-day City Hall Park. In Heath's memoir's it is noted that on April 2, 1776, the general reviewed troops on what was called the Green or Common. Hale most likely was part of this review.

Captain Hale, like many soldiers, was involved in building fortifications to thwart the British attack they knew was coming, and going out on patrols. In his diary quoted in one of his many biographies, Hale wrote to his brother Enoch, "The army is everyday improving in discipline, and it is hoped will soon be able to meet the enemy at any kind of play. . . ."[245]

George Washington decided to ride by horseback to New York City instead of taking the troop transports. He arrived on April 13, 1776. The Continental army went about fortifying an area that was near impossible to defend against one of the most well-trained professional armies in the world as well as one of the largest navies. Washington knew that an attack on his army would come from both land and sea.

*On June 28, 1776, as independence was being debated by the Continental Congress, General George Washington noted that "we have certain Advice" about the British troops heading in the direction of*

*New York City. His men had counted the staggering number of 130
ships, and they carried British General Sir William Howe and many
thousands of British regulars.*[246]

The British finally arrived in late June 1776, landing their troops on
Staten Island. Washington wrote to John Hancock.

*Since I had the honor of addressing you and on the same day, several
Ships more arrived within the Hook, making the number that came in
then a hundred & Ten, and there remains no doubt of the whole of the
Fleet from Hallifax being now here . . . yesterday evening fifty of them
came up the Bay, and Anchored on the Staten Island side. their views
I cannot precisely determine, but am extremely apprehensive as part
of 'em only came, that they mean to surround the [Staten] Island.*[247]

On July 9, 1776, Hale heard the news that the Continental Congress
had signed the Declaration of Independence, creating a new country
named the United States. The Declaration of Independence was read to
all the troops.

Washington knew that the attack would probably be focused on
Manhattan. He decided, however, that his best course of action would
be to divide his force between Brooklyn and Manhattan Island. Most
historians point to this as a mistake. He also continued to build fortifications, including Fort Washington and Fort Constitution, which later was
renamed Fort Lee. As historian Ziyad Rahaman Azeez wrote, "Washington suffered from a severe lack of intelligence by way of spies."

Howe ordered the attack to commence on August 27, 1776. The battle itself lasted until August 29, 1776. By nightfall, the Continental army
was trapped on Brooklynn Heights with the East River at their backs.
General Howe, instead of attacking, allowed Washington to retreat across
the East River and save his army. "He began the evacuation at night, leaving campfires burning, muffling wagon wheels, and forbidding soldiers
from speaking."[248] The Continental army made it across the East River
from the evening of August 29 to the early morning hours of August 30.

As far as we know, Hale did not participate in the Battle of Long Island. It is believed he was stationed at an area known as Bayard's Mount. However, prior to the Battle of Long Island, in the second week of August 1776, George Washington created an elite group of rangers under the command of Lieutenant Colonel Thomas Knowlton from Ashford, Connecticut. They became known as Knowlton's Rangers. The rangers would be composed of New England men predominantly from Connecticut, Rhode Island, and Massachusetts. It would be made up of roughly 130 men and 20 officers. Hale was made an officer of one of the companies. Their main missions were to be an elite infantry fighting force that was used on scouting missions and to harass the British.

"On September 10, 1776, Knowlton briefed his officers regarding the proposed spy mission."[249] When volunteers were requested, Hale did not immediately raise his hand. Instead he sought the counsel of a friend, Captain William Hull, who was also a Yale classmate. Hull's advice to his friend was to remain a soldier. A soldier's life, he explained to Nathan, was an honorable one. A spy's life was the opposite of an honorable life. It was a life of deceit and generally a dishonorable pursuit. Hull remembered telling Hale that if caught, he was sure to die an inglorious death. Nathan Hale listened intently to his friend's line of reasoning. In the end, he opted to go against his friend's counsel. Hale volunteered.

Hale and First Sergeant Stephen Hempstead left New York for Norwalk, Connecticut. Once in Norwalk, they traveled by an armed sloop across Long Island Sound, coming ashore at Huntington or Oyster Bay. The mission changed while Hale was en route. Washington was advised by the Continental Congress not to defend lower New York City and instead occupy northern Manhattan. They also ordered him not to burn New York City.

During the time that the Battle of Harlem Heights was taking shape, Hale was coming ashore on Long Island. His disguise, it was decided, would be a Dutch schoolteacher who had recently graduated Yale. He carried his diploma and would explain, if questioned, that he was Dutch and hailed from Connecticut. He would continue to explain that he was a Loyalist who wanted to teach under the protection of the British. It was not too farfetched a story because many citizens from his home state had fled to New York City. Hale believed his ruse might be a good one. Hale had no idea that with that many Connecticut natives heading to New York City someone might recognize him.

By September 16, 1776, Washington withdrew most of his troops to the northern part of Manhattan near Harlem Heights. The general was anxious to know what the British plans were and when he could possibly expect to engage them in battle. He sent Knowlton's Rangers to scout. While out and about they saw about 150 British soldiers advancing toward the Patriot lines. A skirmish started and after some fighting the rangers fell back toward Washington's camp with the British in pursuit. Hearing the gunfire, Washington gathered about a thousand soldiers and counterattacked, driving the British to retreat, a victory to boost morale. However, Knowlton died in the clash with the British.

Nathan Hale was not present during the battle that took the life of his commanding officer. From September 16 to 20, Captain Nathan Hale took notes, made maps of New York Island, continuing even after New York City caught fire on September 20, 1776. Probably while trying to make it back to the American lines, he was apprehended on September 21, 1776.

When Hale was caught, he was brought before General James Robertson, a brigade commander. When asked who he was, Hale used the ruse he had practiced of being a Dutch schoolteacher, until, some believe, he saw his Uncle Samuel Hale. Samuel Hale was a Loyalist from Portsmouth, New Hampshire, and was also General Howe's deputy commissary of prisoners. Samuel positively identified his nephew Nathan as a captain in the Continental army. After Nathan was searched, sketches, notes, and other information were found in his shoes. Nathan was promptly marched to the Beekman Mansion, now General Howe's headquarters. There wasn't a court-martial. Howe hastily sentenced Hale to death. He was to be executed the following morning, hanged by the neck until dead. Until the morning of his execution, he was confined to the greenhouse on the Beekman estate.

Captain John Montresor tried to make his time as comfortable as possible as he sat and talked with him. It has been written that he tried

View from the Southeast Morris-Jumel Mansion / HABS/HAER Library of Congress, Washington, DC

to make Hale's last moments on earth less scary. However, others did not feel as compassionate toward the spy. When Hale asked for the benefit of clergy or a Bible, both were refused.

The morning came and Hale was marched near "Dove's Tavern (near present day 66th Street and 3rd Ave.)"[250] He was hanged at 11 a.m. Nathan had written a letter to his brother Enoch and Colonel Knowlton (Hale did not know he had been killed during the Battle of Harlem Heights). After he was hanged, his body was left hanging for days and then cut down to be buried in an unmarked grave, the location of which is not exactly known.

On September 22, 1776, British officers, under a flag of truce, approached the American line to discuss the use of musket balls with nails placed through them. "General Washington sent his adjutant general, Colonel Joseph Reed, accompanied by General Israel Putnam and Captain Alexander Hamilton, to meet the party." Captain Hull also was a member of the party. Captain Montresor, who was with the British, told them of Hale's death. As a witness to the execution, the captain told Hull what he saw.

Nathan Hale Execution / Library of Congress, Washington, DC

*Captain Hale entered: he was calm, and bore himself with gentle dignity, in the consciousness of rectitude and high intentions. He asked for writing materials, which I furnished him: he wrote two letters . . . He was shortly after summoned to the gallows. But a few persons were around him, yet his characteristic dying words were remembered. He said, "I only regret, that I have but one life to lose for my country."*[251]

They then returned to the British lines.

Who betrayed Hale has long been assumed to be his Uncle Samuel Hale. His father, Deacon Hale, in a letter, talked about the betrayal. However, maybe Captain Hale was not cut out for the spy business or was outwitted by a better spy also posing as a double agent. Consider Tiffany recorded his version of events leading up to Hale's capture.

Consider Tiffany was a Connecticut storekeeper and Loyalist. He wrote that Major Robert Rogers, "a British hero from the French and Indian war" tricked Hale. Tiffany believed that Rogers and Hale probably knew each other. Captain Hale agreed to meet Rogers at his headquarters in New York City, convincing him that he too was working for the Americans. While eating at Roger's headquarters, "British soldiers surrounded the house and arrested Hale."[252] David McCullough, in his book *1776*, holds a popular view that, "the mission was doomed from the start, ill-planned and pathetically amateurish." Perhaps Hale told "the wrong people about his mission."[253]

Nathan Hale's life was eventually all but forgotten until his home went up for sale. A man by the name of George Dudley Seymour became fascinated by the life and spy story of Nathan Hale. He purchased the home in 1914 and began to restore it as well as fill it with antiques relating to the period and to Hale's life. Eventually, Seymour created a large book dedicated to all that was known about Nathan Hale at the time. He also convinced the federal government to create a stamp to honor this hero. Hale was not the only schoolteacher turned spy. Ann Bates, a lesser-known spy, was also a schoolteacher around the same time, but in Philadelphia.

# Thomas Hickey

*The reflection upon my Situation, & that of this Army, produces many*
*an uneasy hour when all around me are wrapped in Sleep.*[254]

GEORGE WASHINGTON

John Adams, a delegate to Congress, wrote to his wife Abigail Adams, on June 17, 1775, "I can now inform you that the Congress have made Choice of the modest and virtuous, the amiable, generous and brave George Washington Esqr., to be the General of the American Army, and that he is to repair as soon as possible to the Camp before Boston."[255]

George Washington received his commission on June 19, 1775. He traveled to Cambridge, Massachusetts, arriving on July 2, 1775, where he eventually took up his headquarters at the Vassal House. The home sat alongside the Kings Highway. John Vassal's mansion had been confiscated because he was a prominent Tory. When Washington arrived, he was tasked with creating a professional fighting force out of undisciplined troops. He summed up the predicament in a letter to Lieutenant Colonel Joseph Reed in 1776, Reed was one of Washington's aide-de-camps and one of his most trusted advisors.

*The reflection upon my Situation, & that of this Army, produces many*
*an uneasy hour when all around me are wrapped in Sleep. Few People*
*know the Predicament we are In, on a thousand Accts—fewer still*
*will beleive, if any disaster happens to these Lines, from what causes*
*it flows—I have often thought, how much happier I should have been,*
*if, instead of accepting of a command under such Circumstances I had*
*taken my Musket upon my Shoulder & enterd the Ranks, or, if I could*

*have justified the Measure to Posterity, & my own Conscience, had*
*retir'd to the back Country, & livd in a Wig-wam. . . .*[256]

In addition to creating a disciplined fighting force, General Washington also needed to create a personal guard. There is no indication that Washington worried excessively about his safety. However, on March 11, 1776, from his headquarters in Cambridge, he issued his General Orders for March 11, 1776, in which he created, "a Guard for himself, and baggage." The colonels or commanding officers were instructed to furnish him with four men to appear at his headquarters on March 12, 1776, at noon. For anyone to be considered, he wrote, the men needed to be of good moral character and known for their "sobriety, honesty, and good behavior." In addition, they needed to be from "five feet, eight Inches high, to five feet, ten inches."[257]

According to Mount Vernon Historic Site in Virginia, the official name of Washington's new unit was His Excellency's Guard or the General's Guard. Enlisted men referred to the unit as The Life Guards, Washington's Life Guards, or Washington's Body Guard. Captain Caleb Gibbs of the Fourteenth Massachusetts was chosen as the commandant of the guard, and Washington's nephew George Lewis the lieutenant. Gibbs would be promoted to the rank of major. These men would be known for their undying loyalty to General Washington. However, a deserter from the British army, hailing from Wethersfield, Connecticut, in roughly two months, would be hung for plotting against the commander-in-chief.

After the Siege of Boston, the British fleet set sail for Halifax, Nova Scotia. Prior to evacuating Boston, on March 17, 1776, George Washington sent Major General Charles Lee to New York City in January 1776, to start setting up fortifications and readying the army for the movement south to the city. Washington, in a letter to Connecticut Governor Jonathan Trumbull on January 7, 1776, was sure the British were going to shift the focus of the war to New York City and the vital Hudson.

*Having undoubted intelligence, of the fitting out a Fleet at Boston and*
*of the embarkation of Troops from thence, which from the Season of*
*the year and other circumstances must be destined for some expedition*

*South of this; and having such information as I can depend upon,*
*that the Inhabitants of Long Island in the Colony of New York, or a*
*great part of them, are Inimical to the rights and Liberties of America,*
*and from their conduct and professions, have discovered an apparent*
*Inclination. . . .*[258]

The Continental army headed south from New England in the middle of April 1776. They moved toward New York City by troop transports while Washington with his guard left Cambridge on April 4, 1776, traveling not by transports, but by horseback. He arrived in New York City by April 14, 1776. Three days later General Washington wrote to the Committee of Safety of New York about a problem that left him in dismay. Loyalists living in and around the city were freely interacting with the British men-of-war, giving vital intelligence and even giving them needed supplies. Clearly frustrated, he wrote,

*That a continuance of the intercourse, which has hitherto subsisted*
*between the Inhabitants of this Colony and the Enemy, on board the*
*Ships of War, is injurious to the Common Cause, requires no extraor-*
*dinary abilities to prove. . . . To tell you, Gentlemen, that the advan-*
*tages of an intercourse of this kind, are altogether on the side of the*
*Enemy, whilst we derive not the smallest benefit from it, would be*
*telling what must be obvious to every one. It is, indeed, so glaring,*
*that even the Enemy themselves must despise us for suffering it to be*
*continued; for, besides their obtaining supplies of every kind, by which*
*they are enabled to continue in your harbours, it also opens a regular*
*Channel of intelligence; by which they are, from time to time, made*
*acquainted with the number and extent of our Works, our Strength,*
*and all our movements; by which they are enabled to regulate their*
*own Plans, to our great disadvantage and Injury.*[259]

Even before General Washington arrived in New York City, rumors of plots began to surface that Loyalists in the city were going to join the attack against the Rebels once battles commenced. Matthew Adgate, Chairman of the King's District Committee located in Albany County, wrote in a letter to General Washington on May 13, 1776, that there seemed to be a plot "seldom appeared in the world since the fall of Adam." Adgate believed that recruiting was going on among Loyalists throughout the colonies to send as many soldiers to New York City as possible. He was also told by sources he did not name that many Patriots currently serving in the army, as well as most of the Provincial Congress, would switch sides once the British fleet arrived. While at the time this included the noted patriot Philip Schuyler, it was later proven false in his case. Adgate called the plan "as dark as hell."[260]

Still another letter arrived from Jonathan Sturgis, the Chairman of the Committee of Safety for Suffolk County on Long Island. In his letter he reported that numerous Tories were being apprehended. He wrote of a Captain Seth Harding, Commander of the brig *Defence*, which was an American vessel. Captain Harding, he continued, captured a small sloop on the Long Island Sound. Aboard the sloop were many Tories going to "join the Ministerial Troops." Sturges believed the Tories were coming from Reading, Connecticut, to Long Island via Long Island Sound. Sturges concluded that "we think we know enough to convince us that a horrid plot is ledd by the Tories to destroy the people of the country."[261]

After reading the intelligence letter, Washington found time to reply, two days later, "I will lend any aid in my power, that shall be thought within the line of my department, to root out or Secure such abominable pests of Society, but as you have neither pointed out the names or places of abode of the persons alluded to, by your Informants, on Long Island, I must beg the favour of a more explicit description." Why Sturges did not provide names is not known.

Benjamin Tupper, Lieutenant Colonel of the Twenty-First Continental Regiment wrote to General Washington the same day, May 16, 1776, located on board the sloop *Hester* near Amboy, which is off the shore of Staten Island and New Jersey on Raritan Bay. In the letter he wrote that he believed there was a plot afoot with Loyalists seeking to help the British, in force, to help defeat the Americans. Tupper continued in the letter that he had seized a woman by the name of Mrs. Darbage. She was caught after she was observed going on board a British man-of-war. After she left the ship she was promptly arrested. When Tupper tried to interrogate Darbage, she became obstinate, refusing to talk. Tupper wrote to General Washington,

*She has absolutely refused to give any account, or answer any questions, both to the Committee of the town as well as to myself, and says she will do the same to your Excellency; but it is my opinion a little smell of the black-hole will set her tongue at liberty. It is the opinion of our friends in this town that she is able to bring out a number of rascals and villains in sundry towns nigh here.*[262]

A black hole was a prison or jail that sometimes employed torture as a means to extract needed information.

The idea of some kind of Loyalist plot was becoming more and more a reality to Washington. He also received a letter with information from eleven committees meeting in Berkshire County on May 18, 1776. They reported that intelligence indicated four battalions, or more than three thousand men, had already been raised in New York alone and additional soldiers were being raised in the towns of Newton, New Milford, and Canaan, Connecticut. Forces were also being recruited from Goshen and Cornwall in the Hudson Highlands. These soldiers would be used when the time was right to attack and secure forts along the Hudson River.

Growing concern prompted General Washington to address the issue with the New York Provincial Congress on June 10, 1776. Washington wrote to the president of the New York Congress that he suspected dangerous individuals in New York and even more troubling to him was that these people had not been secured. It was his opinion that the plot contained both internal and external enemies to the American cause. Many, including Washington, believed that the Royal Governor William Tryon was most assuredly behind the efforts at organizing the Loyalists.

*The encouragements given by Governour Tryon to the disaffected, which are circulated no one can well tell how; the movements of this kind of people, which are more easy to perceive than describe; the confident report which is said to have come immediately from Governour Tryon, and brought by a frigate from Halifax, that the troops at that place were embarking for this; added to a thousand incidental circumstances, trivial in themselves but strong from comparison,—leaves not a doubt upon my mind but that troops are hourly expected at the Hook.*[263]

William Tryon was the last Royal Governor of the Province of New York. While he was in England in 1774, the American Revolution had commenced. When Tryon returned to New York City, in June 1775, he did not expect his city to be under the influence of the rebels. The governor also feared for his life that the rebels in the city might try to kill him or throw him in jail. He realized that his safety could not be guaranteed so, on October 18, 1775, he fled the governor's mansion in the dead of night. "The next day, Tryon and an entourage made their way to the East River and took a ferry to a British transport ship called the *Halifax*. Several days later, he moved to a boat, the *Duchess of Gordon*, which was docked alongside a 64-gun warship that could guarantee his protection."[264]

John Bakeless, in his book *Turncoats, Traitors, and Heroes*, writes that he believes there were three plots being hatched during this time that Washington had not yet put together. The first plot was a plan to kidnap the general. It was never realized. A second plot involved raising armed forces made up of Tories that would rise up in New York City, Long Island, and along the Hudson River as far north as the Highlands. The uprising would commence when the Howe brothers launched their attacks on the Continental army. It is the plot that Washington's intelligence stumbled upon very early. Part of this plot involved Tories not only blowing up ammunition stockpiled by the Continental army, but also seizing Rebel artillery. The captured artillery would be used to shell the frantic Rebels. Finally, as the plan progressed, Loyalist troops would cut the King's Bridge, effectively cutting off any opportunity of the Rebels to escape. In theory, if all worked out, while the Howe brothers attacked Washington's front, the Tories would attack from the rear. The final plot, which the existence of can never be known for sure, was an attempt to poison Washington at the hands of one of his Life Guards. It has also been asserted that he was not going to be poisoned by one of his Life Guards but instead Washington would be stabbed.

Frustrated, Washington issued a threat to the population of New York City and Long Island, which included modern-day Brooklyn. He stated that if anyone was caught going on board the *Duchess of Gordon*, Tryon's ship, they would be seen as committing treason. However, many ignored Washington's proclamation. Citizens continued to sell supplies to and purchase supplies for Governor Tryon. It was just too lucrative financially to stop. There were also a large number of Tories hoping to oust the Rebels with the British army. General Washington, it seems, may have underestimated the support the British enjoyed in the port city and beyond. Washington's discovery of the second plot was quite by accident in many ways or at least the scope of it. Individuals were involved in a counterfeiting ring that would be eventually traced back to the Royal Governor Tryon, confirming Washington's suspicions about Tryon.

Two men sat in the city hall jail. One was Israel Youngs, who ran a press that he used to print counterfeit money and other papers of credit. Youngs worked with another well-known local counterfeiter, Isaac Ketcham, who secured paper to print counterfeit Continental money on Young's press. Ketcham, who would figure prominently in the second plot, was arrested in May 1776. Bakeless described the charge of counterfeiting as relatively common and not particularly serious. The plot took a new twist in the middle of June.

On June 15, 1776, two Continental soldiers were arrested. They stood charged on oath with attempting to pass counterfeit money, or bills of credit, which pass current in this colony. They were Private Michael Lynch and Sargent Thomas Hickey. Again, it was considered a low-level crime and the men would have been released at some point. However, as some historians have pointed out, Hickey turned a small-time crime into a major one because he could not stop shooting his mouth off to anyone who would listen. He told Ketcham, a cellmate, that he was done fighting for the American cause and that when the time came many men would rise up and defeat the Rebels. Ketcham listened with an eager ear. If this did not get the attention of both Young and Ketcham, Hickey's attempt at recruiting Ketcham to his cause did. Ketcham saw the chance to save himself or maybe lessen any punishment coming his way. What the two men found even more astonishing is they spoke of being members of General Washington's Life Guards.

It was during this time that some historians believe the plot to poison Washington had been in motion. Some believe it was more talk than actual action. If this assassination was planned it was probably planned at the Sargent of Arms Tavern. A waiter by the name of William Corbie testified that Washington would be killed, his staff taken, and the rebellion, the conspirators believed, would be over quickly. It was believed that a member of his elite guards would stab him as well as other officers.

The coconspirators met regularly, according to Carlos E. Godfrey's book, which is an early history of the commander-in-chief's guard, at the tavern where Corbie worked. It was situated southeast of Washington's headquarters. It was also the assigned rendezvous for the coconspirators. All plans, of course, were vetted through Governor Tryon. Some historians believe that Washington was not going to be stabbed, but taken captive when the Loyalists rose up to assist Howe in the defeat of the rebels. However, some have also alluded to the fact, as in the *History of Fraunces Tavern*, that the plan was hatched by Thomas Hickey to poison General Washington, which he tried to do just before he was arrested.

According to some of the stories, Hickey approached Washington's housekeeper Mary Smith, asking if she would help him kill the general by way of a poison. She agreed to help Hickey, but only to expose the plot. According to the same sources, she feigned an allegiance until she knew the full depth of the plan. Once she was assured of the plan and its details, she alerted Washington.

General George Washington loved peas. It was arranged on June 15, 1776, that the general would be served peas at dinner. Prior to him eating them, Hickey would place the poison on Washington's dish. Knowing ahead of time about the plot, Washington politely declined the peas and the Patriot cause averted disaster. Afterward, still another story states, the discarded peas were fed to chickens that, after consuming them, died, confirming something was indeed wrong with the food.

Many historians do not believe this actually happened because there is not a definitive document showing that this plan was actually in place. It is not unrealistic that there was a desire to kidnap Washington and parade him through the streets, which would no doubt be a coup for the British. Recent historians also point out that there is no direct mention of the plot to poison him in any of Washington's surviving papers, or even the reports of the committee. Instead, it is pointed out that it is quoted from a letter written by Dr. William Eustis, army surgeon, to Dr. David Townsend, a regimental and hospital surgeon for the Continental Army. In the letter he discusses the plot to kill Washington and even goes as far as to coin a new word, *sacricide*, to describe the killing of Washington.

Meanwhile, back in jail, seeing a chance at securing his own freedom, Ketcham sent a letter to the New York Provincial Congress alluding to the fact that he had information they might find of interest. Ketcham's letter was read before the New York Provincial Congress on June 17, 1776. The testimony was damning to be sure. It was decided to pursue Ketcham's allegations.

During his testimony, Ketcham "informed the Provincial Congress that he believed two fellow prisoners, Continental soldiers, Thomas Hickey and Michael Lynch, belonged to some 'corps.'" In his letter to the New York Provincial Congress, the cellmate of Hickey told the lawmakers that "he spoke freely when they were confined."[265] Later, Israel Youngs confirmed what Ketcham stated, that both men spoke of never fighting for the American cause again. He told the Provincial Congress that Hickey and Lynch told Ketcham that they were also receiving money from the British.

Ketchem was of the opinion that,

*They have not as yet fixed any plan of operation; that sometimes they talk; when the fleet arrives, of cutting down King's Bridge; that as many of them as would go over to the regulars, and that such as should be obliged to stay do more executions than five times the number out of the army.*[266]

He also believed a man whom Hickey and Lynch referred to as Colonel Webb was traveling throughout New England as a civilian in order to bribe upper class men to lead others to New York City to help defeat the Rebels. The Loyalist regiments were to land in three areas of New

York: Long Island, Staten Island, and New York Island. Hickey also told Ketcham that the King of England would show mercy by giving a blanket pardon to all the men who joined the British. The only stipulation was they had to join before the fighting started. Once they beat the Rebels they could also count on a generous payment and an equally generous land grant confiscated from the defeated Rebels.

Ketcham explained to a stunned Provincial Congress that a large number of soldiers were also enlisted to help the King of England defeat the Rebels in New York City. When Howe's fleet appeared off Sandy Hook, which was expected in June or July, that would be the signal to the Loyalists waiting.

The Provincial Congress formed a secret committee chaired by John Jay and formed at the direction of General Washington to find and root out information about those still or believed to be loyal to the King of England. The next witness to be examined by the committee was William Leary.

During the time that Ketcham was testifying to the Provincial Congress, William Leary was sent south to look for a worker who had fled Ringwood Iron-Works operated by Robert Erskine. His orders were to bring the individual back to the ironworks who might have been bound by some sort of indenture. Leary reported in his testimony before the secret committee on June 20, 1776, that he did find the runaway worker at the home of a gentleman named Forbes. Forbes, he testified, got a pistol for the man named William Benjamin to defend himself against Leary. Leary easily seized the pistol and took the man into custody.

Leary escorted the man to the Paulus Hook Ferry with the intent of bringing him back to the ironworks. However, he lost him at the ferry when a sergeant grabbed the worker and signed him up for service in Captain Roosevelt's Company. At the ferry, Leary met another individual who used to be employed at the ironworks. His name was James Mason.

Mason, according to historian Douglas Southall Freeman, told Leary there were more men whom the two knew, and that Leary might be interested in meeting with them. If he agreed to meet with them, Leary must swear not to say anything about the meeting or turn in any of the men. Leary refused to comply with this wish, but was still interested in meeting the men and hearing what they had to say. What Leary heard shocked him. The individuals spoke of soldiers quitting the American cause and that they were all being paid from Tryon's ship by way of a gunsmith named Gilbert Forbes. When the men became suspicious of Leary they fled back into the city. Leary believed, like Washington, that the Mayor of New York City, David Matthews, had some involvement.

With each individual who came to the secret committee, more names were given with more people to search out and arrest. The committee next arrested James Mason, the man who originally spoke to Leary. Maybe he could shed light on this increasingly large plot.

Mason, perhaps to save himself, turned in a man named William Forbes. Mason explained that he was told that any man who enlisted before the fighting would be given five guineas and a generous land grant. He continued that Gilbert Forbes not only paid Mason, but also enlisted him as a recruiter for the British army. Mason also gave names of those who were recruiting for the King of England's army as well as a former schoolmaster in Goshen located in Orange County, New York. Mason knew him as Clarke but it was probably an alias. This man had convinced Mason to join and was in the process of enlisting a large company of Tories to head to New York City to join the fight. Finally, Mason told the committee that Thomas Hickey, who was currently still in jail, was involved in the plot along with other members of the guard.

He spoke of Gilbert Forbes; William Green, a drummer in the guard; James Johnson, a fifer; a soldier in the guard named John Barnes; and one William Forbes. Leary, and later Mason, also implicated New York City Mayor David Matthews who he claimed, "contributed 100 British pounds to the plot." He concluded his testimony before John Jay and Gouverneur Morris, that he believed, "Gilbert Forbes is at the head here, and the Mayor and the Governour." Based on the testimony of Leary and Mason it was ordered that both Gilbert Forbes and David Matthews be arrested.

On June 21, 1776, William Corbie gave the names of those he knew were involved in the conspiracy. He gave this information, according to Godfrey's book, to Joseph Smith, "a prominent man of the city."[267] Smith took the information to the Provincial Congress on June 21, 1776, and an arrest warrant was sent to General Washington by Philip Livingston, John Jay, and Gouverneur Morris.

*Sir: Whereas David Matthews, Esquire, stands charged with dangerous designs and treasonable conspiracies against the rights and liberties of the United Colonies of America: We do, in pursuance of a certain resolve of the Congress of the Colony of the 20th of June instant, authorize and request you to cause the said David Matthews to be, with all his papers, forthwith apprehended and secured, and that return be made to us of the manner in which the warrant shall be executed. . . .*[268]

Once again, Godfrey writes that at 2 a.m. on June 22, 1776, "a party of men under the command of Captain John Laboyteaux, proceeded . . . to the house of [Gilbert] Forbes, on Broadway, where they placed him under arrest and seized several incriminating papers, including a copy of the constitution of the conspirator's association."[269] Forbes, described as "a short, thick man who wears a white coat,"[270] was placed in chains and brought to the city jail. About an hour prior to Forbes's arrest, David Matthews, appointed mayor of New York City by Royal Governor Tryon about four months earlier, was also arrested.

After the arrest of Matthews, the next day, Major General Nathanael Greene, in a letter to Washington, told his superior that he sent a detachment under the command of Colonel James Varnum "who surrounded his house and seized his person precisely at the hour of one this morning."[271] They searched for Matthews's papers but none could be found. Perhaps he was tipped off and the papers removed or destroyed. Matthews was taken in chains from his Flatbush home to the jail in New York City. William Green, James Johnson, John Barnes, and William Forbes were all also arrested at this time.

Gilbert Forbes refused to talk. A minister went to meet with him in his jail cell. Several sources report that the minister explained to Forbes that the situation he was facing was a dire one that probably would end in his execution. He explained that while it might not be possible to stave off execution, there still was the possibility of saving his soul by confessing.[272]

Maybe Gilbert even thought he could possibly save his own skin. The minister convinced him to spill his guts to the committee.

The Mayor of New York City was brought before Philip Livingston, John Jay, and Gouverneur Morris on or around June 23, 1776. He stated, "that about six or seven weeks ago he went on board the *Duchess of Gordon,* by permission of General Israel Putnam." He wanted to obtain permission for Lord Drummond to go to Bermuda; that as the examinant [Mayor Mathews] was about to leave the HMS Duchess, "the Governour took him into his private room, and put a bundle of paper money in his hands. . . ."[273] Matthews testified that he was told by Tryon to take out five pounds and give it the prisoners in the jail and the rest would go to "Gilbert Forbes, for some rifles and round-bored guns which he made for him, and for others which the said Forbes was to make. . . ."[274] The Mayor of New York City testified that he was surprised to hear Forbes was part of this. He also explained that he knew he should not be involved in this situation but decided to do it anyway.

Matthews testified that when he met with Gilbert Forbes, he was alarmed that Gilbert spoke of plans to take the batteries at New York when Howe's fleet arrived. They also planned to cut off the Rebel's escape by cutting down King's Bridge. Matthews told Forbes this would be a grave mistake. Gary Shattuck, wrote in his article *Plotting the "Sacricide" of George Washington,* asserted that the committee listening to Matthews's testimony did not believe his attempt to portray himself as the unwitting pawn in the whole scheme. They did not, however, have any concrete proof linking him to a crime.

The plan to defeat the Rebels, according to Freeman, was hatched by an old soldier who had served in the French and Indian War. He was a former sergeant in the British Artillery. Freeman writes that Mason believed him to be an old pensioner. He also writes that Gilbert Forbes did not testify on record until June 29, 1776. Although, he believed that Gilbert was almost surely questioned before that date, because the committee clearly understood the implications of the plan.

Washington's drummer in the Life Guard was William Green. He was brought before the committee and admitted he was involved in recruiting, being paid by the British, and enlisted in the British army. He asked the committee to have mercy on him. He agreed to testify against the others and shed light on Thomas Hickey's involvement in the plot. Gilbert Forbes, also testified against others and to their involvement in the plot to rise up when the British attacked.

A court-martial for the trial of Thomas Hickey and other soldiers was convened on June 26, 1776. It was held at the American headquarters. Those present included Colonel Samuel H. Parsons, President; William Tudoe, Judge Advocate; Lieutenant Colonel William Sheppard; Major Levi Wells; Captains Joseph Hoyt, Abel Pettibone, Samuel Warren, James Mellin, Warham Parks, William Reed, Joseph Pettigil, David Lyon, David Still, and Timothy Purcival. Hickey was charged with "exciting and joining in a mutiny and sedition, and of treacherously corresponding with, inlisting among and receiving pay from the enemies of the United American Colonies."[275] Hickey plead not guilty to the charges and represented himself.

In his testimony, Hickey implicated David Matthews and Gilbert Forbes. He admitted to enlisting in the British army but explained that at the time he believed it was a good opportunity to dupe the Tories. Hickey pointed out that he received some free money, as he looked at it. When it looked as if he would not garner any sympathy, Hickey added that in the process of looking out for himself, he was also gaining valuable intelligence from the British. When he accumulated enough intelligence, he had every intention of telling General Washington when the time was right. Finally, he felt that playing both sides also assured his own safety in the event the British defeated the Americans. Testimony from Gilbert Forbes, Israel Youngs, and William Green sealed Hickey's fate when they pinned him as the ringleader. Hickey called no witnesses.

Southhall and other historians believe that the court-martial, with the support of George Washington, wished to make an example of Hickey. Historians also believe Hickey's defense was pitiful. The court was quick and unanimous in its opinion "that the prisoner is guilty of the charges against him, and of a breach of the fifth and of the thirtieth articles of the Rules and Regulations for the government of the Continental forces." The court sentenced Thomas Hickey to "suffer death for said crimes by being hanged by the neck till he is dead."[276]

On June 27, 1776, from his headquarters in New York, General Washington confirmed Thomas Hickey's death sentence in the General Orders for the day. The execution was set for 11 a.m. on June 28. "All the officers and men off duty, belonging to Gen Heath's, Spencer's, Lord Stirling's and Genl Scott's Brigades, to be under arms, on their respective parades, at Ten o'Clock tomorrow morning . . . to attend the execution of the sentence."[277] Some twenty thousand individuals assembled to watch the execution. It was hoped it would serve as a warning to others in the Continental Army. Solomon Nash, a solider witnessing the execution, wrote in his journal that "the day [was] clear and Pleasant." He mentioned that Hickey was a member of General Washington's Life Guard and that he was being executed, "for turning a Torie."[278]

Prior to the execution, General Washington penned a letter to the Continental Congress.

*I doubt not, you will have heard of the Plot that was forming among many disaffected persons in this City and Government for aiding the King's Troops on their arrival. The matter I am in hopes, by a timely discovery, will be suppressed, and put a stop to, many Citizens and others, among whom is the Mayor are now in confinement.*[279]

Washington continued that he was sure the plot could be traced to Governor Tryon and that the mayor was a principal agent in the plot. Finally, he wrote that members of his own guard were involved. One of the principal agitators was to be hanged the very day he was communicating this to Congress.

Washington, on the day of the execution, included an admonishment to the army as a whole.

*The unhappy Fate of Thomas Hickey, executed this day for Mutiny, Sedition and Treachery, the General hopes will be a warning to every Soldier, in the Army, to avoid those crimes, and all others, so disgraceful to the character of a Soldier, and pernicious to his country, whose pay he receives and Bread he eats—And in order to avoid those Crimes the most certain method is to keep out of the temptation of them, and particularly to avoid lewd Women, who, by the dying Confession of this poor Criminal, first led him into practices which ended in an untimely and ignominious Death.*[280]

When Hickey was approached by a minister for his last rites and to pray, he dismissed him, saying ministers were "all cutthroats."[281] According to eyewitness accounts, Hickey wept as the noose was placed around his neck. He quickly regained his composure and his last words were, "unless Green was very cautious, the design would as yet be executed on him." A reference to the individual who testified against him and a man he believed was involved in the plot.

Gilbert Forbes, on the next day, was examined again by the secret committee. No others would be punished, but others were to remain in jail. Mayor David Matthews was one such example. When the attack by the British seemed imminent, Matthews was moved to Litchfield, Connecticut, for safekeeping. He would escape and be back in British-held New York City by December 1776. In the summer of '76, New York City and Long Island had slipped from the grasp of the Americans, not to be regained until the end of the war in 1783.

# BIBLIOGRAPHY

**Diaries, Memoirs, and Travelers' Accounts**

De Chastellux, Marquis. *Travels in North America in the Years 1780, 1781, and 1782.* Edited by Howard C. Rice Jr. 2 vols. Chapel Hill: University of North Carolina Press, 1963.

Ford, Chauncey Worthington, ed. *Correspondence and Journals of Samuel Blachley Webb.* Vol. 1. New York: Wickersham Press, 1893.

Hardenbergh, John L. *The Journal of Lt. John L. Hardenbergh.* Edited by John S. Clark. Auburn, NY: Cayuga County Historical Society, 1879.

Martin, Joseph Plumb. *Ordinary Courage: The Revolutionary War Adventures of Joseph Plumb Martin.* Edited by James Kirby Martin. St. James, NY: Brandywine Press, 1993.

Nash, Solomon. *Journal of Solomon Nash, a Soldier of the Revolution 1776–1777.* Edited by Charles I. Bushnell. New York: privately printed, 1861.

Riedesel, Friederike Charlotte Luise. *Letters and Journals Relating to the War of the American Revolution, and the Capture of the German Troops at Saratoga.* Translated by William Leete Stone. Albany, NY: J. Munsell, 1867.

Symmes, Rebecca D., ed. *A Citizen-Solider in the American Revolution: The Diary of Benjamin Gilbert in Massachusetts and New York.* Cooperstown, NY: New York State Historical Society, 1980.

Wallenstein, James, trans. *Letters and Memoirs Relating to the War of American Independence and the Capture of the German Troops at Saratoga.* New York: G&C Carvill, 1827.

**Archives and Unpublished Manuscripts**

Ann Bates Claim for Compensation, March 17, 1785. British Treasury Papers, In-Letters, T1/611. British National Archives London, England.

Bruyn, Charles, to Court of Common Pleas, 1818. Grantee Index of Deeds. Ulster County Clerk's Office, Kingston, New York. Book D, Liber XXIII.

"An Estimate or List of the Estates, Real and Personal of all the Free-holders and Inhabitants of the Precinct of Newburgh for 1767." Ulster County Clerk's Office, Kingston, New York.

Hasbrouck, Cornelius, to Dickerson, John, 1789. Grantee Index of Deeds. Ulster County Clerk's Office, Kingston, New York. Book D, Liber LL.

Hasbrouck, Cornelius, to Hasbrouck, Isaac, 1788. Grantee Index of Deeds. Ulster County Clerk's Office, Kingston, New York. Book D, Liber II.

Hasbrouck, Cornelius, to Hasbrouck, Isaac, 1800. Jonathan Hasbrouck Family Papers (1751–1904). Historic Huguenot Street, New Paltz, New York.

Hasbrouck, Cornelius, to Sudam, John, 1818. Grantee Index of Deeds. Ulster County Clerk's Office, Kingston, New York. Book D, Liber XXIII.

Hasbrouck, Jonathan. "Acc't Ledger 1776–1789." New York State Office of Parks, Recreation and Historical Preservation. Washington's Headquarters State Historic Site, Newburgh, New York.

———. Family Papers (1751–1904). Historic Huguenot Street, New Paltz, New York.

Hasbrouck, Rachel. Letter, June 15, 1818. Historic Huguenot Street, New Paltz, New York. Foreclosure Notice filed by Ulster County Sheriff Bruyn, Book D, Liber 23.

King's American Regiment Orderly Book, 1777. William L. Clements Library, University of Michigan, Ann Arbor.

New York State Library. New York State Treasurer Acc'ts and Assessment Tax Lists 1722–1788. Box 1.

Miscellaneous documents relating to the acquisition of the Hasbrouck house by the State of New York. Washington's Headquarters State Historic Site, Newburgh, New York.

Revolutionary War Battalions and Militia Index Cards. Historical Society of Pennsylvania, Philadelphia.


**Primary Sources Published**

Clinton, George. *Public Papers of George Clinton, First Governor of New York, 1777–1795, 1801–1804.* Edited by Hugh Hastings. Vols. 1–7. Albany: State of New York, 1899.

*Collections of the New York Historical Society for the Year 1891.* New York: New York Historical Society, 1894.

*Collections of the New York Historical Society for the Year 1891.* "Muster Rolls of New York Provincial Troops 1755–1764." New York: New York Historical Society, 1892.

*Collections of the New York Historical Society for the Year 1903.* New York: New York Historical Society, 1904.

Fernow, Berthold. *New York in the Revolution.* Vol. 1. Albany, NY: Weed, Parsons and Company, 1887.

Force, Peter, ed. *American Archives.* 9 vols. Washington, DC: Government Printing Office, 1837–53. Hasbrouck, Abraham. "Diary and Scrapbook (1734–1846)." In *Earliest Records of the Hasbrouck Family in America, with European Background,* compiled by Kenneth E. Hasbrouck. New Paltz, NY: Hasbrouck Family Association and Huguenot Historical Society, 1992.

Hasbrouck, Kenneth E., comp. *The Hasbrouck Family in America, with European Background.* Vols. 1 and 2. 3rd ed. New Paltz, NY: Huguenot Historical Society, 1986.

Hoes, Roswell R., trans. and ed. *Baptismal and Marriage Register of the Old Dutch Church of Kingston, Ulster County, New York, 1660–1809.* Albany, NY: Genealogical Publishing, 1997.

*Journals of the Provincial Congress, Provincial Convention, Committee of Safety and Council of Safety of the State of New-York, 1775-1776-1777.* 2 vols. Albany, NY: Thurlow Weed, Printer to the State, 1842.

Lincoln, Charles Z. *The Colonial Laws of New York from the Year 1664 to the Revolution.* 4 vols. Albany, NY: James B. Lyon, State Printer, 1894.

*Minutes of the Committee and First Commission for Detecting Conspiracies 1776–1778; Minutes of the Council of Appointment 1778–1779.* New York: New York Historical Society, 1925.

New York State Legislature. *Journal of the Legislature Council of the Colony of New York Began the 9th Day of April, 1691; and ended the 27th of September, 1743.* Albany, NY: Weed, Parsons & Co., 1861.

New York State. *Calendar of Council Minutes 1668–1783.* Albany: University of the State of New York, 1902.

O'Callaghan, E. B., comp. *The Documentary History of the State of New York.* Albany, NY: Weed, Parsons & Co., 1850.

———. *Documents Relative to the Colonial History of the State of New York.* 15 vols. Albany, NY: Weed, Parsons & Co., 1856–61.

———. *Calendar of New York Colonial Manuscripts Indorsed Land Papers in the Office of the Sec. of State of New York 1643–1803.* Harrison, NY: Harbor Hill Books, 1987.

Washington, George. *The Writings of George Washington from the Original Manuscript Sources, 1745–1799.* Edited by John C. Fitzpatrick. Washington, DC: Government Printing Office, 1931–44.

**Government Publications**

Bureau of Historic Sites and Preservation. *Washington Slept . . . But Where Did He Sleep?* Newburgh, NY: Bureau of Historic Sites and Preservation, 1975.

*Heads of Families at the First Census of the United States Taken in the Year 1790: New York.* Washington, DC: Government Printing Office, 1908.

*Journals of Congress: Containing the Proceedings from Sept. 5, 1774, to 1776.* Philadelphia: Printed and sold by R. Aitken, 1777.

National Archives and Records Service. *Revolutionary War Pension and Bounty Land Warrant Application Files.* Washington, DC: General Services Administration, National Archives and Records Service, 1970.

United States Senate. *The Pension Roll of 1845.* 4 vols. Baltimore, MD: Genealogical Publishing, 1992.

Waite, John G., and Paul R. Huey. *Washington's Headquarters, the Hasbrouck House: An Historic Structure Report.* Albany: New York Historic Trust, 1971.

**Maps**

Bruyn, Johs. *Map of the Town of Shawangunk, Ulster County.* Certified February 1st, 1798, by Joseph J. Hasbrouck, Supervisor. New York, 1798.

Clinton, Charles. *Map of the Town of New Windsor, Ulster County, December 1797.* Albany, New York, 1797.

Culles, Christopher, and Walter R. Ristow. *A Survey of the Roads of the United States of America in 1789.* Cambridge, MA: Harvard University Press, 1961.

De Witt, Simeon. *The Winter Cantonment of the American Army and Its Vicinity for 1783.* Place of publication and publisher not identified.

Faden, William. *A Plan of New York Island, with Part of Long Island, Staten Island & East New Jersey, with a Particular Description of the Engagement on the Woody Heights of*

*Long Island, between Flatbush and Brooklyn, on the 27th of August 1776, between His Majesty's Forces Commanded by General Howe and the Americans under Major General Putnam, with the Subsequent Disposition of Both Armies.* London, 1776.

*A Map of Jonathan Hasbrouck's Building Lots in the Village of Newburgh, November 28, 1830.* Newburgh, New York, 1830.

Sauthier, Claude Joseph, and William Faden. *A Map of the Province of New York, Reduced [. . .].* London: William Eaden, 1776.

## Booklets

Corning, Amos Elwood. *Newburgh in the Revolutionary War.* Vol. 1. Newburgh, NY: privately published., 1953.

———. *The Story of Hasbrouck House: Washington's Headquarters, Newburgh, New York.* Newburgh, NY: Board of Trustees, State of New York of Washington's Headquarters, 1950.

———. *Washington at Temple Hill.* Newburgh, NY: Lanmere, 1932.

Pratt, George. *An Account of the British Expedition Above the Hudson River, and of the Events Connected with the Burning of Kingston in 1777.* Marbletown, NY: Ulster County Historical Society, 1977.

## Secondary Sources—Books

Bailey, Rosalie Fellows. *Pre-revolutionary Dutch Houses and Families in Northern New Jersey and Southern New York.* Irvine, CA: Reprint Services Corporation, 1993.

Bailyn, Bernard. *The Ideological Origins of the American Revolution.* Cambridge, MA: Harvard University Press, 1968.

Bakeless, John. *Turncoats, Traitors, and Heroes: Espionage in the American Revolution.* New York: De Capo Press, 1998.

Barnum, H. L. *The Spy Unmasked; or, Memoirs of Enoch Crosby, Alias Harvey Birch, the Hero of the "Spy, a Tale of the Neutral Ground," by Mr. Cooper.* New York: J. & J. Harper, 1829.

Berkin, Carol. *Revolutionary Mothers: Women in the Struggle for America's Independence.* New York: Vintage Books, 2009.

Bonomi, Patricia U. *A Factious People: Politics and Society in Colonial New York.* Ithaca, NY: Cornell University Press, 2014.

Cohen, David S. *The Dutch-American Farm.* New York: New York University Press, 1992.

Conely, Sheldon. *The Battle of Fort Montgomery: A Short History.* Fleischmanns, NY: Purple Martin Press, 2002.

Countryman, Edward. *A People in Revolution: The American Revolution and Political Society in New York, 1760–1790.* New York: ACLS History E-Book Project, 2005.

Dempsey, Janet. *Washington's Last Cantonment: "High Time for a Peace."* Monroe, NY: Library Research Associates, 1987.

Diamant, Lincoln. *Chaining the Hudson: The Fight for the River in the American Revolution.* New York: Fordham University Press, 2004.

Division of Archives and History. *The American Revolution in New York: Its Political, Social and Economic Significance.* Albany: University of the State of New York, 1926.

Doster, Joanne Marshall. *Pioneer Families of Barry County, Michigan: Genealogies and Family Histories of 60 Families of Barry*. Decorah, IA: Anundsen Publishing Co., 1995.

Duerden, Tim. *A History of Delaware County, New York: A Catskill Land and Its People, 1797–2007*. Fleischmanns, NY: Purple Mountain Press, 2007.

Eager, Samuel W. *An Outline History of Orange County: With an Enumeration of the Names of Its Towns, Villages, Rivers, Creeks, Lakes, Ponds, Mountains, Hills and Other Known Localities and Their Etymologies or Historical Reasons Therefore; Together with Local Traditions and Short Biographical Sketches of Early Settlers, Etc.* Salem, MA: Higginson Book, 2000.

Ellet, Elizabeth F. *Revolutionary Women in the War for American Independence: A One-Volume Revised Edition of Elizabeth Ellet's 1848 Landmark Series*. Edited and annotated by Lincoln Diamant. Westport, CT: Praeger, 1998.

Emery, Rufus, and Edward Manning Ruttenber. *A Record of the Inscriptions in the Old Town Burying Ground of Newburgh, N.Y.* Newburgh, NY: Historical Society of Newburgh Bay and the Highlands, 1898.

Fleming, Thomas. *The Perils of Peace*. New York: Harper Collins, 2007.

Freeman, Douglas Southall. *Leader of the Revolution*. Vol. 4 of *George Washington: A Biography*. New York: Charles Scribner's and Sons, 1951.

Gallagher, John J. *The Battle of Brooklyn, 1776*. Westminster, MD: Heritage Books, 2004.

Greene, Nelson, ed. *History of the Valley of the Hudson River of Destiny 1609–1930*. Chicago: S. J. Clarke Publishing, 1931.

Hodges, Graham Russell. *Root and Branch: African Americans in New York and East Jersey 1613–1863*. Chapel Hill and London: University of North Carolina Press, 1999.

Humphrey, Thomas J. *Land and Liberty: Hudson Valley Riots in the Age of Revolution*. DeKalb: Northern Illinois University Press, 2004.

Johnston, Henry Phelps. *Nathan Hale 1776 Biography and Memorial*. New Haven, CT: Yale Press, 1814.

Kaminski, John P. *George Clinton: Yeoman Politician of the New Republic*. Madison, WI: Madison House, 1993.

Kammen, Michael G. *Colonial New York: A History*. New York: Oxford University Press, 1996.

Keller, Allan. *Life along the Hudson*. New York: Fordham University Press, 1997.

Kelsay, Isabel Thompson. *Joseph Brant, 1743–1807: Man of Two Worlds*. Syracuse, NY: Syracuse University Press, 2007.

Kohn, Richard H. *Eagle and Sword: The Federalists and the Creation of the Military Establishment in America, 1783–1802*. New York: Free Press, 1996.

Le Fevre, Ralph. *History of New Paltz, New York and Its Old Families (from 1678 to 1820): Including the Huguenot Pioneers and Others Who Settled in New Paltz Previous to the Revolution; With an Appendix Bringing Down the History of Certain Families and Some Other Matter to 1850*. Baltimore, MD: Clearfield Company, 1996.

Lossing, Benson John. *The Hudson, from the Wilderness to the Sea*. Hensonville, NY: Black Dome Press, 1860.

Lossing, Benson John———. *The Two Spies: Nathan Hale and John André*. Charleston, SC: Nabu Press, 2010.

Martin, James Kirby, and Sean Hannah. *Leading with Character: George Washington and the Newburgh Conspiracy*. Mount Vernon, VA: George Washington's Mount Vernon, 2016.

McCullough, David G. *1776*. New York: Simon & Schuster Paperbacks, 2006.

———. *1776: Excerpts from the Acclaimed History, with Letters, Maps, and Seminal Artwork*. New York: Simon & Schuster, 2007.

Misencik, Paul R. *The Original American Spies: Seven Covert Agents of the Revolutionary War*. Jefferson, NC: McFarland & Company, 2014.

Monell, John James. *Historical Sketches: Washington's Headquarters, Newburgh, New York, and Adjacent Localities*. Newburgh, NY: E. M. Ruttenber, 1872.

*New Windsor Centennial: Temple Hill, June 22d, 1883*. Newburgh, NY: E. M. Ruttenber & Son, 1883.

Reynolds, Helen Wilkinson. *Dutch Houses in the Hudson Valley before 1776*. New York, Dover Publications, 1965.

Richards, David T. *Swords in Their Hands: George Washington and the Newburgh Conspiracy*. Candler, NC: Pisgah Press, 2014.

Ruttenber, Edward Manning. *City of Newburgh: A Centennial Historical Sketch*. Newburgh, NY: E. M. Ruttenber & Son, 1876.

Ruttenber, Edward Manning, and L. H. Clark, comp. *History of Orange County, New York*. Philadelphia: Everts & Peck, 1881.

Schenkman, A. J. *Washington's Headquarters in Newburgh: Home to a Revolution*. Charleston, SC: History Press, 2009.

———. *Wicked Ulster County: Tales of Desperados, Gangs & More*. Charleston, SC: History Press, 2012.

Schoonmaker, M. *History of Kingston, N.Y.: From Its Early Settlement to the Year 1820*. New York, 1888.

Seymour, George Dudley. *Documentary Life of Nathan Hale*. New Haven, CT: privately published, 1941.

Snow, Dean. *1777: Tipping Point at Saratoga*. New York: Oxford University Press, 2018.

Sylvester, Nathaniel Bartlett, and Jonathan W. Hasbrouck. *History of Ulster County, New York, with Illustrations and Biographical Sketches of Its Prominent Men and Pioneers*. Philadelphia: Everts & Peck, 1880.

Trelease, Allen William. *Indian Affairs in Colonial New York: The Seventeenth Century*. Ithaca, NY: Cornell University Press, 1960.

Waite, John G., and Paul R. Huey. *Washington's Headquarters, the Hasbrouck House: An Historic Structure Report*. Albany: New York State Historic Trust, 1971.

Williams-Myers, Albert James. *Long Hammering: Essays on the Forging of an African American Presence in the Hudson River Valley to the Early Twentieth Century*. Trenton, NJ: Africa World, 1994.

Woodward, Ashbel. *Memoir of Col. Thomas Knowlton, of Ashford, Connecticut*. London: Forgotten Books, 2015.

**Journals and Magazines**

Brink, Benjamin Meyer, ed. *Olde Ulster: An Historical and Genealogical Magazine*. 10 vols. Kingston, NY: B. M. Brink, 1905–14.

Countryman, Edward. "Split Wide and Split Deep: The Revolutionary Hudson Valley." *Hudson River Valley Review* 20, no. 1 (Summer 2003): 1–13.

Fowler, Robert Ludlow. "Historic Houses and Revolutionary Letters." *Magazine of American History* 2 (August 1890): 81–99.

Kohn, Richard H. "The Inside History of the Newburgh Conspiracy: America and the Coup d'Etat" *William and Mary Quarterly* 27, no. 2 (April 1970): 187–220.

Maier, Pauline. "Popular Uprisings and Civil Authority in Eighteenth-Century America." *William and Mary Quarterly* 27, no. 1 (January 1970): 3–35.

Maker, Mary Beth. "Nathan Hale: Icon of Innocence." *Connecticut History* 45 (Spring 2006): 1–30.

Miller, Henry Edward. "The Spy of the Neutral Ground." *New England Magazine* 24, no. 3 (May 1898): 307–19.

Pickering, James H. "Enoch Crosby, Secret Agent of the Neutral Ground: His Own Story." *New York History* 47, no. 1 (January 1966): 61–73.

Skeen, C. Edward, and Richard H. Kohn. "The Newburgh Conspiracy Reconsidered." *William and Mary Quarterly* 31, no. 2 (April 1974): 273–98.

Wermuth, Thomas S. "The Women! In This Place Have Risen a Mob." *Hudson River Valley Review* 20, no. 1 (Summer 2003): 71–77.

Wermuth, Thomas S., and James H. Johnson. "The American Revolution in the Hudson River Valley—An Overview." *Hudson River Valley Review* 20, no. 1 (Summer 2003): 5–13.

**Websites**

Associated Press. "Nathan Hale Blundered Into a Trap, Papers Show." *New York Times*, September 21, 2003. www.nytimes.com/2003/09/21/us/nathan-hale-blun-dered-into-a-trap-papers-show.html.

Devoss, David. "Divided Loyalties." *Smithsonian Magazine*, January 1, 2004. www.smithsonianmag.com/history/divided-loyalities-107489501.

DeWan, George. "The Plot to Kidnap George Washington." *Newsday*, February 28, 2019. www.newsday.com/long-island/history/george-washington-long-island-our-story-1.18452352.

Diamond, Anna. "The Plot to Kill George Washington." *Smithsonian Magazine*, December 1, 2018. www.smithsonianmag.com/history/plot-kill-george-washington-180970729.

"From George Washington to Alexander Hamilton, 4 March 1783." Founders Online, National Archives and Records Administration. Accessed August 1, 2019. https://founders.archives.gov/documents/Washington/99-01-02-10767.

"From George Washington to David Brooks, 3 June 1779." Founders Online, National Archives and Records Administration. Accessed August 1, 2019. https://founders.archives.gov/documents/Washington/03-21-02-0032.

"From George Washington to David Rittenhouse, 16 February 1783." Founders Online, National Archives and Records Administration. Accessed August 1, 2019. https:// founders.archives.gov/documents/Washington/99-01-02-10654.

"From George Washington to Joseph Jones, 14 December 1782." Founders Online, National Archives and Records Administration. Accessed August 1, 2019. https:// founders.archives.gov/documents/Washington/99-01-02-10202.

"From George Washington to Joseph Jones, 18 March 1783." Founders Online, National Archives and Records Administration. Accessed August 1, 2019. https://founders. archives.gov/documents/Washington/99-01-02-10858.

"From George Washington to Lewis Nicola, 22 May 1782." Founders Online, National Archives and Records Administration. Accessed August 1, 2019. https://founders. archives.gov/documents/Washington/99-01-02-08501.

"General Orders, 29 October 1782." Founders Online, National Archives and Records Administration. Accessed August 1, 2019. https://founders.archives.gov/ documents/Washington/99-01-02-09824.

"George Washington to the Assistant Clothier at Newburgh, 7 September 1779" Founders Online, National Archives and Records Administration. Accessed August 1, 2019. https://founders.archives.gov/documents/Hamilton/01-02-02-0437.

Ghering, Cynthia. "Women Spies—Ann Bates." William L. Clements Library, University of Michigan. Accessed August 1, 2019. https://clements.umich.edu/ exhibit/spy-letters-of-the-american-revolution/stories-of-spies/ann-bates/.

"History & Culture." Valley Forge National Historical Park, National Park Service. Accessed August 1, 2019. www.nps.gov/vafo/learn/historyculture/index.htm.

Hutson, James. "Nathan Hale Revisited: A Tory's Account of the Arrest of the First American Spy." *Library of Congress Information Bulletin* 62, no. 7/8, July/August 2003. www.loc.gov/loc/lcib/0307-8/hale.html.

Levine, David. "How a Shoemaker Turned Into a Spy." *Hudson Valley Magazine*, May 28, 2014. www.hvmag.com/Hudson-Valley-Magazine/June-2014/ How-a-Shoemaker-Turned-Into-a-Spy.

Michaud, Jon. "Walking the Heights." *The New Yorker*, June 20, 2017. www.newyorker. com/books/page-turner/walking-heights.

"Newburgh Address: George Washington to Officers of the Army, March 15, 1783." Digital Encyclopedia, George Washington's Mount Vernon. Accessed August 1, 2019. www.mountvernon.org/education/primary-sources-2/article/ newburgh-address-george-washington-to-officers-of-the-army-march-15-1783.

Putnam Graveyards. Accessed August 1, 2019. www.putnamgraveyards.com.

"Proclamation for the Cessation of Hostilities, 18 April 1783." Founders Online, National Archives and Records Administration. Accessed August 1, 2019. https:// founders.archives.gov/documents/Washington/99-01-02-11104.

"Revolutionary Spies." National Women's History Museum, November 9, 2017. www. womenshistory.org/articles/revolutionary-spies.

Ruppert, Bob. "His Excellency's Guards." *Journal of the American Revolution*, August 18, 2014. www.allthingsliberty.com/2014/08/his-excellencys-guards.

Severo, Richard. "Revolutionary Fort Held Hostage to Decay and Apathy." *New York Times*, May 24, 1998. www.nytimes.com/1998/05/24/nyregion/revolutionary-fort-held-hostage-to-decay-and-apathy.html.

Shattuck, Gary. "Plotting the 'Sacricide' of George Washington." *Journal of the American Revolution*, July 25, 2014. https://Allthingsliberty.com/2014/07/plotting-the-sacricide-of-george-washington.

"To George Washington from Major General Riedesel, 17 January 1779." Founders Online, National Archives and Records Administration. Accessed August 1, 2019. https://founders.archives.gov/documents/Washington/03-19-02-0013.

### Illustrations—National Portrait Gallery

Clarke, William. *George Washington*. 1800. National Portrait Gallery, Smithsonian Institution, Washington, DC; Gift of Eleanor Morein Foster in memory of Charles Harry Foster.

De Saint-Mémin, Charles Balthazar Julien Févret. *James Clinton*. 1797. National Portrait Gallery, Smithsonian Institution, Washington, DC; Gift of Mr. and Mrs. Paul Mellon.

Polk, Charles Peale, after Charles Willson Peale. *Henry Knox*. After 1783. National Portrait Gallery, Smithsonian Institution, Washington, DC.

Peale, James, after Charles Willson Peale. *Horatio Gates*. 1782. National Portrait Gallery, Smithsonian Institution, Washington, DC; Gift of Mr. Lawrence A. Fleischman and Gallery Purchase.

Reich, Jacques. *John Burgoyne*. Circa 1899–1920. National Portrait Gallery, Smithsonian Institution, Washington, DC.

Sharples, James, Jr., and Felix Thomas Sharples. *George Clinton*. 1806. National Portrait Gallery, Smithsonian Institution, Washington, DC; Gift of Charles N. Andreae.

Stuart, Gilbert, and John Trumbull. *John Jay*. Begun 1784; completed by 1818. National Portrait Gallery, Smithsonian Institution, Washington, DC.

Unidentified artist. *George Washington*. 1783. National Portrait Gallery, Smithsonian Institution, Washington, DC.

Unidentified artist, after Ezra Ames. *Thayendanegea (Joseph Brant)*. After 1806. National Portrait Gallery, Smithsonian Institution, Washington, DC.

Waldo, Samuel Lovett, and William Jewett. *Enoch Crosby*. 1830. National Portrait Gallery, Smithsonian Institution, Washington, DC.

### Illustrations—Library of Congress

*DuMond House, Main Street (State Highway 6), Hurley, Ulster County, NY*. 1933. Historic American Buildings Survey (Fed.), Library of Congress, Washington, DC.

*General Philip Schuyler House, Troy Road Vicinity, Colonie, Albany County, NY*. 1933. Historic American Buildings Survey (Fed.), Library of Congress, Washington, DC.

MacFarland, E. P. *View from South. First Dutch Reformed Church, Main Street, Fishkill, Dutchess County, NY*. April 23, 1934. Historic American Buildings Survey (Fed.), Library of Congress, Washington, DC.

Mixon, Stanley P. *Exterior General View from South West. Nathan Hale Schoolhouse, Nathan Hale Park (moved from Village Green).* July 17, 1940. Historic American Buildings Survey (Fed.), Library of Congress, Washington, DC.

———. *Int., Reception Room and Parlor, Paneled End and Mantel, (1770) Addition. Hasbrouck House, Washington, Liberty, Lafayette, Colden Streets, Newburgh, Orange County, NY.* July 23, 1940. Historic American Buildings Survey (Fed.), Library of Congress, Washington, DC.

Moses, Arnold. *View from the Southwest. Morris-Jumel Mansion, Edgecomb Avenue & 160th–162nd Streets, New York County, NY.* September 10, 1936. Historic American Buildings Survey (Fed.), Library of Congress, Washington, DC.

*Nathan Hale, Captain in Regular Army, U.S.A., Executed as Spy by the British.* Circa 1913. Library of Congress, Washington, DC.

# ENDNOTES

### Tories and Mohawks Raid New York's Western Frontier

1 George Clinton, *Public Papers of George Clinton, First Governor of New York, 1777–1795, 1801–1894*, ed. Hugh Hastings, vol. 7 (Albany, NY: Oliver A. Quayle, 1904), 191–92.

2 Colin G. Calloway, "The American Revolution," National Park Service, U.S. Department of the Interior, accessed February 9, 2020, www.nps.gov/revwar/about_the_revolution/american_indians.html.

3 Fort Stanwix Staff, "The Clinton-Sullivan Campaign of 1779," National Park Service, U.S. Department of the Interior, accessed February 9, 2020, www.nps.gov/fost/learn/historyculture/the-western-expedition-against-the-six-nations-1779.htm.

4 Albert Pawling's Pension Application, Pension #S19016 M804, Revolutionary War Pension and County Land Warrant Application, NARA Record Group 15, Roll 1891. U.S. Senate, *The Senate of the U.S. 1st Session of the 28th Congress, Dec. 4, 1843*, vol. 3 (Washington, DC: Gales and Seaton, 1844), 145–46.

5 Donald C. Holmes, "Formation of Butler's Rangers," United Empire Loyalists' Association of Canada, www.uelac.org/PDF/Formation-of-Butlers-Rangers.pdf.

6 Silas Bowker, Jr., Pension Application File, NARA M804, #303, File No. W21684.

7 Ibid.

8 Clinton, *Public Papers*, vol. 7, 194.

9 Ibid., 190–91.

10. Ibid., 195.

11 Ibid., 191–92.

12 Ibid., 192.

### A Massacre at the Hands of Mohawk Chief Joseph Brand

13 "From George Washington to General Sullivan, May 31, 1779," Founders Online, National Archives and Records Administration, accessed February 9, 2020, https://founders.archives.gov/documents/washington/03-20-02-0661.

14 George Clinton, *Public Papers of George Clinton, First Governor of New York, 1777–1795, 1801–1894*, ed. Hugh Hastings, vol. 4 (Albany, NY: Oliver A. Quayle, 1904), 798.

15 Fort Stanwix Staff, "The Clinton-Sullivan Campaign of 1779," National Park Service, U.S. Department of the Interior, accessed February 9, 2020, www.nps.gov/fost/learn/historyculture/the-western-expedition-against-the-six-nations-1779.htm.

16 "To George Washington from George Clinton, 15 October 1778," Founders Online, National Archives and Records Administration, accessed February 9, 2020, https://founders.archives.gov/documents/washington/03-17-02-0407.

17 John L. Hardenbergh, *Lt. John L. Hardenbergh Journal* (Auburn, NY: Knapp & Peck, 1879), 23.

18 A. V. Blake, *Life of Joseph Brant-Thayendanegea*, vol. 2 (New York, 1838), 460.

19 Clinton, *Public Papers*, vol. 4, 798.
20 "From George Washington to General Sullivan, May 31, 1779."
21 Fort Stanwix Staff, "Clinton-Sullivan Campaign of 1779."
22 *Kingston Daily Freeman*, May 7, 1903, vol. 32, no. 17, 2.

## The Convention Army Travels South after Saratoga
23 Walter C. Anthony, *Washington's Headquarters, Newburgh* (Newburgh, NY: Historical Society of Newburgh Bay and the Highlands, 1928), 31.
24 "From George Washington to Major General Horatio Gates, 30 October 1777," Founders Online, National Archives and Records Administration, accessed February 9, 2020, https://founders.archives.gov/documents/washington/03-12-02-0049.
25 Charles Ramsdell Lingley, "The Treatment of Burgoyne's Troops Under the Saratoga Convention," *Political Science Quarterly* 22, no. 3 (September 1907): 441.
26 Ibid.
27 Lorraine McMullen, "Massow, Friederike Charlotte Louise von," in *Dictionary of Canadian Biography*, vol. 5, University of Toronto/Université Laval, accessed February 9, 2020, www.biographi.ca/en/bio/massow_friederike_charlotte_louise_von_5E.html.
28 Ibid.
29 Ibid.
30 Ibid.
31 Marvin L. Brown, ed., "Baroness on the Battlefield," *American Heritage* 16, no.1 (December 1964): 65–79.
32 Friederike Charlotte Luise Freifrau von Riedesel, *Letters and Journals Relating to the War of the American Revolution, and the Capture of the German Troops at Saratoga, by Mrs. General Riedesel*, trans. William L. Stone (Albany, NY: Joel Munsell, 1867), 127.
33 Brown, "Baroness on the Battlefield."
34 David Head, "Hessians," Digital Encyclopedia, George Washington's Mount Vernon, accessed February 5, 2020, www.mountvernon.org/library/digitalhistory/digital-encyclopedia/article/hessians.
35 von Riedesel, *Letters and Journals*, 135.
36 Paul R. Huey and John G. Waite, *Washington's Headquarters, the Hasbrouck House: An Historic Structure Report* (Albany: New York State Historic Trust, 1971), 21.
37 George Clinton, *Public Papers of George Clinton, First Governor of New York, 1777–1795, 1801–1894*, ed. Hugh Hastings, vol. 4 (Albany, NY: Oliver A. Quayle, 1904), 434.
38 Ibid.
39 von Riedesel, *Letters and Journals*, 138.
40 Anthony, *Washington's Headquarters, Newburgh*, 31.
41 Ibid.
42 Clinton, *Public Papers*, vol. 4, 434.
43 von Riedesel, *Letters and Journals*, 154.
44 Brown, "Baroness on the Battlefield."

## *Nous y Voici* (We Are Here)

45 Edward C. Boynton, *General Orders of George Washington, Commander-in-Chief of the Army of Revolution, Issued at Newburgh on the Hudson, 1782–1783* (Harrison, NY: Harbor Hill Books, 1973), 100.

46 "The Battle of Saratoga—Sept and Oct 1777," Saratoga.com, accessed February 9, 2020, www.saratoga.com/aboutsaratoga/battle-of-saratoga.

47 "Oriskany," American Battlefield Trust, accessed February 9, 2020, www.battlefields.org/learn/articles/oriskany.

48 Jan Sheldon Conley, *The Battle of Fort Montgomery: A Short History* (Fleischmanns, NY: Purple Mountain Press, 2002), 13.

49 "To George Washington from Lord Stirling, 1 June 1776," Founders Online, National Archives and Records Administration, accessed February 9, 2020, https://founders.archives.gov/documents/Washington/03-04-02-0336.

50 John P. Kaminski, *George Clinton: Yeoman Politician* (Madison, WI: Madison House, 1993), 21.

51 William Abbott, ed., *Memoirs of Major General William Heath* (New York: W. Abbatt, 1901), 120.

52 George Clinton, *Public Papers of George Clinton, First Governor of New York, 1777–1795, 1801–1894*, ed. Hugh Hastings, vol. 2 (Albany, NY: Oliver A. Quayle, 1904), 393–94.

53 E. M. Ruttenber and L. H. Clark, comp., *History of Orange County, New York* (Philadelphia: Everts & Peck, 1881), 224.

54 Benson J. Lossing, *The Pictorial Field Book of the Revolution*, vol. 2 (New Orleans: Pelican Publishing, 2008), 116.

55 Boynton, *General Orders of George Washington*, 100.

56 Clinton, *Public Papers*, vol. 2, 398–99.

57 Ibid., 443.

58 Ibid., 444.

59 Ibid.

60 "The Livingstons and Their Riverfront House," Friends of Clermont, accessed February 2, 2020, www.friendsofclermont.org/the-livingstons.

61 Ralph LeFevre, *History of New Paltz, New York and Its Old Families from 1678 to 1820* (Albany, NY: Brandow, 1909), 339.

62 Benjamin Meyer Brink, ed., *Olde Ulster: An Historical and Genealogical Magazine, VIII*, vol. 1 (Kingston, NY: B. M. Brink, 1905), 245.

63 "The Spy and the 'Guard' House," accessed February 21, 2020, www.hurleyheritage society.org/history/spy-and-guard-house.

## The Pennsylvania Mutiny of 1783 and the Newburgh Connection

64 George Clinton, *Public Papers of George Clinton, First Governor of New York, 1777–1795, 1801–1894*, ed. Hugh Hastings, vol. 6 (Albany, NY: Oliver A. Quayle, 1904), 143.

65 Paul R. Huey and John G. Waite, *Washington's Headquarters, the Hasbrouck House: An Historic Structure Report* (Albany: New York State Historic Trust, 1971), 22.

66 Ibid., 23.

67 Clinton, *Public Papers*, vol. 6, 143.

68 Ibid., 144.

69. Ibid., 145.

70 Ibid.

71 Ibid.

72 Ibid.

73 "Stories from the People's House; Chasing Congress Away," History House, June 1, 2015, https://history.house.gov/Blog/2015/June/6-1-Chasing-Congress/.

74 "To George Washington from Henry Carbery, 25 July 1789," Founders Online, National Archives and Records Administration, accessed February 9, 2020, https://founders.archives.gov/documents/washington/05-03-02-0172.

75 James Madison, *The Papers of James Madison*, vol. 7, 3 May 1783–20 February 1784, eds. William T. Hutchinson and William M. E. Rachal (Chicago: University of Chicago Press, 1971), 180.

76 John Adams, *The Adams Papers: Papers of John Adams*, vol. 15, June 1783–January 1784, eds. Gregg L. Lint, C. James Taylor, et al. (Cambridge, MA: Harvard University Press, 2010), 121.

## Jacob Middaugh and the Marbletown Disaffection

77 George Clinton, *Public Papers of George Clinton, First Governor of New York, 1777–1795, 1801–1894*, ed. Hugh Hastings, vol. 1 (Albany, NY: Oliver A. Quayle, 1904), 783.

78 Ibid., 784.

79 "James Clinton to Officer Commanding at Ramapough," Donald F. Clark Collection, New York Historical Society, MS 118, #306.

80 Philip Heslip, ed., *King's American Regiment Orderly Book (1776–1777)*, William L. Clement Library, University of Michigan, accessed April 2011, https://quod.lib.mich.edu/c/clementsead/mich-wcl-M-744kin?is=navbarbrowselink;view=text.

81 *Calendar of Historical Manuscripts, Relating to the War of the Revolution, in the Office of the Secretary of State, Albany, N.Y.*, vol. 2 (Albany, NY: Weed, Parsons and Company, 1868), 128.

82 Ibid., 113.

83 Ibid., 123.

84 Clinton, *Public Papers*, vol. 1, 758.

85 Gould, *History of Delaware County*.

86 "The Journal of Cadwallader Colden 1776–1779," Huntington Library, accessed February 2, 2020, https://hdl.huntington.org/digital/collection/p15150coll7/id/29262.

87. "James Clinton to Officer Commanding at Ramapough."

88 Clinton, *Public Papers*, vol. 1, 783.

89 Ibid., 762.

90 Ibid., 783.

91 *Journals of the Provincial Congress, Provincial Convention, Committee of Safety and Council of Safety of the State of New-York, 1775-1776-1777*, vol. 1 (Albany, NY: Thurlow Weed, Printer to the State, 1842), 928.

92 *Calendar of Historical Manuscripts, Relating to the War of the Revolution, in the Office of the Secretary of State, Albany, N.Y.*, vol. 2 (Albany, NY: Weed, Parsons and Company, 1868), 160.

93 "Traitors in Kingston," *The Squaredealer*, April 10, 2016, https://thesquaredealer.wordpress.com/2016/04/10/traitors-in-kingston.

94 Clinton, *Public Papers*, vol. 3, 626.

95 John D. Monroe, *Chapters in the History of Delaware County, New York* (Delhi, NY: Delaware County Historical Association, 1949), 61.

96 *Second Report of the Bureau of Archives for the Province of Ontario* (Toronto: L. K. Cameron, 1905), 1256.

**The Mutiny on Temple Hill in 1783**

97 "To Alexander Hamilton from George Washington, 4 April 1783," Founders Online, National Archives and Records Administration, accessed February 9, 2020 https://founders.archives.gov/documents/Hamilton/01-03-02-0202.

98 Charles L. Fisher, "Archaeology at New Windsor Cantonment: Construction and Social Reproduction at a Revolutionary Encampment," *Northeast Historical Archaeology* 12, no. 1 (1983): 15.

99 A. Elwood Corning, *Newburgh in the Revolutionary War*, vol. 1 (Newburgh, NY: Newburgh, 1953), 2.

100. Ron Chernow, *Washington: A Life* (New York, NY: Penguin, 2010), 430–31.

101 Richard Haggard, "The Nicola Affair: Lewis Nicola, George Washington, and American Military Discontent during the Revolutionary War," *Proceedings of the American Philosophical Society* 146, no. 2 (June 2002): 148.

102 "From George Washington to Lewis Nicola, 22 May 1782," Founders Online, National Archives and Records Administration, https://founders.archives.gov/documents/Washington/99-01-02-08501.

103 Fisher, "Archaeology at New Windsor Cantonment," 5.

104 Ibid.

105 Katie Benz, "New Windsor Cantonment," Digital Encyclopedia, George Washington's Mount Vernon, accessed February 9, 2020, www.mountvernon.org/library/digitalhistory/digital-encyclopedia/article/new-windsor-cantonment.

106 "From George Washington to James McHenry, 17 October 1782," Founders Online, National Archives and Records Administration, accessed February 9, 2020, https://founders.archives.gov/documents/washington/99-01-02-09750.

107 George Bancroft, *History of the United States of America from the Discovery of the Continent*, vol. 6 (New York: D. Appleton and Co., 1858), 59.

108 U.S. Congress, *Address and Recommendations to the States by the U.S. in Congress Assembled* (Philadelphia, 1783), 39.

109 Edward C. Boynton, *General Orders of George Washington, Commander-in-Chief of the Army of Revolution, Issued at Newburgh on the Hudson, 1782–1783* (Harrison, NY: Harbor Hill Books, 1973), 108.

110 Ibid.

111 Ibid., 110.

112 Ibid., 69–70.

113 Ibid., 70.

114 Mary Stockwell, "Newburgh Address," Digital Encyclopedia, George Washington's Mount Vernon, accessed February 9, 2020, www.mountvernon.org/library/digitalhistory/digital-encyclopedia/article/newburgh-address.

115 "From George Washington to Officers of the Army, 15 March 1783," Founders Online, National Archives and Records Administration, accessed February 9, 2020, https://founders.archives.gov/documents/Washington/99-01-02-10840.

116 "From George Washington to David Rittenhouse, 16 February 1783," Founders Online, National Archives and Records Administration, accessed February 9, 2020, https://founders.archives.gov/documents/Washington/99-01-02-10654.

117 Michael Hattem, "Newburgh Conspiracy," Digital Encyclopedia, George Washington's Mount Vernon, accessed February 2, 2020, www.mountvernon.org/library/digitalhistory/digital-encyclopedia/article/newburgh-conspiracy.

118 Kohn, "Inside History of the Newburgh Conspiracy," 213.

119 Hattem, "Newburgh Conspiracy."

120 "Proclamation for the Cessation of Hostilities, 18 April 1783," Founders Online, National Archives and Records Administration, accessed February 2, 2020, www.founders.archives.gov/documents/washington/99-01-02-11104.

**Cornelius Hasbrouck**

121 "Judge Robert Yates to George Clinton as to the Criminal Conduct of C. Hasbrouck, Jr., Witness Depositions by John Stillwell and John Simpson, January 13, 1781." New York State Archives, Gov. George Clinton Gubernatorial Personal Records, Box 24, Manuscript Vol. 12, Doc. 3489.

122 Ibid.

123 Ibid.

124 Ibid.

125 Ibid.

126 George Clinton, *Public Papers of George Clinton, First Governor of New York, 1777–1795, 1801–1894*, ed. Hugh Hastings, vol. 6 (Albany, NY: Oliver A. Quayle, 1904), 573–74.

127 John P. Butler, ed., *Journal of the Continental Congress 1774–1789*, vol. 16 (Washington, DC: U.S. Government Printing Office, 1978), 127.

128 Clinton, *Public Papers*, vol. 7, 492.

129 "Cornelius and Tryntje Hasbrouck and Samuel Fowler, Jr. Bond," Jonathan Hasbrouck Family Papers (1751–1904), Historic Huguenot Street, New Paltz, New York.

130 "Cornelius Hasbrouck Selling Land to Isaac Hasbrouck in the former Kipp Patent 1800, May 17," Jonathan Hasbrouck Family Paper (1751–1904), Historic Huguenot Street, New Paltz, New York.

131 *New York Evening Post*, March 21, 1803, 4–4.

132 Gustave Anjou, *Ulster County, N.Y. Probate Records in the Office of the Surrogate, and in the County Clerk's Office at Kingston, N.Y.*, vol. 1 and 2 (New York: self-published, 1906), 161.

133 *New York Herald*, August 24, 1816, 4–4.

134 Ibid.

135 Ibid.

136 Deed of sale from Cornelius Hasbrouck to John Sudam Kingston, New York Deed Book D, Liber 23, p. 110, Ulster County Clerk's Archive, Kingston, New York.

137 Ibid.

138 Gordon Pim of Ontario Heritage Trust to A. J. Schenkman, August 17, 2010.

**The Tory Ettrick**

139 "From John Adams to Thomas Jefferson, 2 February 1816," Founders Online, National Archives and Records Administration, accessed February 9, 2020, https://founders.archives.gov/documents/Adams/99-02-02-6575.

140 Paul R. Huey and John G. Waite, *Washington's Headquarters, the Hasbrouck House: An Historic Structure Report* (Albany: New York State Historic Trust, 1971), 24–25.

141 Janet Dempsey, *Washington's Last Cantonment: "High Time for a Peace"* (Monroe, NY: Library Research Associates, 1990), 28.

142 Huey and Waite, *Washington's Headquarters*, 25.

143 Carlos E. Godfrey, *The Commander-in-Chief Guard* (Washington, DC: Stevenson-Smith Co., 1904), 87–89.

144 E. M. Ruttenber and L. H. Clark, comp., *History of Orange County, New York* (Philadelphia: Everts & Peck, 1881), 284.

145 Godfrey, *Commander-in-Chief Guard*, 88.

146 John C. Fitzpatrick, ed., *The Writings of George Washington 1745–1799*, vol. 4 (Washington, DC: U.S. Government Printing Office, 1931), 338.

147 Ibid., vol. 7, 452.

148 E. M. Ruttenber, *History of Newburgh*, 138.

149 John C. Fitzpatrick, ed., *The Writings of George Washington 1745–1799*, vol. 7 (Washington, DC: U.S. Government Printing Office, 1938), 111.

**Tories from Newburgh**

150 *Journals of the Provincial Congress, Provincial Convention, Committee of Safety and Council of Safety of the State of New-York, 1775-1775-1777*, vol. 2 (Albany, NY: Thurlow Weed, Printer to the State, 1842), 444.

151 A. Elwood Corning, *Newburgh in the Revolutionary War*, vol. 1 (Newburgh, NY: Newburgh, 1953), 2. E. M. Ruttenber, *History of the Town of Newburgh* (Newburgh, NY: E. M. Ruttenber & Co., 1859), 91.

152 *Journals of the Provincial Congress*, vol. 2, 444.

153 Ibid., 453.

154 Ibid.

155 Ibid., 454.

156 Ibid.

157 *Calendar of Historical Manuscripts, Relating to the War of the Revolution, in the Office of the Secretary of State, Albany, N.Y.*, vol. 2 (Albany, NY: Weed, Parsons & Company, 1868), 74.

158 Ibid.

159 Ibid.

160 Ibid., 75.

161 Ibid.

162 Ibid.

163 Ibid.

164 Ibid., 76.

165 Ibid., 173.

166 Ibid.

167 Ibid., 80.

168 Ibid.

169 *Journals of the Provincial Congress*, vol. 2, 453.

170 Ibid., 454.

171 *Calendar of Historical Manuscripts*, vol. 2, 79.

172 George Clinton, *Public Papers of George Clinton, First Governor of New York, 1777–1795, 1801–1894*, ed. Hugh Hastings, vol. 4 (Albany, NY: Oliver A. Quayle, 1904), 588.

173 Charles Dewey, "Terror in the Ramapos," *Journal of the American Revolution*, March 21, 2019, www.allthingsliberty.com/2019/03/terror-in-the-ramapos.

**Enoch Crosby**

174 H. L. Barnum, *The Spy Unmasked; or, Memoirs of Enoch Crosby, Alias Harvey Birch, the Hero of the "Spy, a Tale of the Neutral Ground," by Mr. Cooper* (New York: J. & J. Harper, 1829), 105.

175 John C. Dann, ed., *The Revolution Remembered: Eyewitness Accounts of the War for Independence* (Chicago: University of Chicago, 1980), 340. Enoch Crosby Pension, October 15, 1832, #S10505, National Archives and Records Administration, Washington, DC.

176 Nathan Wuertenberg, "Quebec Campaign," Digital Encyclopedia, George Washington's Mount Vernon, accessed January 1, 2020, www.mountvernon.org/library/digitalhistory/digital-encyclopedia/article/quebec-campaign.

177 Affidavit of Enoch Crosby, October 15, 1832; File #S10505, Case Files of Pension and Bounty-Land Warrant Applications Based on Revolutionary War Service; Pension and Bounty Land Warrant Application Files, 1800–1960; Department of Veterans Affairs, Record Group 15, National Archives, Washington, DC; National Archives and Records Administration microfilm publication M804, roll 0697.

178 Ibid.

179 John Bakeless, *Turncoats, Traitors, and Heroes* (New York: Da Capo Press, 1959), 144.

180 Affidavit of Enoch Crosby, October 15, 1832.

181 Harry Edward Miller, "The Spy of the Neutral Ground," *New England Magazine* 18 (1898), 314

182 Affidavit of Enoch Crosby, October 15, 1832.

183 Ibid.

184 Ibid.

185 James H. Pickering, "Enoch Crosby, Secret Agent of the Neutral Ground: His Own Story," *New York History* 47, no. 1 (January 1966): 61–73.

186 Barnum, *Spy Unmasked*, 76.

187 Fine Dictionary, "Crupper," www.finedictionary.com/crupper.html.

188 *Minutes of the Committee and of the First Commission for Detecting and Defeating Conspiracies in the State of New York: December 11, 1776–September 23, 1778*, vol. 1 (New York: New York Historical Society, 1924), 165.

189 Barnum, *Spy Unmasked*, 70

190 Bakeless, *Turncoats, Traitors, and Heroes*, 144.

191 Ibid.

192 Affidavit of Enoch Crosby, October 15, 1832.

193 "Enoch Crosby Obituary," *Pittsfield Sun*, June 26, 1835, no. 1816 edition, vol. 35, 2.

**Ann Bates**

194 Carol Berkin, *Revolutionary Mothers: Women in the Struggle for America's Independence* (New York: Knopf Doubleday, 2005), 140.

195 Martha K. Robinson, "British Occupation of Philadelphia," The Encyclopedia of Philadelphia, accessed May 5, 2020, https://philadelphiaencyclopedia.org/archive/british-occupation-of-philadelphia.

196 Ann Bates Pension Application, London Treasury Doc T1/611, March 17, 1785.

197 John Bakeless, *Turncoats, Traitors, and Heroes* (New York: Da Capo Press, 1959), 252.

198 Ibid.

199 Ann Bates Pension Application.

200 Ibid.

201 Ibid.

202 Bakeless, *Turncoats, Traitors, and Heroes*, 254.

203 Ibid., 254–55.

204 Ibid.

205 Ibid.

206 H. L. Landers, *The Virginia Campaign and the Blockade and Siege of Yorktown 1781* (Washington, DC: U.S. Government Printing Office, 1931), 144.

207 Bakeless, *Turncoats, Traitors, and Heroes*, 259.

208 Ann Bates Pension Application.

209 Bakeless, *Turncoats, Traitors, and Traitors*, 261.

210 Ann Bates Pension Application.
211 Bakeless, *Turncoats, Traitors, and Heroes*, 262.
212 Ann Bates Pension Application.

**Margaret Corbin**
213 "From George Washington to John Hancock, 16 November 1776," Founders Online, National Archives and Records Administration, accessed February 9, 2020, https://founders.archives.gov/documents/Washington/03-07-02-0118.
214 "Lord Howe's Conference with the Committee of Congress, 11 September 1776," Founders Online, National Archives and Records Administration, accessed February 9, 2020, https://founders.archives.gov/documents/Franklin/01-22-02-0358.
215 "Letter from John Adams to Abigail Adams, 14 September 1776," Adams Family Papers, Massachusetts Historical Society, accessed January 17, 2020, www.masshist.org/digitaladams.
216 "George Washington to Continental Congress, 16 September 1776," Library of Congress, accessed February 2, 2020, www.loc.gov/resource/mgw3a.001/?sp=419. And "The American Revolution : Timeline : Articles and Essays : George Washington Papers : Digital Collections : Library of Congress,"
217 DIA Public Affairs, "Knowlten's Rangers: 'But one life to give,'" Defense Intelligence Agency, May 4, 2014, www.dia.mil/News/Articles/Article-View/Article/566972/knowltons-rangers-but-one-life-to-give.
218 "Thomas W. Knowlton Killed in Action at the Battle of Harlem Heights 1776," *Harlem World Magazine*, December 14, 2019, www.harlemworldmagazine.com/thomas-w-knowlton-killed-in-action-at-the-battle-of-harlem-heights-1776.
219 David G. McCullough, *1776* (New York: Simon & Schuster Paperbacks, 2006), 218.
220 David Osborn, "The Battle of Pell's Point," National Park Service, U.S. Department of the Interior, accessed January 1, 2020, www.nps.gov/sapa/learn/historyculture/upload/Pellspoint-revised2.pdf.
221 "From George Washington to John Augustine Washington, 6–19 November 1776," Founders Online, National Archives and Records Administration, accessed February 7, 2020, https://founders.archives.gov/documents/Washington/03-07-02-0070.
222 "Battle of Pell's Point," Friends of Pelham Bay Park, accessed February 7, 2020, www.pelhambaypark.org/battle-of-pells-point.
223 Ibid.
224 Joseph C. Scott, "Battle of White Plains," Digital Encyclopedia, George Washington's Mount Vernon, accessed January 4, 2020, www.mountvernon.org/library/digitalhistory/digital-encyclopedia/article/battle-of-white-plains.
225 Ibid.
226 "From George Washington to John Augustine Washington, 6–19 November 1776."
227 Jared Sparks, ed., *The Writings of George Washington*, vol. 4 (Boston: Little, Brown and Co., 1855), 178.
228 "From George Washington to John Augustine Washington, 6–19 November 1776."
229 Megan Brett, "Margaret Cochrane Corbin and the Papers of the War Department," The 18th-Century Common, October 20, 2014, www.18thcenturycommon.org/corbin.

230 Edward Hagaman Hall, *Margaret Corbin: Heroine of the Battle of Fort Washington, 16th November 1776* (New York: American Scenic and Historic Preservation Society, 1932), 14.

231 Ibid., 15.

232 Ibid., 19–20.

233 Carol Berkin, *Revolutionary Mothers: Women in the Struggle for America's Independence* (New York: Knopf Doubleday, 2005), 139.

234 "1926 DAR Efforts," Daughters of the American Revolution, April 18, 2018, www.dar.org/national-society/1926-dar-efforts.

235 Michael Hill, "Where's Capt. Molly? Search on for Revolutionary Hero's Grave," *Army Times*, April 30, 2018, www.armytimes.com/news/your-army/2018/04/30/wheres-capt-molly-search-on-for-revolutionary-heros-grave.

## Nathan Hale

236 Albert A. Lovell, "Librarians Report," *Worcester Society of Antiquity* 2 (1881): 136.

237 Henry Phelps Johnston, *Nathan Hale, 1776: Biography and Memorials* (New Haven, CT: Yale University Press, 1914), 269.

238 Ibid., 44.

239 George Dudley Seymour, *Documentary Life of Nathan Hale, Comprising All Available Official and Private Documents Bearing on the Life of the Patriot, Together with an Appendix, Showing the Background of His Life* (New Haven, CT: privately published, 1941), 25.

240 Paul R. Misencik, *The Original American Spies: Seven Covert Agents of the Revolutionary War* (Jefferson, NC: McFarland & Company, 2014), 7.

241 Ibid.

242 Johnston, *Nathan Hale*, 71.

243 "Abigail Adams to John Adams, 1–10 March 1776," Adams Family Papers, Massachusetts Historical Society, accessed February 7, 2020, www.masshist.org/digitaladams.

244 Andrew P. Peabody, "Prof. Peabody's Oration in Cambridge," *New England Historical and Genealogical Register* 29 (October 1875): 422.

245 Seymour, *Documentary Life of Nathan Hale*, 122.

246 "From George Washington to the Massachusetts General Court, 28 June 1776," Founders Online, National Archives and Records Administration, accessed February 9, 2020, https://founders.archives.gov/documents/Washington/03-05-02-0092.

247 George Washington, *Official Letters to the Honourable American Congress*, vol. 1 (London, 1795), 178.

248 "The Role of Governors Island in the American Revolution," National Park Service, U.S. Department of the Interior, last updated February 26, 2015, www.nps.gov/gois/learn/historyculture/battle-of-brooklyn.htm.

249 Misencik, *Original American Spies*, 15.

250 David Kirby, "Nathan Hale Was Here . . . and Here . . . and Here," *New York Times*, November 23, 1997, www.nytimes.com/1997/11/23/nyregion/making-it-work-nathan-hale-was-here-and-here-and-here.html. Misencik, *Original American Spies*, 21.

251 George D. Seymour, "The Last Days and Valiant Death of Nathan Hale," *American Heritage* 15, no. 3 (April 1964), www.americanheritage.com/last-days-and-valiant-death-nathan-hale.

252 James Hutson, "Nathan Hale Revisited: A Tory's Account of the Arrest of the First American Spy," *Library of Congress Information Bulletin* 62, no. 7/8 (July/August 2003), www.loc.gov/loc/lcib/0307-8/hale.html.

253 David G. McCullough, *1776* (New York: Simon & Schuster Paperbacks, 2006), 223–25.

## Thomas Hickey

254 "From George Washington to Lieutenant Colonel Joseph Reed, 14 January 1776," Founders Online, National Archives and Records Administration, accessed February 9, 2020, https://founders.archives.gov/documents/Washington/03-03-02-0062.

255 "Letter from John Adams to Abigail Adams, 11–17 June 1775," Adams Family Papers, Massachusetts Historical Society, www.masshist.org/digitaladams.

256 "From George Washington to Lieutenant Colonel Joseph Reed, 14 January 1776."

257 "General Orders, 11 March 1776," Founders Online, National Archives and Records Administration, accessed February 9, 2020, https://founders.archives.gov/documents/washington/03-03-02-0326.

258 "Series 3, Varick Transcripts, 1775–1785," George Washington Papers, Library of Congress," www.loc.gov/collections/george-washington-papers/articles-and-essays/series-notes/series-3-varick-transcripts.

259 "From George Washington to the New York Committee of Safety, 17 April 1776," Founders Online, National Archives and Records Administration, accessed February 6, 2020, https://founders.archives.gov/documents/washington/03-04-02-0061.

260 "To George Washington from the King's District Committee of Correspondence, 13 May 1776," Founders Online, National Archives and Records Administration, accessed February 9, 2020, https://founders.archives.gov/documents/washington/03-04-02-0229.

261 "From George Washington to Jonathan Sturges, 16 May 1776," Founders Online, National Archives and Records Administration, accessed February 9, 2020, https://founders.archives.gov/documents/Washington/03-04-02-0256.

262 "To George Washington from Lieutenant Colonel Benjamin Tupper, 13 May 1776," Founders Online, National Archives and Records Administration, accessed February 9, 2020, https://founders.archives.gov/documents/Washington/03-04-02-0232.

263 John Carey, ed., *Official Letters to the Honourable American Congress*, vol. 1 (New York: Samuel Campbell, 1796), 151.

264 Larry Getten, "How a New York Governor Once Plotted to Assassinate George Washington," *New York Post*, December 29, 2018, https://nypost.com/2018/12/29/how-a-new-york-governor-once-plotted-to-assassinate-george-washington.

265 *American Archives: Consisting of a Collection of Authentick Records, State Papers, Debates, and Letters and Other Notices of Publick Affairs, the Whole Forming a Documentary History of the Origin and Progress of the North American Colonies; of the Causes and Accomplishment of the American Revolution; and of the Constitution of Government for the*

*United States, to the Final Ratification Thereof*, vol. 6 (Washington, DC: M. St. Clair Clarke and Peter Force, 1843), 1410. Douglass Southall Freeman, *Washington* (New York: Simon & Schuster, 1992), 275–76.

266 *Journals of the Provincial Congress, Provincial Convention, Committee of Safety and Council of Safety of the State of New-York, 1775-1775-1777*, vol. 1 (Albany, NY: Thurlow Weed, Printer to the State, 1842), 497.

267 Carlos E. Godfrey, *The Commander-in-Chief Guard* (Washington, DC: Stevenson-Smith Co., 1904), 23.

268 "Arrest Warrant from a Secret Committee of the New York Provincial Congress, 21 June 1776," Founders Online, National Archives and Records Administration, accessed February 9, 2020, https://founders.archives.gov/documents/Washington/03-05-02-0042.

269 Godfrey, *Commander-in-Chief Guard*, 24.

270 *Calendar of Historical Manuscripts, Relating to the War of the Revolution, in the Office of the Secretary of State, Albany, N.Y.*, vol. 1 (Albany, NY: Weed, Parsons & Company, 1868), 351.

271 *American Archives*, 1158.

272 *Calendar of Historical Manuscripts*, 355.

273 Ibid., 351.

274 *American Archives*, 1164.

275 "General Orders, 27 June 1776," Founders Online, National Archives and Records Administration, accessed February 9, 2020, https://founders.archives.gov/documents/Washington/03-05-02-0073.

276 Godfrey, *Commander-in-Chief Guard*, 30.

277 Ibid., 30–31.

278 Solomon Nash and Charles I. Bushnell, *Journal of Solomon Nash: A Soldier of the Revolution, 1776–1777; Now First Printed from the Original Manuscript* (New York: privately printed, 1861), 21.

279 Worthington Chauncey Ford, ed., *The Writings of George Washington*, vol. 4, 1776 (New York: G.P. Putnam Sons, 1889), 187.

280 *American Archives*, 1148–50.

281 "Dr. William Eustis to Dr. David Townsend," *New England Historical and Genealogical Register* 23, no. 1 (1869): 206–9.

# INDEX

# ABOUT THE AUTHOR

A. J. Schenkman is a social studies teacher in Ulster County, New York, and a freelance writer. He is the author of the popular *Wicked Ulster County: Tales of Desperadoes, Gangs and More* as well as two earlier publications, *Washington's Headquarters: Home to a Revolution* and *Murder and Mayhem in Ulster County.* He has published numerous articles on Hudson Valley history as well as appearing on multiple podcasts, radio stations, and television. A. J. is the historian for the Town of Gardiner, New York.